Yury Arzhanov

Porphyry, *On Principles and Matter*

Scientia Graeco-Arabica

Herausgegeben von
Marwan Rashed

Band 34

Yury Arzhanov

Porphyry, *On Principles and Matter*

A Syriac Version of a Lost Greek Text with an English Translation, Introduction, and Glossaries

DE GRUYTER

ISBN 978-3-11-127466-9
e-ISBN (PDF) 978-3-11-074702-7
ISSN 1868-7172

Library of Congress Control Number: 2021940470

Bibliographic information published by the Deutsche Nationalbibliothek
The Deutsche Nationalbibliothek lists this publication in the Deutsche Nationalbibliografie; detailed bibliographic data are available on the Internet at http://dnb.dnb.de.

This volume is text- and page-identical with the hardback published in 2021.
Printing and binding: CPI books GmbH, Leck
Printed in Germany

www.degruyter.com

Acknowledgements

My acquaintance with the Syriac text of the treatise published in the present volume became possible due to the generous help of Elizabeth Sobczynski, the founder and Chief Executive of the London-based Levantine Foundation. Her long-term project on the preservation and conservation of manuscripts in the Coptic monastery Dayr al-Suryan in Egypt made the majority of the codices still held in the monastery library available to scholars. I was lucky to accompany her and her colleagues during two preservation campaigns, in December 2016 and November 2019, when a team of conservators began working on a number of Syriac manuscripts. Before 2016 ms. DS 27 was not in good shape; but, fortunately, it was among those codices which were chosen to be stabilised, thus making it possible for me to read it. Bishop Mattheos gave his blessing to my visits to the monastery and my work with Syriac manuscripts, providing another key which opened the doors of Dayr al-Suryan's library to me. Both the former librarian, Abouna Bigoul, and his young successor, Abouna Amoon, supported me in my work. Thus, my special thanks go to the monks of the Dayr al-Suryan, who kept their precious codices, and to Ms. Sobczynski and the Levantine Foundation, who for many years have organised the work of conserving and stabilising them.

I would like to thank Lucas Van Rompay, whose description of ms. DS 27 in the catalogue of 2014, prepared together with Sebastian Brock, attracted my attention to this interesting codex for the first time. Prof. Van Rompay generously provided me with his copy of several folios of ms. DS 27, which he made for his private use.

I owe a lot to my conversations with Jonathan Greig, who helped me to better understand many passages in the philosophical treatise published in this volume. Parts of this book were also discussed with John Dillon, Andrew Smith, John Watt, George Karamanolis, Carlos Steel, and Alexandra Michalewski.

Sami Aydin and Martin Heimgartner read the draft version of my edition and translation and made multiple critical notes, which allowed me to avoid plenty of errors and to improve the translation of the treatise. However, it goes without saying that the positions taken and any shortcomings in the following text remain mine alone.

It is my pleasure to thank Marwan Rashed for including my book in his series (hopefully it will one day have the title, "Scientia Graeco-Syro-Arabica"); Florian Ruppenstein from the publishing house, De Gruyter, for setting the book's layout; and Penelope Hay for proof-reading the English text.

Finally, I would like to thank my wife, Olga, for her constant support for my work and for inspiring me on new discoveries.

https://doi.org/10.1515/9783110747027-201

Preface

The Syriac treatise published in this volume is in many respects a unique text. Though it has been preserved anonymously, there remains little doubt that it belongs to Porphyry of Tyre. Accordingly, it enlarges our knowledge of the views of Plotinus' famous disciple. The text is an important witness to Platonist discussions of First Principles and of Plato's concept of Prime Matter in the *Timaeus*. It contains extensive quotations from Atticus, Severus, and Boethus, and thus provide us with new textual witnesses to these philosophers, whose legacy remains very limited. Additionally, the treatise is a rare example of a Platonist work preserved in the Syriac language. Syriac reception of Plato and Platonic teachings has left rather scant traces, and the question of what precisely Syriac Christians knew about Plato and his philosophy remains a debated issue. The treatise provides new evidence of the close acquaintance of Syriac scholars with Platonic cosmology and with philosophical commentaries on the *Timaeus*.

Before turning to the description of the Syriac text, some preliminary notes are necessary:

The author: The text has come down to us without the author's name. However, the latter calls himself a disciple of Longinus and Plotinus, and thus it is most probable that the treatise derives from Porphyry of Tyre. Comparison with extant fragments of Porphyry's writings leaves no doubt that the treatise goes back to Plotinus' disciple.

The title: The Syriac text has been preserved without title. The comparison with the extant evidence of, and about, Porphyry's writings does not allow one to identify with certainty the Syriac version as part of any known Greek work of this author. The treatise focuses on two topics: First Principles and Prime Matter evaluated in the light of Plato's *Timaeus*. Thus, in order to give an idea of the contents of this Syriac text, it is published as Porphyry's *On Principles and Matter* (abbreviated as *PM*).

The main aim of this book is the publication of the Syriac text, making it available for specialists in late ancient philosophy. Hence, it is not meant to provide an exhaustive commentary on the details of the text, but it does seek to establish the evidence necessary to demonstrate that the text belongs to Porphyry. It is hoped that with the release of this edition, the important work of elaborating multiple details within the text will be taken up by historians of philosophy and Porphyry scholars.

The structure of the Introduction reflects the main purpose of the book, i.e. the publication of the Syriac version of the treatise. The Introduction contains two parts, the first of which suggests a detailed description of the preserved text and tries to contextualize it within the history of Syriac literature. The second part gives an

https://doi.org/10.1515/9783110747027-202

overview of the contents of the treatise and lists its main arguments, allowing one to ascribe the Greek source to Porphyry with great certainty. The glossary at the end of the book is an attempt to reconstruct the terminology of the Greek original, which is based on the extant ancient Syriac translations from the Greek.

Transliteration: Syriac words are vocalized according to the East Syriac vocalization system, but long and short vowels remain undifferentiated.

Table of Contents

Introduction

https://doi.org/10.1515/9783110747027-001

1 The Syriac Text and its History

1.1 Description by Timothy I (d. 823)

The earliest reference to the Syriac treatise *On Principles and Matter* (hereafter: *PM*) dates from the last decades of the eighth century AD. At that time, Timothy I, who had just assumed his position as the head of the Church of the East (East Syrian Catholicos-Patriarch between 780–823)[1], wrote a letter to Mar Pethion, the head of the school of the monastery of Mar Abraham at Bashosh near Mosul[2]. Pethion died in 782/783, so that it must have been 781 or early 782 when Timothy wrote his letter, asking Pethion to do him a favor and to search for a number of books[3].

The place where these books could have been found was not the East Syriac monastery of Mar Abraham where Pethion lived, but the West Syriac convent Mar Mattai, which was situated not far from Mosul and possessed a large library[4]. Timothy asked Pethion to make his inquiries concerning books secretly, for he supposed that, if his request became public, the Syrian Orthodox community would not be eager to share their book treasures with the head of the Church of the East.

Timothy's first years as Catholicos were marked by active scholarly work. Following the request of the caliph al-Mahdi, Timothy (who had received a solid training in the school of Pethion's predecessor, Abraham bar Dashandad[5]) started to translate Aristotle's *Topica* into Arabic[6]. The difficulties in understanding this Aristotelian

---

1 For Timothy I, see especially Berti, *Vita e studi di Timoteo I*. See further Heimgartner, "Der ostsyrische Patriarch Timotheos I. (780–823) und der Aristotelismus".

2 Letter 43 in the collection of letters of Timothy. The Syriac text has been preserved in ms. Baghdad, Chaldean Monastery 509 (dated to 1299), which served as the basis for a number of later copies; cf. Heimgartner, *Die Briefe 42–58: Textedition*, vii–xii. The Syriac text of Letter 43 was published twice on the basis of the modern copies of the Baghdad codex: Braun, "Briefe", 4–11 (Syriac with a German transl.); Pognon, *Une version syriaque*, xvi–xx (Syriac with a French transl.). Sebastian Brock published an English translation of it: Brock, "Two Letters of the Patriarch Timothy", 235–237. The modern critical edition of the letter is: Heimgartner, *Die Briefe 42–58: Textedition*, 65–68. German translation: Heimgartner, *Die Briefe 42–58: Übersetzung*, 47–52.

3 For the date of the letter, see Berti, *Vita e studi di Timoteo I*, 50–62; Heimgartner, *Die Briefe 42–58: Übersetzung*, li.

4 Cf. Berti, "Libri e biblioteche cristiane nell'Iraq".

5 Cf. Berti, *Vita e studi di Timoteo I*, 122–132.

6 Timothy writes that he worked together with the scholar Abu Nuḥ and that he himself translated only part of the text from Syriac into Arabic, while Abu Nuḥ finished the translation. Timothy's description of this project is not quite clear and it has caused various interpretations of it. Cf. Heimgartner, *Die Briefe 42–58: Übersetzung*, 47–48, n. 219.

work made Timothy ask Pethion to look for commentaries and scholia not only on the *Topica*, but also on other works of Aristotle (in the Syriac or Greek languages)[7].

Additionally, among the works that attracted the attention of the Catholicos was one text, which Timothy described as follows[8]:

> Further, search for the treatises on the natural principles of bodies, written by someone according to the Platonic teachings (*dogma plaṭoniqos*), whose beginning is: "Concerning natural principles of bodies some said..." In the first part (*memra*), he (i.e. the author) lists the views of all the ancient philosophers and explains the Platonic (*plaṭoniqo*)[9] Ideas (*ideos*) and Forms (*tapnke*). In the second part (*memra*), he starts to speak about matter, species, and negation according to the Aristotelian teachings (*dogma arisṭoṭeliqos*). He makes ca. five chapters in it, but gives no conclusion to the treatise.

Timothy's account suggests that the version of the text known to him was anonymous, though it makes clear that the author of the treatise aimed to expound the Platonic views of the material, combining it with elements of Aristotelian philosophy. While presenting the main points of the text, Timothy uses several terms characteristic of Platonic philosophy: *ideos* = αἱ ἰδέαι; *tapnke* = τὰ εἴδη, thus stressing that they formed the core of the argument.

Concerning the form of the text, Timothy stated that the treatise was incomplete. Its beginning, which the Catholicos quoted verbatim, does not look like a usual introduction to a philosophical work, which would explain its aim and ascribe it to particular author. Similarly, as Timothy noted, the text did not contain a proper conclusion, so that it looked rather like a fragment, which, however, was large enough to include several parts (*memre*), one of which contained a number of chapters.

Since the first publication of Timothy's letter to Mar Pethion, scholars have failed to identify the text that attracted the interest of the Catholicos in 781/782, in spite of

7 Letter 43.5, see Heimgartner, *Die Briefe 42–58: Textedition*, 66; Heimgartner, *Die Briefe 42–58: Übersetzung*, 49–50.

8 Syriac text: ܒܥܘ ܕܝܢ ܘܡܛܠ ܡܐܡܪܐ ܕܥܠ ܪܫܐ ܟܝܢܝܐ ܕܓܘܫܡܐ. ܕܡܬܚܬܡܝܢ ܠܐܢܫ ܡܢ ܕܘܓܡܐ ܦܠܛܘܢܝܩܘܣ. ܕܐܝܬܘܗܝ ܪܫܝܬܗ ܗܢܐ. ܥܠ ܪܫܐ ܟܝܢܝܐ ܕܓܘܫܡܐ ܐܝܬ ܕܐܡܪܘ.. ܘܡܢܝܐ ܗܘ ܕܥܬܐ ܕܟܠܗܘܢ ܦܝܠܘܣܘܦܐ ܩܕܡܝܐ ܒܡܐܡܪܐ ܩܕܡܝܐ. ܘܡܦܫܩ ܠܐܝܕܐܘܣ ܘܠܛܦܢܟܐ ܦܠܛܘܢܝܩܘ. ܒܡܐܡܪܐ ܕܝܢ ܕܬܪܝܢ ܫܪܐ ܕܢܐܡܪ ܡܛܠ ܗܘܠܐ ܘܐܕܫܐ ܘܠܡܣܬܠܩܢܘܬܐ. ܐܝܟ ܕܘܓܡܐ ܐܪܝܣܛܘܛܠܝܩܘܣ. ܘܐܡܪ ܒܗ ܐܝܟ ܚܡܫܐ ܪ̈ܫܢܐ. ܘܠܐ ܥܒܕ ܠܗ ܫܘܠܡܐ ܠܡܐܡܪܐ. (Heimgartner, *Die Briefe 42–58: Textedition*, 67.36–68.6). English translation is mine. Cf. Brock, "Two Letters of the Patriarch Timothy", 237.

9 For the Syriac *waw* (ܘ) representing the Greek plural ending οι, see Butts, *Language Change*, 91, 99.

his detailed description of the treatise[10]. This situation changed in 2014, when Sebastian Brock and Lucas Van Rompay published a catalogue of Syriac manuscripts now preserved in the Egyptian monastery Dayr al-Suryan[11]. The authors of the catalogue did not notice the similarity between one of the items in ms. 27 and the text refered to in Timothy's letter. However, their description of the codex included the *incipit* of a treatise, which coincided nearly verbatim with the quotation preserved in Timothy's Letter 43. Thanks to this description, it became possible for the present author to establish the connection between the two texts[12].

1.2 Treatise in Ms. Dayr al-Suryan Syr. 27 (9th cent.)

In 1951, the Coptic scholar Murad Kamil visited the "Monastery of the Syrians" (Dayr al-Suryan) in the Egyptian desert of Scetis, where the abbot showed him the Syriac manuscripts (34 in number) that were still preserved in the monastic library[13]. Kamil briefly studied the contents of the codices and described the results of his analysis in Arabic, in a hand-written catalogue, which remained unpublished. Around 1960, Kamil's text was translated into English by Piet B. Dirksen, whose work was also never published[14]. The codex containting *PM* was listed under number 29 in this catalogue and, according to Kamil, it combined two different manuscripts, which he dated to the seventh and the tenth centuries respectively.

The first published description of the codex containing *PM* appeared in 2014 in the afore-mentioned catalogue of Brock and Van Rompay, where ms. 29 of Kamil received the shelf-mark 27 (hereafter: ms. DS 27)[15]. Similar to Kamil, Lucas Van Rompay, who was mainly responsible for the description of ms. DS 27, distinguished two large parts in it, which he marked as A and B. Part A covers folios 1–94. It contains poetical works of Ephrem the Syrian, Isaac of Antioch, and Jacob of Sarug, and it may be dated as early as the sixth century. Part B covers the rest of the codex (fols. 95–127) and includes, in turn, remains from several other manuscripts.

Van Rompay identified five different "unrelated" manuscripts that formed Part B[16]. However, it is likely that this number should be reduced. There is no doubt that

---

10 Cf. Brock, "Two Letters of the Patriarch Timothy", 243; Berti, *Vita e studi di Timoteo I*, 320; Heimgartner, *Die Briefe 42–58: Übersetzung*, 51, n. 238.

11 Brock & Van Rompay, *Catalogue*.

12 The identification was suggested for the first time in the Russian publication: Arzhanov, "Syriac Natural Philosophy". See also Arzhanov, *Syriac Sayings of Greek Philosophers*, 129–130.

13 Brock & Van Rompay, *Catalogue*, xviii.

14 Kamil, *Catalogue*.

15 Brock & Van Rompay, *Catalogue*, 159–177.

16 Brock & Van Rompay, *Catalogue*, 164–177.

the last folios of DS 27, i.e. fols. 124–127 (= "[Ms. 5]" of Van Rompay[17]) originate from a separate codex that is, like the rest of Part B, dated to the ninth/tenth century. These folios are written in one column in the traditional Estrangela script and thus clearly differ from the ductus and from the layout of the rest of Part B.

Two folios, i.e. fols. 96–97 (= "[Ms. 2]" of Van Rompay) are characterized by some unique elements[18] that differentiate them from the ductus of fols. 95 + 98–123. However, they share the same layout of the pages as the latter and are dated to the ninth century. The differences between fols. 96–97 on the one hand, and fols. 95 + 98–123 on the other, may be explained by the assumption that different scribes worked on the same codex, which would reduce the number of manuscripts in Part B to two, though this question demands further clarification.

What seems to be much more certain is the relation between the rest of the folios in Part B. Van Rompay identified three different codices there (= "[Ms. 1]", "[Ms. 3]", and "[Ms. 4]"). The text of *PM* gives good reasons for revising this identification. The first mention of the treatise, which in Syriac starts with the words: "Among those who did research on natural principles…" (cf. the description by Timothy I above) appears on folio 100r, which Van Rompay considered part of "[Ms. 4]". At the end of the fragment of an unidentified text, there stands a short note: "After this — 'On those who did research on natural principles…'." This note is elliptical and it may be understood as: "After this, follows…" However, the next piece in the manuscript is not the abovementioned treatise, but the epistle of Severus Sebokht to Yonan concerning questions of Aristotelian logic. The text of *PM* begins on fol. 114v, which Van Rompay ascribes to "[Ms. 1]". Folios 98–99, which Van Rompay identified as a separate work ("Explanation of Plato's thoughts on matter") and as part of another codex, "[Ms. 3]", in reality contain the last portion of *PM*.

Thus, "[Ms. 1]", "[Ms. 3]", and "[Ms. 4]", as identified by Van Rompay turn out to be connected through the treatise *On Principles and Matter*, which is scattered through different parts of ms. DS 27. The dating, layout, and the ductus of the three allegedly separate manuscripts also speak in favor of their interrelation:

- All three parts are dated by Van Rompay to the ninth/tenth centuries.
- Their layout is nearly identical: the area of writing is 18/19 × 12/12.5 cm, written in two columns, with 32 to 40 lines per column (this number varies throughout the ms.).
- The form of writing is very similar. It combines elements of Estrangela (e.g., in the letters *Beth*, *Gamal*, *Mim*, *Qaph*, and *Shin*) and Serto (e.g., in the letters *Alaph*, *Dalath*, *He*, *Rish*, and *Taw*).

17 Cf. the table in Brock & Van Rompay, *Catalogue*, 177.
18 Cf. Brock & Van Rompay, *Catalogue*, 166.

– The similarities between the three parts of the ms. do not rule out the obvious differences between them. Rather, they can be explained as different scribal habits, so that a number of hands may be detected in the same codex.

Thus, we have enough arguments to consider "[Ms. 1]", "[Ms. 3]", and "[Ms. 4]" as identified by Van Rompay, as originally belonging to the same manuscript, although a number of scribal hands may be determined there. Based on its paleographical features, combining Estrangela and Serto scripts[19], this manuscript may be dated with the help of the "Digital Analysis of Syriac Handwriting" (DASH) tool[20] to the last half of the ninth century[21].

Though the exact date and place of the production of the codex remain unknown due to the loss of its colophon, a scribal note at the bottom of folio 111r informs us about the time and circumstances of its coming to Egypt[22]:

> This book belongs to the Monastery of the Mother of God in the desert of Scetis (i.e. Dayr al-Suryan). Patriarch Abraham donated it to the monastery in the days of Abbot Ṣaliba. Anathema will fall on everyone who removes it from the desert of Scetis.

This note refers to the Coptic patriarch of Syriac origin, Abraham b. Zurʿa, who occupied the Alexandrian see in 975–978[23] and who must have brought a number of Syriac mss. with him to Egypt[24].

It is now difficult to reconstruct the original volume of the codex that Abraham donated to the monastery in the late tenth century. Given the evidence listed above, we may put the preserved folios of the codex in the following order:

19 This is particularly evident in the specific combination of the following letters: Serto *Alaph*, Estrangela *Gamal*, Serto *He*, Estrangela *Qaph*, and Serto *Taw*.

20 <http://dash.stanford.edu/>, accessed 01.10.2020. This powerful tool supplements and at some points replaces the main reference work, i.e. Hatch, *Album of Dated Syriac Manuscripts*.

21 The comparison with the DASH-database has made clear that the style of handwriting of those folios of ms. DS 27 that include *PM* turns out to be closest to mss. BL Add. 14668, fols. 40–43 (dated to 866), BL Add. 14650 (dated to 874–875), BL Add. 12167 (dated to 876), BL Add. 17130 (dated to 876–877), BL Add. 18819 (dated to 883–884), and BL Add. 17194 (dated to 885–886).

22 Syriac: ܐܝܬܘܗܝ، ܟܬܒܐ ܗܢܐ ܕܕܝܪܐ ܕܒܝܬ ܝܠܕܬ ܐܠܗܐ ܕܒܡܕܒܪܐ ܕܐܣܩܝܛܐ ܥܒܕܗ ܠܕܝܪܐ ܐܒܪܗܡ ܦܛܪܝܪܟܐ ܒܝܘܡܝ ܪ̄ ܨܠܝܒܐ ܘܚܪܡܐ ܢܗܘܐ ܥܠ ܟܠ ܕܢܦܩ ܠܗ ܡܢ ܡܕܒܪܐ ܕܐܣܩܝܛܐ (Brock & Van Rompay, *Catalogue*, 172).

23 See den Heijer, "Les Patriarches coptes d'origine syrienne", 49–57.

24 Cf. Brock & Van Rompay, *Catalogue*, 172.

a	fols. 100r–103v + fols. 106r–107v	Letters of Severus Sebokht to Yonan[25] and to Aitallaha[26] concerning some questions of Aristotle's *De Interpretatione* and *Analytica Priora*
b	fols. 107v–113v	Anonymous treatise *On the Division of Substance, on the Division of Creatures, and on the Mixtures of Bodies*, which contains a commentary on the main terms of Porphyry's *Isagoge*[27]
c	fol. 95r	Ps.-Aristotle *On Virtue*[28]
d	fols. 95r–v + 114r	Prophecies of Pagan Philosophers about Christ[29]
e	fols. 114r–v	List of Syriac particles
f	fol. 114v + fols. 104r–105v + fols. 115r–116v + fols. 98r–99v	Treatise *On Principles and Matter*
g	fols. 117r–118r	Treatise on names deriving from actions
h	fols. 118r–v	Treatise on the types of statements according to Aristotle
i	fol. 118v	Ephrem the Syrian, A dispute with a poet
j	fols. 118v–123r	Treatise *On the Soul* divided into seven sections and derived mainly from the pseudepigraphical tract *On the Soul* ascribed to Gregory Thaumaturgus[30]

25 Hugonnard-Roche, "Questions de logique au VIIe siècle". Cf. Reinink, "Severus Sebokts Brief".

26 Hugonnard-Roche, "L'épître de Sévère Sebokht à Aitilaha" (the author did not use ms. DS 27 for his edition).

27 Cf. the note on fol. 113v, col. b: ܫܡܗ̈ܐ ܗܟܝܠ ܝܘܢܝ̈ܐ ܕܒܟܬܒܐ ܗܢܐ ܕܐܝܣܓܘܓܐ ܠܟ ܡܫܟܚܝܢ ܐܝܬܝܗܘܢ ܗܠܝܢ – "Now, the Greek terms, that are found in this treatise *Isagoge*, are…" A similar collection of definitions entitled "On the division of substance" is found in ms. BL Add. 14658, fols. 168ra–172rb, cf. Wright, *Catalogue*, part 3, 1159.

28 An unidentified pseudepigraphon, whose full text is quoted in Brock & Van Rompay, *Catalogue*, 164.

29 Brock, "A Syriac Collection of Prophesies". Cf. Brock, "Some Syriac Excerpts from Greek collections of Pagan Prophecies"; Arzhanov, *Syriac Sayings of Greek Philosophers*, 103–110.

30 The text of this treatise has been published twice. The first edition based on ms. Sinai Syriac 16: Lewis, *Catalogue of the Syriac MSS*, 19–26. Another one based on ms. BL Add. 14658: Furlani, "Syriac Version of the λόγος κεφαλαιώδης περὶ ψυχῆς πρὸς Τατιανόν". See also Zonta, "*Nemesiana Syriaca*". A third witness to this treatise is ms. Mardin, Church of the Forty Martyrs (CFMM) 404, available online in the database of *vHMML*, <https://www.vhmml.org/>, assessed on 01.03.2020.

k	fols. 123r–v	A collection of texts, bearing the title *On Virtue According to the Philosophers and on the Definition of Names* and including a selection from *Sayings of Greek Philosophers*[31] and *Pythagorean Sentences*[32]

The compendium that is reconstructed in the proposed form begins with questions on Aristotelian logic (items *a* and *b*, see also *c* and *h*), includes some works on grammar (items *e* and *g*), and a treatise on natural philosophy (*f*). These works appear side by side with various pieces that may be characterized as "popular philosophy" (*d* and *i*), or moral philosophy in the gnomic form (*j* and *k*), which mostly appear at the end of the compendium. Such a combination of logic, grammar, physics, and moral philosophy is characteristic of another large philosophical anthology, ms. BL Add. 14658, dating from the seventh century, which until the beginning of the 19th century had also been preserved in the library of Dayr al-Suryan[33].

The treatise *On Principles and Matter* occupies a central position in this compendium. Now, various portions of it are disseminated through Part B of ms. DS 27. The correct order of folios is: 114v; 104r–105v; 115r–116v; 98r–99v.

Both the beginning of the treatise (on fol. 114v) and its end (on fol. 99v) have been preserved in the codex. The description of Timothy I (see above) and the reference to the treatise on fol. 100r corroborate the assumption that the Syriac version of the treatise (already at the end of the eighth century, when Timothy was looking for it) contained no specific title, but was referred to by its first sentence.

The references by Timothy (ܥܠ ܪ̈ܫܝܬܐ ܟܝܢ̈ܝܬܐ ܕܦܓܪ̈ܐ – "On natural principles of bodies") and the reference on fol. 100r of the codex (ܥܠ ܐܝܠܝܢ ܕܒܨܘ ܒܥܘܩܒܐ ܥܠ ܪ̈ܫܝܬܐ ܟܝܢ̈ܝܬܐ – "On those who did research on natural principles") in various ways make use of the first sentence of the treatise, which runs as follows: ܐܝܠܝܢ ܕܒܨܘ ܒܥܘܩܒܐ ܥܠ ܪ̈ܫܝܬܐ ܟܝܢ̈ܝܬܐ. ܐܝܬ ܡܢܗܘܢ ܕܐܡܪܘ ܕܚܕܐ ܗܝ ܪܫܝܬܐ ܩܕܡܝܬܐ. ܘܐܝܬ ܡܢܗܘܢ ܕܐܡܪܘ. ܕܣܓܝ̈ܐܐ ܐܢܝܢ ܪ̈ܫܝܬܐ ܕܒ̈ܝ ܟܝܢܐ ܟܝܢ̈ܝܬܐ – "Among those who did research on natural principles, some said that the first principle is one, and some said that the principles of natural things are many". While the Catholicos picks up the last words of this sentence, the scribe of the codex quotes its beginning. At present, it is difficult to say whether, originally, the Syriac version of the treatise started with these words and lacked any formal introduction, or whether some part of the treatise had been lost before Timothy came across it at the end of the eighth century.

31 Cf. Arzhanov, *Syriac Sayings of Greek Philosophers*, 34–37.

32 For various collections of this gnomic anthology, see Arzhanov, *Syriac Sayings of Greek Philosophers*, 84–90.

33 For the content of this ms. and the idea of the *enkyklios paideia* reflected in it, see part 1.4 of the Introduction.

In the restored form, the treatise runs without breaks, so that no lacunas can be detected between the preserved folios. Thus, we can assume that ms. DS 27 contains the treatise in a very similar form, as it became known to Timothy, although the codex of Dayr al-Suryan contains no division into parts and chapters, which Timothy anticipates in his description.

The East Syrian Catholicos made clear that the treatise had no formal conclusion. This is also the case with the version of ms. DS 27 which ends with a quotation from Boethus. This quotation runs until the end of the second column of fol. 99v, and after it we find a blank space that could be filled with ca. two lines of text (if we compare this column with the first one on the same page). A graphic sign ⁘ marks the end of the treatise, confirming the assumption that no part of the text has been lost due to the loss of folios in ms. DS 27.

The structure of the treatise preserved in the codex of Dayr al-Suryan is also confirmed by the 13th-century witness of Grigorios Bar ʿEbraya, or Barhebraeus, who preserved an abridged version of it.

1.3 Epitome by Barhebraeus (d. 1286)

The Syrian Orthodox Maphrian and polymath, one of the main figures of the so-called "Syriac Renaissance" of the 12th–13th centuries, Grigorios Abu l-Farağ Bar ʿEbraya, or Barhebraeus, was born in 1225/1226 in Melitene[34]. He studied in Antioch, Tripoli, and possibly in Damascus, before entering the office of bishop and later on, in 1264, that of the "Maphrian of the East", the second highest office of the Syrian Orthodox Church, which he held until his death in 1286. His regular place of residence as Maphrian was the monastery of Mar Mattai near Mosul. Thus, Barhebreaus had constant access to the convent's library, which served as a rich source of material for his works. Additionally, he often resided in Maragha, which at that time became the usual residence of Ilkhans and a new center of learning. Maragha was the place where Barhebraeus met leading Muslim scholars of his day, among others Naṣir al-Din al-Ṭusi, whose works made a great impact on him[35].

Barhebraeus left an enormous corpus of writings, which to a large extent have the form of compendia and encyclopedias. Their contents vary from issues of theology to meteorology and natural sciences. The Syrian Orthodox Maphrian draw on a large variety of sources, both Syriac and Arabic, compiling them in such a way that

34 For Barhebraeus, his life and works, see Takahashi, *Barhebraeus: A Bio-Bibliography*.
35 Cf. Borbone, "*Marāgha Mdittā Arškitā*".

allowed him to create his own, quite original, works[36]. Some of his sources provided him with the literary forms that he was eager to fill with new materials[37].

The *Candelabra of Sanctuary* (*Mnarat Qudshe*) is a compendium of mainly theological contents[38]. Its title refers to the image of a candelabra with twelve bases for candles, and each part, or *Base*, focuses on a particular branch of knowledge. The second *Base*, which deals with the structure of the universe, was the earliest part of this huge compendium[39]. Barhebraeus composed it in 1266/1267 after a long stay in the monastery of Mar Mattai[40]. During his work, the Maphrian was thus able to make use of the monastery's rich library, which at that time must still have contained the *PM*, which Timothy I had been searching for there several centuries before.

The second *Base* bears the title ܡܛܠ ܟܝܢܘܬܐ ܕܗܘܝܐ ܟܠ – "On the Nature of the Universe"[41]. It contains an excursus on Greek natural philosophy, which turns out to be an abridged version of the treatise that came down to us in ms. DS 27. It starts with an introductory sentence on the diversity of opinions among ancient philosophers concerning the nature of the universe, which has no parallel in the version of ms. DS 27 and was probably introduced by Barhebraeus for the sake of coherence. In the next sentence, he turns to the views of Thales (cf. *PM* §5) and other Greek philosophers. The version of Barhebraeus contains the following three parts:

1. Classification of the views of ancient philosophers on First Principles. The list includes: Thales, Anaximenes, Diogenes, Hippasus, Heraclitus, Theophrastus, Xenophanes, Parmenides, Melissus, Anaxagoras, Leucippus, Democritus, Epicurus, Empedocles, Aristotle, the Stoics, and Pythagoras.
2. An exposition of Plato's thought on First Principles based on the interpretation of the *Timaeus* by Atticus, Severus, Plutarch, and Boethus.
3. A short reference to the teachings of Bardaiṣan and Mani on First Principles.

The third part of Barhebraeus' account finds no parallels in the version of ms. DS 27. There, the Syrian Orthodox Maphrian refers to two main local "heresies", which all Syriac authors, starting from Ephrem the Syrian, were eager to refute[42]. However, the

36 Cf. Takahashi, *Aristotelian Meteorology in Syriac*, 3–4.

37 Cf. the analysis of the sources of several parts of the second *Base* of the *Candelabra of Sanctuary* in Takahashi, "The Greco-Syriac and Arabic Sources of Barhebraeus' Mineralogy and Meteorology".

38 See Takahashi, *Barhebraeus: A Bio-Bibliography*, 175–190.

39 This part of Barhebraeus' work was published several times. Based on ms. Berlin Syr. 190 (Sachau 81): Gottheil, "A Synopsis of Greek Philosophy". On the basis of mss. Vat. Syr. 168, Berlin Syr. 190 (Sachau 81), and Paris Syr. 210: Bakoš, *Le candélabre du sanctuaire*. Based on ms. Jerusalem, St. Mark's Monastery, Syr. 135: Çiçek, *Mnorath Kudshe*.

40 For the date of the composition of the second *Base* of the *Candelabra*, see Takahashi, *Bio-Bibliography*, 23, 91.

41 See Bakoš, *Le candélabre du sanctuaire*, 542.2 = Çiçek, *Mnorath Kudshe*, 46.2 = Gottheil, "A Synopsis of Greek Philosophy", 249, line 1 of the Syriac text.

42 For Bardaiṣan and Ephrem, see section 1.4 of the Introduction.

two other parts of Barhebraeus' epitome match the opening and the closing sections of the treatise in ms. DS 27, thus confirming the volume of the treatise in the form preserved in the codex of Dayr al-Suryan, i.e. without any additions at the beginning and at the end.

In spite of differences between the versions of Barhebraeus and ms. DS 27, they clearly go back to the same version of the text, as a comparison of the two passages below demonstrate:

PM §§11–12

ܠܘܩܝܦܘܣ ܕܝܢ ܐܦ ܗܘ. ܠܐ ܡܫ̈ܘܚܢܐ ܐܡܪ
ܕܐܝܬܝܗܘܢ ܪ̈ܫܐ. ܘܕܩܢܝܢ ܥܡ ܫܘܚܠܦܐ
ܘܗܘܝܐ ܐܡܝܢܐ. ܬܘܒ ܕܝܢ ܐܡܪ. ܕܠܝܬ
ܡܕܡ ܕܝܬܝܪܐܝܬ ܐܝܬܘܗܝ، ܐܘ ܠܐ
ܐܝܬܘܗܝ، ܠܗܢܐ ܕܝܢ ܢܦܩ ܕܝܡܘܩܪܝܛܘܣ.
ܐܡܪ ܐܦ ܗܘ ܕܠܐ ܡܫ̈ܘܚܢܐ ܐܝܠܝܢ ܪ̈ܫܐ.
ܒܕ ܒܓܢܣܐ ܚܕ ܐܡܪ ܕܐܝܬܝܗܘܢ.
ܒܐܣ̈ܟܡܐ ܕܝܢ ܘܒܐܕܫܐ ܦܪܝܫܝܢ. ܐܘ
ܒܕܠܘܩܒܠܘܬܐ.
ܠܗܠܝܢ ܕܝܢ ܕܗܟܢܐ ܕܥܠܡ ܘܐܦ ܐܦܝܩܘܪܘܣ:
ܐܦ ܗܘ ܣܒܪ ܠܐ <ܡܫ̈ܘܚܢܐ> ܐܡܪ
ܕܐܝܬܝܗܘܢ ܪ̈ܫܐ ܘܠܐ ܡܬܦܫܩܢܐ.
ܡܬܬܐܡܪܝܢ ܕܝܢ ܗܠܝܢ ܒܣܦܝܩܘܬܐ ܠܐ
ܡܫܝܚܬܐ. ܘܐܝܬ ܠܗܘܢ ܨܘܪ̈ܬܐ
ܘܐܣܟܡ̈ܐ ܘܟܘܪܐ. ܘܡܬܪܡ ܠܗܘܢ ܕܠܐ
ܡܢܗܘܢ ܡܢ ܚܠܐ. ܘܗܠܝܢ ܒܕ ܡܬܒܪܢܝܢ
ܘܕܟܝܢ ܒܢ̈ܕܕܐ ܡܫܟܠܝܢ ܠܗ ܠܒܠܚܕ
ܘܠܗܠܝܢ ܕܒܗ.

Barhebraeus[43]

ܐܦ ܣܒܪ ܘܠܘܩܝܦܘܣ ܪ̈ܫܐ ܠܐ ܡܫ̈ܘܚܢܐ
ܐܡܪ. ܐܠܐ ܕܩܢܝܢ ܥܡ ܫܘܚܠܦܐ ܘܗܘܝܐ
ܐܡܝܢܐ. ܘܠܝܬ ܡܕܡ ܕܝܬܝܪܐܝܬ
ܐܝܬܘܗܝ، ܐܘ ܠܐ ܐܝܬܘܗܝ، ܐܝܬܘܗܝ،
ܘܕܝܡܘܩܪܝܛܘܣ ܬܘܒ ܪ̈ܫܐ ܠܐ ܡܫ̈ܘܚܢܐ
ܐܡܪ ܐܣܦܝܪ̈ܝܢ ܐܣܟܡܝܢܐ ܕܒܗܘܢܐ
ܒܠܚܘܕ ܘܠܐ ܒܣܘܥܪܢܐ ܡܬܦܠܓܝܢ.

ܘܐܦܝܩܘܪܘܣ ܬܘܒ ܠܐ ܡܫ̈ܘܚܢܐ ܘܠܐ
ܡܬܦܫܩܢܐ ܕܡܬܬܐܡܪܝܢ ܒܣܦܝܩܘܬܐ ܠܐ
ܡܫܝܚܬܐ. ܘܐܝܬ ܠܗܘܢ ܨܘܪ̈ܬܐ
ܘܐܣܟܡܐ ܘܟܘܪܐ. ܐܡܪ ܠܪ̈ܫܐ.

Leucippus, too, says that principles are infinite and that they have change and continuous generation. Further, he said that something that exists is not more than something that does not exist. This was supported by Democritus. He, too, said that principles are infinite, declaring that they are one in genus but different in shapes, species, or in opposition.

Leucippus also assumed that principles are infinite, though they have change and continuous generation, and that something that exists is not more than something that does not exist. Further, Democritus said that principles are infinite, have spherical shape, and that they can be divided only in thought, but not in actuality.

43 Bakoš, *Le candélabre du sanctuaire*, 544.5–9 = Çiçek, *Mnorath Kudshe*, 47.9–19 = Gottheil, "A Synopsis of Greek Philosophy", 250.15–20.

Also Epicurus seems to have agreed with them. He, too, said that the principles were in⟨finite⟩ and indivisible, that they were moving in the infinite void, that they have size, shape, and weight, and further that they are similar to something without parts. When they interweave with and adhere to one another, they complete the world and what is in it.

Further, Epicurus said that principles were infinite and indivisible, moving in the infinite void, and that they have size, shape, and weight.

The underlined elements in the two Syriac passages coincide verbatim, and these parallels are numerous enough to show that the two texts are related to each other. Given, however, the differences between them, the nature of this relation could be explained by two different scenarios:

(1) Barhebraeus was familiar with a version of the text other than that preserved in ms. DS 27; i.e. both texts go back to a version that predates the direct prototype of ms. DS 27, which has not come down to us.
(2) Barhebraeus was familiar with the same version of the text, which he altered according to the needs of his compendium, and while composing this part of the *Candelabra of Sanctuary*, he made use not only of the Syriac treatise now found in ms. DS 27, but also of other Syriac and Arabic sources.

Though the first scenario cannot be ruled out, there seem to be no positive arguments in favor of it. One remark of the Maphrian speaks in favor of the second scenario, where he makes clear that he abridged and altered the original text of *PM*, thus adjusting it to his composition[44]:

> Severus, then, whom Plotinus followed, and Boethus, who was followed by Longinus, the teacher of Porphyry, have said a lot concerning the aim of the teachings of Plato. *But we omit their (words) in order not to make our exposition too long.*

Scenario two is corroborated by the fact that most of the elements in the text of Barhebraeus, which are not present in the treatise preserved in ms. DS 27, find parallels in the doxographical materials, first of all in the Arabic translation of Ps.-Plutarch's

44 The English translation and cursive are mine. Syriac: ܠܣܘܝܪܘܣ ܕܝܢ ܗܘ ܕܠܗ ܢܩܦ ܦܠܘܛܝܢܘܣ ܘܠܒܘܐܬܘܣ ܗܘ ܕܠܗ ܢܩܦ ܠܘܢܓܝܢܘܣ ܡܠܦܢܗ ܕܦܘܪܦܘܪܝܘܣ ܣܓܝܐܬܐ ܐܡܝܪ̈ܢ ܥܠ ܢܝܫܐ ܗܘܐ ܕܝܘܠܦ̈ܢܘܗܝ ܕܦܠܛܘܢ. ܘܕܠܐ ܬܐܪܟ ܡܠܬܐ ܫܒܩܢ ܐܢܝܢ. (Bakoš, *Le candélabre du sanctuaire*, 547.3–4 = Çiçek, *Mnorath Kudshe*, 48.35–49.6).

Placita Philosophorum[45]. While using the text of *PM*, Barhebraeus was mainly interested in its doxographical parts containing the views of ancient philosophers on First Principles. That was probably the reason he picked fragments from the treatise mainly from the first and from the last part of it, i.e. from the doxography regarding the ancient philosophers and from the discussion of the Platonic interpretation of Matter which included the views of the Middle Platonists Atticus, Severus, Plutarch and others (see *PM* §§1–16 and §§68–97). To this list of the views of Greek philosophers, Barhebraeus finally added two main "Syriac philosophers", Bardaiṣan and Mani.

Another argument corroborates the assumption that Barhebraeus was acquainted with the ms. that served as the direct source for ms. DS 27. Part B of the latter contains a collection of "Prophecies of Pagan Philosophers about Christ"[46]. This florilegium has been preserved in Syriac in various forms, one of which is represented by mss. DS 27 and SMMJ 124[47]. The "Prophecies" appear also in the *Candelabra of Sanctuary* of Barhebraeus, i.e. in the same work that contains the abridged version of *PM*[48]. One characteristic relates the text of ms. DS 27 closely to Barhebraeus: after the "Prophecies", DS 27 has preserved for us a note of the translator of the Greek text of the "Prophecies" into Syriac, who complained that there was one more prophecy which he was unable to translate, "because it was similar to the speech of Homer"[49]. The same remark on the missing prophecy that was "similar to the speech of Homer" appears in Barhebraeus, which makes it very probable that the Syrian Orthodox Maphrian was acquainted with the same codex that had served as source for Part B of ms. DS 27 in the late ninth century.

1.4 Natural Philosophy in Syriac Schools

The Syriac version of the treatise *On Principles and Matter* serves as an important witness to the study of Greek science and philosophy in Syriac schools in the pre- and early Islamic periods. Its translation into Syriac forms part of the process of reception

45 Hans Daiber pointed out to a number of parallels between Barhebraeus and the Arabic Ps.-Plutarch (Aetius): Daiber, *Aetius Arabus*, 338, 358, 359.

46 See the structure of the ms. in 1.2, above.

47 See Arzhanov, *Syriac Sayings of Greek Philosophers*, 103–110.

48 The *Prophecies* appear in two parts of the work, *Base* 3 (Graffin, *Le Candélabre du Sanctuaire*, 582–584) and *Base* 4 (Khoury, *Le Candélabre du Sanctuaire*, 18–21).

49 The full text of the translator's note: "These testimonies and oracles were collected from the book of the Pope Anastasius, patriarch of Alexandria. They were translated from Greek into Syriac by the humble Nona, in accordance with my ability, for the praise of God and for the benefit of those who come across them. They are eleven in number. There was one more, but because it was similar to the speech of Homer, I was not able to translate it properly" (see Arzhanov, *Syriac Sayings of Greek Philosophers*, 106).

of Greek natural philosophy by Syrian Christian intellectuals[50]. It seems important to dwell for a short time on this process before we turn to the question of the probable historical background of the Syriac translation of the treatise.

We may differentiate three large periods in the development of the Syriac philosophical tradition[51]:

(1) The early stage between ca. the third and fifth centuries AD, which may to some extent be characterised as authentically Syriac;
(2) The time between the sixth and ninth centuries AD, when Syriac philosophy comes to be largely dependent on the Alexandrian tradition and can therefore be called Graeco-Syriac;
(3) The period after the ninth century, which may be called Syro-Arabic[52].

The formative period of Syriac philosophy does not look like a homogeneous tradition, but appears to modern scholars in a plurality of various forms. It includes such indigenous writers as Aphrahaṭ (first half of the fourth century), and Ephrem the Syrian (d. 373), who seem to have remained uninfluenced by Greek philosophy and thus appear as "essentially Semitic" thinkers[53]. On the other hand, it includes the figure of Bardaiṣan (d. 222), who was greatly dependent on Hellenic culture[54]. Also, Ephrem's knowledge of and references to Greek ideas[55] were to a large extent due to the need for polemic against influential intellectual groups of his time, like the followers of Bardaiṣan.

The latter figure stands out in this period, as the influence of his ideas reached even to the time of Barhebraeus (cf. above). Virtually none of Bardaiṣan's writings has survived until today; however, the preserved *Book of the Laws of the Countries* composed by his pupil Philip, and references to Bardaiṣan's views by Eusebius of

50 For the Syriac reception of Greek natural philosophy, see Arzhanov & Arnzen, "Die Glossen in Ms. *Leyden Or. 583*".

51 For general overviews of Syriac philosophy, or philosophy in Syriac, see Endress, "Philosophie und Wissenschaften bei den Syrern"; Daiber, "Die syrische Tradition in frühislamischer Zeit"; Hugonnard-Roche & Watt, "Philosophie im syrischen Sprachbereich"; Watt, "Syriac Philosophy"; Fiori & Hugonnard-Roche, *La philosophie en syriaque*.

52 This classification differs from the one proposed by Sebastian Brock, who suggested the following periodisation of the process of creative adaptation of Hellenic culture, or the "Hellenization of Syriac culture": (1) the fourth century, when "Syriac culture is still essentially Semitic in its outlook", (2) the fifth and sixth centuries that form a period of transition, and (3) the period after the seventh century (Brock, "From Antagonism to Assimilation").

53 The expression of S. Brock, see Brock, "From Antagonism to Assimilation", 17.

54 Cf. Furlani, "Sur le stoïcisme de Bardesane d'Édesse"; Beck, "Ephräms Rede gegen eine philosophische Schrift des Bardaisan"; Possekel, "Bardaisan of Edessa: Philosopher or Theologian?"; Ramelli, *Bardaisan of Edessa: A Reassessment*.

55 Cf. Possekel, *Evidence of Greek Philosophical Concepts*.

Caesarea[56] suggest that "the Aramaic philosopher", as Ephrem calls him[57], had a good knowledge of contemporary philosophy, especially Stoic ethics[58].

Some elements of Platonic teachings may be identified in Bardaiṣan's views, and it thus seems not altogether surprising to find a reference to him made by Porphyry[59], who calls Bardaiṣan "a Babylonian man"[60]. Porphyry states that Bardaiṣan put a figure of Christ in the form of a cross in the center of the universe, who thus represents the whole cosmos but who also serves as a "model" (παράδειγμα) for God in His creative activity[61]. The latter notion (if it really comes from "the Aramaic philosopher" and not from Porphyry himself) suggests that Bardaiṣan must have been familiar with the central Platonic concept of the First Forms, which God was contemplating during the creation of the world, a concept which Bardaiṣan has modified in a Christian way[62].

Bardaiṣan's knowledge of Platonic philosophy is corroborated by his later critic, Ephrem the Syrian, who mentions that Bardaiṣan composed a polemical treatise addressed to the "house of Plato"[63]. Further, Ephrem's disciple Aba wrote in the treatise *On the Mind* that, according to Plato, "the mystery and sign of everything that exists is with the King of the Universe"[64]. That is, he was familiar with this image, which appears in the Second Epistle of Plato and which became a frequent reference text for Christian apologists.

Thus, we have good reason to assume that elements of Platonic cosmology were known to educated Syrians in the early stage of the Syriac philosophical tradition. Though we are not able to establish with certainty what Bardaiṣan or Ephrem, who

56 The preserved witnesses have been collected and analysed in Drijvers, *Bardaiṣan of Edessa*.

57 Syr. ܦܝܠܘܣܘܦܐ ܕܐܪ̈ܡܝܐ, literally "the philosopher of the Arameans", see Mitchell, *Ephraim's Prose Refutations*, vol. 2, 7–8.

58 Stoic moral philosophy is present in the *Letter of Mara Bar Serapion to his Son*, a Syriac treatise written in the genre of consolation probably in the fourth century. The full text of the *Letter* was published with an English translation in: Cureton, *Spicilegium Syriacum*, 70–76 (English), 43–48 (Syriac). German translation: Schulthess, "Der Brief des Mara bar Sarapion". The most recent analysis of the *Letter*, which includes the earlier bibliography: Merz & Tieleman, *The Letter of Mara bar Sarapion in Context*. For the dating of the *Letter*, see especially McVey, "A Fresh Look".

59 Fragments from Porphyry's lost work *De Styge* have been transmitted by Stobaeus, see Porphyry, Fr. 372–378 (442–461 Smith).

60 Cf. Ramelli, *Bardaisan of Edessa: A Reassessment*, 91–109; Tanaseanu-Döbler, "Bemerkungen zu Porphyrios und Bardaiṣan".

61 Stobaeus, *Eclogae* I.3.96 (I 66.24–70.13 Wachsmuth) = Porphyry, Fr. 376 (447–461 Smith).

62 Cf. a detailed analysis of this passage by Porphyry in Ramelli, *Bardaisan of Edessa: A Reassessment*, 91–108.

63 See Ephrem the Syrian, "A Discourse made by the Blessed Mar Ephrem against the Discourse which is called 'About DMNWS' which was composed by Bardaiṣan against the house of Plato": Mitchell, *Ephraim's Prose Refutations*, vol. 2, i–xxii (English), 1–49 (Syriac).

64 The Syriac text of Aba's treatise has been preserved in ms. Dayr al-Suryan Syr. 20. See fol. 184v: ܐܘ ܗܝ، ܕܐܡܪ. ܕܠܘܬ ܗܘ ܡܠܟܐ ܕܟܘܠܐ ܐܝܬܘܗܝ، ܐܪܙܐ ܘܐܬܐ ܕܟܠ ܕܐܝܬ.

lived in Edessa at the beginning of the third and in the second half of the fourth century respectively, meant by the "house of Plato".

The latter expression was used by a later monastic author, John the Solitary, in the first half of the fifth century[65]. His monastery was located in close proximity to Apamea on the Orontes, which became famous for its philosophical school founded by Iamblichus[66]. In the second half of the second century, it became the place of living and teaching for Numenius. In 269, Plotinus' disciple Amelius settled himself there in order to write down the notes he had made of his teacher's lectures. Thus, by the fifth century, Apamea had became an important center of Neo-Platonism, and it is probably this "house of Plato" to which John referred in his letters[67].

By the fifth century, the general negative attitude of Christian intellectuals towards non-Christian ("pagan") philosophical schools (present in the writings of John the Solitary) became especially apparent. As a consequence of this process, the Platonic philosophy that had worked its way into the Syriac philosophical tradition of the third to the fifth centuries became unattractive to Syriac intellectuals. However, another form of it replaced the academic (Neo-)Platonism of such centers as Apamea, namely the monastic ascetic teachings that were based to a large extent on the ideas of Origen. The works of Evagrius Ponticus contributed much to the reception and adaptation of Origenistic ideas in monastic circles[68]. Nearly the whole corpus of Evagrius' writings was translated into Syriac, and his concept of natural philosophy, whose aim he saw as the revelation of the truth hidden in the world,[69] made a great impact on natural philosophy in Syriac schools in the later period.

The knowledge of Greek natural philosophy in Syriac schools also included various forms of doxography, which transmitted for Syriac scholars the views of Greek philosophical schools. The use of doxographical materials was to a large extent dependent on the new models of education, which, since the fourth century, were primarily connected with monasteries[70]. The Syriac ms. BL Add. 14620 has preserved a list of ancient Greek philosophers and sages, which suggests some kind of overview

65 For John the Solitary and his identity, see Hausherr, "Un grand auteur"; Strothmann, *Johannes von Apamea*.
66 Cf. Balty, "Apamea in Syria".
67 Cf. Strothmann, *Johannes von Apamea*, 8 (Syriac), 120 (German).
68 Cf. Arzhanov, "Plato in Syriac Literature", 17–19.
69 Cf. the last part (that has been preserved only in Syriac) of the treatise *Gnostikos*: ܢܝܫܐ ܕܝܢ ܕܝܕܥܬܐ ܕܟܝܢܐ܂ ܕܬܓܠܐ ܫܪܪܐ ܕܛܫܐ ܒܝܢ ܨܒܘܬܐ. – "The aim of physical knowledge (= φυσική) is to reveal the truth hidden in things" (Frankenberg, *Evagrius Ponticus*, 552–553). For the preserved Greek text of the treatise, see Guillaumont & Guillaumont, *Le gnostique*.
70 See Arzhanov, "Greek Philosophers in Monastic Schools". An interesting example of the Oriental reception of the tradition of *Placita Philosophorum* is found in the story of Secundus Taciturnus. Especially the Arabic translation of *Vita Secundi* stands under the sign of the *Placita*, cf. Overwien, "Secundus der schweigende Philosoph".

of Greek philosophy and which transmits for us the picture of classical Greek antiquity as taught in late antique and early medieval Syriac schools[71]. This list contains not only such famous philosophers as Aristotle, Plato and the Seven Sages, but also Zeus, Minus and Rhadamanthus. The latter figures derive from the Greek mythology known to Syriac readers mainly due to the corpus of scholia to the writings of Gregory of Nazianzus attributed to a certain Nonnus[72].

The scholia to the orations of Gregory turned into a rich source of knowledge of the history of Greek philosophy, containing summaries of the Platonic dialogues and rudimentary information on Greek philosophers. Among the scholia, we find the following one[73]:

> Thirty-seventh is the story about the dejection of Heraclitus. It is this. Although Heraclitus and Democritus did not live at the same time, they were natural philosophers who mocked alike at the constant changes of the world, the latter by laughing and the former by weeping. For Democritus laughed continuously at human affairs, while Heraclitus wept. Democritus was an Abderitan, and Heraclitus an Ephesian.

With his writings, Gregory of Nazianzus set up the way for the rejection of the Greek non-Christian school system of the fifth century and for the new Christian system of education which was later adopted by Syriac intellectuals. This transformation marks the transition to a new period of Syriac philosophy, which is dominated by Aristotelian writings and stands under the sign of the Alexandrian tradition.

It starts with the figure of Sergius of Reshʿayna (*Sargis d-Reshʿayna*, d. 536)[74]. In the late fifth century, Sergius spent several years in Alexandria, where he received a philosophical education from Ammonius, son of Hermeias, accompanied by a

---

71 See Arzhanov, *Syriac Sayings of Greek Philosophers*, 131–133.

72 They were translated twice into Syriac, see Brock, *The Syriac Version of the Pseudo-Nonnos Mythological Scholia*. Edition of the Greek corpus: Nimmo Smith, *Pseudo-Nonniani in IV Orationes Gregorii Nazianzeni Commentarii*. English translation: Nimmo Smith, *The Christian's Guide to Greek Culture*.

73 Scholion 4.37: Τριακοστὴ ἑβδόμη ἐστὶν ἱστορία ἡ κατὰ τὴν Ἡρακλείτου κατήφειαν. ἔστι δὲ αὕτη. Ἡράκλειτος καὶ Δημόκριτος οὐκ ἐν τῷ αὐτῷ γεγονότες χρόνῳ, φυσικοὶ δὲ ὄντες, ὁμοίως τὴν τοῦ κόσμου ἀλλεπαλληλίαν διέπαιξαν, ὁ μὲν γελῶν, ὁ δὲ κλαίων. ὁ μὲν Δημόκριτος ἐγέλα συνεχῶς τὰ πράγματα, ὁ δὲ Ἡράκλειτος ἔκλαιεν. ἦν δὲ ὁ μὲν Δημόκριτος Ἀβδηρίτης, ὁ δὲ Ἡράκλειτος Ἐφέσιος. (Nimmo Smith, *Pseudo-Nonniani in IV Orationes*, 103). The English translation is adapted from Nimmo Smith, *The Christian's Guide*, 27. For the Syriac version of the scholion, see Brock, *The Syriac Version of the Pseudo-Nonnos Mythological Scholia*, 99 (English), 231 (Syriac).

74 For Sergius, see Hugonnard-Roche, "Aux origines de l'exégèse orientale et la logique d'Aristote"; Hugonnard-Roche, "Note sur Sergius de Rēšʿainā"; Fiori, "Un intellectuel alexandrin en Mésopotamie"; Aydin, *Sergius of Reshaina*, 3–66.

thorough medical training in the traditions of *iatrosophists*[75]. Having returned to Syria, Sergius began operating in the town of Resh'ayna as a priest and a chief physician (*archiatros*). Being "a man of eloquence, trained in the reading of many books of the Greeks"[76], he started to translate the works of Galen and Aristotle into Syriac, and his translations played an important role in Syriac schools until early Islamic times, as the account of Ḥunayn ibn Isḥaq (d. 873) concerning the translations of Galen makes apparent[77].

Following the requests of his Church colleagues, Sergius wrote two commentaries on Aristotle's *Categories*: a short *Introduction* addressed to Philotheos[78] and a long *Commentary on Categories* addressed to Theodore[79]. Both works of Sergius are composed in the form of the introduction (*prolegomena*) that have come down to us from several Greek authors which belong to the Alexandrian tradition and turn out to be to some extent dependent on the lectures of Sergius' teacher, Ammonius, transmitted through the writings of his pupils: John Philoponus, Simplicius, and Olympiodorus. Thus, besides a detailed commentary on the main logical terms of Aristotle, Sergius' treatises contain an introductory part that offers an overview of the cursus of philosophical education based on the Alexandrian curriculum[80]; e.g., the short treatise addressed to Philotheos suggests the following division of sciences[81]:

75 For the life of Sergius, see Baumstark, *Lucubrationes Syro-Graecae*, 358–384; Aydin, *Sergius of Reshaina*, 3–9. For the Alexandrian *iatrosophists*, see Overwien, "Der medizinische Unterricht der Iatrosophisten". The famous *iatrosophist* Gessius might have been Sergius' teacher, cf. Aydin, *Sergius of Reshaina*, 46.

76 The characteristic of the Syriac Chronicle of Pseudo-Zachariah of Mytilene: ܘ ܓܒܪܐ ܗܘܐ ܗܢܐ ܡܠܝܠܐ. ܘܡܠܦ ܗܘܐ ܒܩܪܝܢܐ ܕܟܬ̈ܒܐ ܣ̈ܓܝܐܐ ܕܝܘ̈ܢܝܐ (Brooks, *Historia Ecclesiastica*, vol. 2, 136.4–6; cf. an English translation in: Greatrex, *The Chronicle of Pseudo-Zachariah Rhetor*, 368).

77 Bergsträsser, *Über die syrischen und arabischen Galen-Übersetzungen*; Lamoreaux, *Ḥunayn ibn Isḥāq on His Galen Translations*.

78 Sami Aydin published it with an English translation on the basis of ms. Berlin, Petermann I 9 (Sachau 88): Aydin, *Sergius of Reshaina*.

79 Unpublished. An Italian summary of the contents in: Furlani, "Sul trattato di Sergio di Rêsh'ainâ circa le categorie". Partial translations into French and English are: Hugonnard-Roche, *La logique d'Aristote du grec au syriaque*, 165–231; Brock, *A Brief Outline of Syriac Literature*, 202–204; Watt, "Sergius of Reshayna on the Prolegomena to Aristotle's Logic".

80 For the division of sciences and philosophy in antiquity as reflected in *prolegomena*-literature, see Hein, *Definition und Einteilung der Philosophie*; Mansfeld, *Prolegomena: Questions to be Settled*.

81 *Introduction to Aristotle and his Categories* addressed to Philotheos, §3: ܐܡܪܝܢ ܓܝܪ ܐܝܠܝܢ ܕܒܚܟܡܬܐ ܥܠ ܚܟܡܬܐ ܡܠܠܘ. ܕܡܬܡܕܥ ܟܝ ܗܝ̇، ܦܝܠܘܣܘܦܘܬܐ ܡܬܦܠܓܐ ܠܬܪ̈ܬܝܢ ܡܢܘ̈ܬܐ. ܗܘ ܕܝܢ ܠܬܐܘܪܝܐ ܘܠܦܪܟܛܝܩܘܬܐ. ܐܦ ܗܝ̇، ܕܝܢ ܬܐܘܪܝܐ ܡܬܦܠܓܐ ܠܬܠ̈ܬ ܕܐܠܗܘܬܐ. ܘܠܡܠܘܬ ܟܝܢܐ ܘܠܝܘ̈ܠܦܢܐ. ܗܘ ܕܝܢ ܕܡܢܝܢܘܬܐ. ܘܕܡܘܣܝܩܝܬܐ. ܘܕܐܣܛܪܘܢܘܡܝܐ. ܘܕܓܐܘܡܛܪܝܘܬܐ. (Aydin, *Sergius of Reshaina*, 96). A slightly different presentation of the educational system appears in the introductory part of Sergius' long *Commentary on Aristotle's Categories* addressed to Theodore, see Hugonnard-Roche, *La logique d'Aristote du grec au syriaque*, 191–192.

> Those who in wisdom speak about wisdom say that, firstly, philosophy is divided into two parts, i.e. into theory and practice. Further, theory, in turn, is divided into theology, into knowledge of natural things, and into mathematical sciences, i.e. into geometry, arithmetic, astronomy, and music.

The same outline of the educational system that includes "knowledge of natural things" (ܡܠܠܘ̈ܬܐ ܟܝ̈ܢܝܐ), i.e. physics, appears in the later Syriac philosophical compendia and schoolbooks[82]. Thus, from the time of Sergius, i.e. from the beginning of the sixth century, the Syriac pedagogical system includes the notion of physics as part of the "theoretical" sciences.

Further evidence corroborates the assumption that Syrians were not only familiar with the notion of Greek *paideia*, but adopted and integrated it into their own pedagogical system. Familiarity with the Greek system of education is apparent in the structure of the Syriac ms. BL Add. 14658, dated to the seventh century[83]. It starts with the afore-mentioned introduction in Aristotle's *Categories* written by Sergius and contains Porphyry's *Isagoge* and the text of *Categories*[84], as well as some treatises on grammar. Another group of texts in the codex is focussed on questions of physics and astronomy, while the rest of it contains various treatises on moral philosophy, some of which have come down as pseudepigraphic works ascribed to Plato[85].

Two texts appear as representatives of natural philosophy in this collection, and both of them are ascribed to Aristotle. The first one is the Syriac version of the pseudepigraphical letter *De Mundo* (Περὶ κόσμου πρὸς Ἀλέξανδρον)[86]. This work was probably composed in the first century BC and thus belongs to the Middle Platonic period[87]. The second treatise that appears in the "physical" part of the BL codex bears the title: "A Memra on the Cause of the Universe Written by Sergius, a Priest from

82 The whole passage from Sergius' treatise is repeated verbatim by Paul the Persian (531–578), see Gutas, "Paul the Persian". A similar one appears in the *Book of Scholia* of Theodore Bar Koni (late 8th century): Hespel, *Théodore bar Koni, Livre des scolies (recension d'Urmiah)*, 45–46.

83 Cf. Wright, *Catalogue*, vol. 3, 1154–1160. The analysis of the content of this codex: Hugonnard-Roche, "Le corpus philosophique syriaque"; King, "Origenism in Sixth Century Syria".

84 Brock, "The Earliest Syriac Translation of Porphyry's Eisagoge"; King, *The Earliest Syriac Translation of Aristotle's Categories*.

85 Thus, the structure of this codex suggests the way from a *prolegomena*-text to what were considered to be works of Plato, the way characteristic of the pedagogical model of Alexandria, cf. Watts, *City and School*.

86 Edition of the Syriac text: de Lagarde, *Analecta Syriaca*, 134–158. Cf. Ryssel, *Über den textkritischen Werth*, Teil 1; McCollum, *A Greek and Syriac Index*; Takahashi, "Syriac and Arabic Transmission of *On the Cosmos*".

87 For an overview of the scholarly evaluation of *De Mundo*, see Thom, "Introduction"; Gregorić & Karamanolis, *Pseude-Aristotle:* De Mundo.

Resh'ayna, According to the Teachings of Aristotle that it is a Sphere"[88]. It turns out to be a Syriac version of Alexander of Aphrodisias' treatise *De Universo*, which has not been preserved in Greek, but has come down to us in several Arabic versions[89].

Both treatises that bear the name of Aristotle in their titles are characterised not only by the pseudepigraphical character, but also by the tendency to present Aristotelian philosophy as a homogeneous theory of the cosmos. While the *De Mundo* stresses the role of God and his power in the world, the *De Universo* aims at harmonizing several passages in Aristotle's writings[90] relating to the motion of bodies and to the role of the Unmoved Mover.

It was this harmonising tendency that probably attracted the interest of Syrian intellectuals who preferred these texts to the complex writings of Aristotle. Additionally, the worldview of the *De Mundo* must have looked attractive to them due to the tendency to stress the role of God in the world[91], a tendency that Sergius of Resh'ayna must have further developed in his translation of the *De Universo*[92]. As noted above, the structure of the manuscript, in which both texts appear, reflects the pedagogical model of the late antique *enkyklios paideia*; and both treatises could have been used for pedagogical purposes.

In his long *Commentary on Categories* addressed to Theodore, Sergius goes into the differences between the Aristotelian and Platonic notion of genera and species[93]:

> In investigating genera and species, philosophers have not agreed with each other, but have introduced various and diverse concepts into the doctrine of them. Plato and all the Academics held a concept about genera and species as follows. They say that everything which exists naturally in the world has some form, (namely that) of its substance, and also possesses a form with its creator, which is its subsistence in itself, by which (form) it was imprinted and came into being here. ⟨...⟩
> So also (they say) the Demiurge of this All formed concepts about the natures of things according to (their) essence. These concepts, as they emanated from Being

88 Syriac: ܡܐܡܪܐ ܕܥܠ ܚܠܠܬܗ ܕܗܘܝܐ ܥܠ ܕܐܡܝܪ ܠܡܪܝ، ܗܘ ܣܪܓܝܣ ܡܥܝܢܐ ܕܪܝܫ ܥܝܢܐ ܐܝܟ ܡܠܦܢܘܬܗ ܕܐܪܣܛܘܛܠܝܣ ܦܝܠܣܘܦܐ ܕܐܝܟ ܟܘܪܐ ܐܝܬܘܗ̇، ܣܦܝܪܐ. The text was published with a French translation in Fiori, "L'épitomé syriaque du traité sur les causes du tout". Cf. Furlani, "Il trattato di Sergio di Resh'ainâ sull'universo".

89 See Miller, "Sargis of Rešaina: On What the Celestial Bodies Know"; Genequand, *Alexander of Aphrodisias On the Cosmos*; Endress, "Alexander Arabus on the First Cause".

90 First of all, *Physics* (chapter 7), *Metaphysics* (book Lambda), and also *De Mundo*. Cf. Genequand, *Alexander of Aphrodisias On the Cosmos*, 6–16.

91 Cf. Moraux, *Aristotelismus bei den Griechen*, vol. 2, 5–82.

92 Cf. King, "Alexander of Aphrodisias' *On the Principles of the Universe*".

93 *Commentary on Categories* addressed to Theodore, ch. 2. The Syriac text is unpublished. The English translation of this passage is adapted from Watt, "Sergius of Reshayna on the Prolegomena to Aristotle's Logic", 37–39 [§8].

(in itself), instantaneously became hypostases, and with them he imprinted, engraved, and provided subsistence to all the things here (in the world), and both until now and eternally with these primary concepts he forms and establishes the nature of all, using his creative art.

This summary of the Platonic teachings on the Demiurge and the concepts that form all natural things in the world most likely goes back to Ammonius, the Alexandrian teacher of Sergius[94]. It is interesting that Sergius integrated it into a commentary on the logical work and thus supposed that the readers of his work should learn these issues not as a separate discipline, but in the course of logical studies[95].

Another example of such a combination is found in Sergius' short *Introduction* addressed to Philotheos. There, before setting out his exposition of Aristotle's category of quantity, Sergius found it necessary to present "the arguments of philosophers about matter"[96]. This presentation is not directly based on Aristotle's *Categories*[97]. Sergius offers the following overview, which is worth quoting *in extenso*[98]:

> They say that the primary foundation of the bodies is Matter, and that it is by nature without quality and without figure, whereby its nature seems to be receptive of any shape and any figure that is a requirement of its manufacture, since it

---

94 Cf. first of all, his commentary on Porphyry's *Isagoge*, where Ammonius suggests a very similar overview of the Platonic teachings on the First Forms: *Ammonius in Porphyrii Isagogen*, 41.10–45.2 Busse. Cf. Watt, "Sergius of Reshayna on the Prolegomena to Aristotle's Logic", 53.

95 For the combination of logic and natural philosophy, see Hugonnard-Roche, "La constitution de la logique tardo-antique".

96 See his short *Introduction to Aristotle and his Categories* addressed to Philotheos, §65: ܡܛܠ ܕܝܢ ܕܐܦ ܡܠܬܗܘܢ ܕܥܠ ܗܘܠܐ ܕܦܝܠܘܣܘܦܐ ܢܩܕܡ ܐܦ ܗܪܟܐ (Aydin, *Sergius of Reshaina*, 132).

97 Aydin, *Sergius of Reshaina*, 222–224. Sami Aydin finds no direct sources for Sergius' excursus. He assumes that it reflects the author's intention to compose not only a commentary on *Categories*, but also a general introduction to philosophy.

98 *Introduction to Aristotle and his Categories* addressed to Philotheos, §65: ܐܡܪܝܢ ܓܝܪ ܕܫܬܐܣܬܐ ܩܕܡܝܬܐ ܕܓܘܫ̈ܡܐ ܐܝܬܝܗ̇ ܗܘܠܐ. ܘܗ̇ܝ ܗܕܐ ܐܝܬܝܗ̇ ܕܠܐ ܚܫܠ ܘܕܠܐ ܐܣܟܝܡ ܒܟܝܢܗ̇. ܗܟܢܐ ܓܝܪ ܠܗ̇ ܡܬܚܙܝܐ ܕܢܗܘܐ ܐܝܬܘܗ̇ܝ, ܟܝܢܗ̇ ܡܩܒܠܢܝܬܐ ܕܟܠ ܕܡ̈ܘܬܐ ܘܕܟܠ ܐܣܟܝ̈ܡܐ ܕܬܒܥ ܣܘܢܩܐ ܕܥܒܕܘܬܐ. ܟܕ ܕܠܐ ܕܡܘܬܐ ܘܐܣܟܝܡܐ ܠܬܚܬܝܢ ܐܝܬܝܗ̇ ܗ̇ܝ. ܘܗ̇ܝ ܠܡ ܗܕܐ ܡܕܡܥܢܬ ܡܬܠܝܟܐ ܡܕܡ ܡܩܒܠܢܐ. ܠܐܘܪܟܐ ܘܠܦܬܝܐ ܘܠܥܘܡܩܐ. ܐܝܟ ܕܐܬܐܡܪ. ܡܟܐ ܕܝܢ ܕܪܕܬ ܠܐܘܪܟܐ ܘܠܦܬܝܐ ܘܠܥܘܡܩܐ. ܘܗܘܘ ܒܗ̇ ܗܠܝܢ ܬܠܬܐ ܡܫܬܝܢ. ܗܕܝܢ ܡܫܡܗܝܢ ܠܗ̇ ܓܘܫܡܐ ܕܬܪܝܢ ܕܓܘܫ̈ܡܐ. ܘܡܢ ܒܬܪ ܗܟܢܐ ܠܡ. ܡܬܬܢܝܐ ܠܡ ܕܡܫܡܠܝܐ ܐܣܟܝ̈ܡܐ ܘܙܢ̈ܝܐ ܘܫܘܠܐ. ܘܡܚܕܪܐ ܠܓܘܫ̈ܡܐ ܡܕ̈ܢܚܐ ܐܪ̈ܟܢܐ. ܗ̇ܢܘܢ ܕܟܢܝܫܐ ܡܬܥܬܕܝܢ ܡܢ ܐܣܛܘܟܣ̈ܐ. ܕܡܢܗܘܢ ܕܗܠܝܢ ܡܬܪܟܒܝܢ ܟܠܗܘܢ ܓܘܫ̈ܡܐ ܕܬܢܢ: ܗ̇ܢܘܢ ܕܡܡܠܠܐ ܘܡܣܟܠܐ ܐܝܬܝܗܘܢ. ܟܕ ܠܡ ܬܦܫܠ ܗ̇ܝ ܗܕܐ ܗܘܠܐ ܕܢܣܒܬ ܚܡܝܡܘܬܐ ܘܝܒܝܫܘܬܐ. ܢܘܪܐ ܗܘܝܐ. ܟܕ ܕܝܢ ܬܩܒܠ ܡܩܪܪܘܬܐ ܘܪܛܝܒܘܬܐ. ܡܝ̈ܐ ܡܫܡܗܐ. ܐܝܕܝܢ ܝܒܝܫܘܬܐ ܘܩܪܝܪܘܬܐ ܬܬܣܒ. ܗ̇ܝ ܕܝܢ ܐܪܥܐ ܡܬܒܢܝܐ. ܘܐܦ ܘܡܫܚܢܘܬܐ ܘܪܛܝܒܘܬܐ ܬܗܘܐ ܒܗ̇. ܐܐܪ ܚܒܪܐ. ܘܗܟܢܐ ܟܠܗ̇ ܕܗܘܠܐ ܢܣܒܐ ܠܟܝܢܗ̇ ܗ̇ܢܘܢ ܕܒܗ̇ ܒܦܝܠܣܘܦܘܬܐ ܟܝܢܝܬܐ ܐܬܕܪܫ. (Aydin, *Sergius of Reshaina*, 132, 134). The English translation is adapted with some modifications from Aydin, *Sergius of Reshaina*, 133, 135.

> seems to be found without shape and figure. Consequently, it first receives a certain extension toward length, breadth, and depth, in order to grow, and when it has attained to length, breadth, and depth, and these three dimensions have occurred in it, then they (i.e. the philosophers) name it the second nature of the bodies. And afterwards, it is considered to receive figures, qualities and faculties, and it makes up four primary bodies, those which by us in common usage are named elements. All bodies that are here are compounded of these (four elements), those (bodies) that undergo generation and corruption. When this Matter, which has acquired magnitude, receives dryness and heat, it becomes fire, when it receives cold and moisture, it produces water, but if it obtains dryness and cold, it forms earth, and if heat and moisture occur in it, it builds air. In this way, those who did research in natural philosophy have tried to speak about matter.

Sergius presents these views as some sort of standard summary of the philosophy of nature. Thus, we may assume that he has learned them during his classes in philosophy in the school of Ammonius Hermeiou in Alexandria. This summary turns out to be very close to *PM*, especially in the following points:

1) Matter is the "primary foundation" of bodies, a characteristic which goes back to Plato (cf. *PM* §§41, 69, 70 etc.);
2) Matter is "without quality and without figure", but is receptive to any quality and figure (this idea constitutes a large part of *PM*, cf., e.g., §69);
3) The four elements ("four primary bodies") are not first principles, for they are generated (cf. §35).

If we assume that the author of the lost Greek original of *PM* was Porphyry, then both *PM* and the short *Introduction* of Sergius derive from the same philosophical tradition of natural philosophy, for Ammonius' teacher Proclus turns out to be familiar with the writings of Porphyry, whom he often quotes in his own commentary on Plato's *Timaeus*.

Sergius' summary of natural philosophy in his short *Introduction* quoted above does not go into further differences between the arguments of "those who did research in natural philosophy". A more extensive overview including excurses into the notions of First Pinciples by Zeno, Pythagoras, Plato, and Stoics appears in chapters 3 and 4 of Sergius' long *Commentary* addressed to Theodore[99].

Other Syriac commentaries on the logical works of Porphyry and Aristotle contain elements of doxography; e.g., a collection of scholia on Aristotle's *Categories* that is attributed to the Alexandrian philosopher Olympiodorus has been preserved in the

---

99 See Aydin, *Sergius of Reshaina*, 73–74.

ninth century Syriac codex BL Add. 18821[100]. It contains an overview of various philosophical schools, including Aristotelians, Platonists, Pythagoreans, Epicureans, and Cyrenaics.

Thus, Syrian scholars were familiar with Greek natural philosophy through the reception of the Alexandrian commentaries on the *Organon* that contained elements of doxography. The logical studies in general form the background of other philosophical and scholarly disciplines, including physics. Syriac manuscripts have preserved for us a number of mostly anonymous treatises that combine questions of natural philosophy with logical categories, probably reflecting the pedagogical practice in Syriac schools in the early medieval period:

- Ms. BL Add. 12155 dated to the seventh/eighth centuries[101] contains on fol. 178r a treatise entitled *A Natural Demonstration (composed) by Sergius the Archiatros*[102]. This short scholion combines definitions of various logical categories (e.g., substance, accident, species, etc.) with terms that derive from natural philosophy (e.g., nature, body, water, etc.). The title of this scholion may be interpreted as an attempt to deal with issues of physics by means of logical definitions, an attempt that most likely reflects the pedagogical practice of the time of the composition of this codex.
- The afore-mentioned scholion finds multiple parallels in the short treatise *On the Division of Substance*[103], which is found in ms. BL Add. 14658 (fols. 168r–172r)[104]. This work contains extracts from Sergius' short *Introduction to Aristotle* addressed to Philotheos[105], and it is possible that it derives from Sergius himself.
- A different version of this collection of logical definitions has been preserved in ms. DS 27 (fols. 107v–113v)[106], where it bears the title *On the Division of Substance, On the Division of Creatures, and On the Mixtures of a Body*[107]. The last part of this title makes clear that physical issues form a considerable portion of this collection. After the initial definitions of the term "substance", it contains a survey of the four elements that constitute physical bodies. The differences between this version of the collection of definitions and the one preserved in the BL ms. may

100 See Furlani, "Pseudo-Olimpiodoro".

101 Wright, *Catalogue*, vol. 2, 921–955.

102 Syr.: ܬܚܘܝܬܐ ܟܝܢܝܬܐ ܕܣܪܓܝܣ ܐܪܟܝܐܛܪܘܣ. Unpublished. An Italian translation: Furlani, "Due scolî filosofici". Furlani considered the ascription of this work to Sergius to be false. However, H. Hugonnard-Roche revised Furlani's arguments and concluded that there were good reasons to take this ascription seriously: Hugonnard-Roche, *La logique d'Aristote du grec au syriaque*, 129. Sami Aydin comes to the similar conclusion: Aydin, *Sergius of Reshaina*, 13.

103 Syriac: ܥܠ ܦܘܠܓ ܐܘܣܝܐ. Unpublished.

104 Cf. Wright, *Catalogue*, vol. 3, 1154–1160.

105 Sami Aydin lists the parallels between two treatises: Aydin, *Sergius of Reshaina*, 12.

106 Cf. Brock & Van Rompay, *Catalogue*, 171–172.

107 Syriac: ܥܠ ܦܘܠܓ ܐܘܣܝܐ ܘܥܠ ܦܘܠܓܐ ܕܒܪܝܬܐ ܘܥܠ ܡܙܓܐ ܠܗܘܢ ܕܦܓܪܐ. Unpublished.

probably be explained by the fact that such a text has not been considered a uniform philosophical treatise, but rather something that could be freely adjusted to the individual pedagogical needs of the users. Nevertheless, both versions of the collection retain the combination of logical terms with the issues of natural philosophy.

- A further example of such a combination is the anonymous philosophical treatise *On Various Kinds of Actions that Differ from Each Other*[108] preserved as part of the codex DS 28 (fols. 160v–164v)[109]. One part of this text bears the sub-title *Natural Treatise*[110], and, similar to the afore-mentioned collections of definitions, it starts with the term "substance" and proceeds to the issues of natural philosophy. It includes a list of the four elements (Syriac ܐܣܛܘ̈ܟܣܐ = Greek τὰ στοιχεῖα), followed by a commentary: "If you would like to know how these four elements, about which we spoke above, are united with each other…"[111] The subsequent explanation deals with the relation between the elements (water, air, fire, and earth) and qualities (dryness, coldness, heat, and wetness), which is very similar to *PM* §§50–55.
- Another *Treatise on Natural Philosophy*[112] has been preserved in ms. BL Add. 17215 (fols. 5–6), dated to 839[113].

These and other examples[114] point to the historical and educational background of the Syriac version of *PM*, which belongs to the same "Graeco-Syriac" period, as the texts described above. The third period, which starts in the ninth/tenth centuries, transcends the scope of the present study and thus may be left aside[115].

---

108 Syriac: ܬܘܒ ܡܡܠܠܐ ܐܚܪܢܐ ܕܦܝܠܣܘܦܘܬܐ ܕܡܛܠ ܣܘ̈ܥܪܢܐ ܡܫ̈ܚܠܦܐ ܕܦܪܝܫܝܢ ܡܢ ܚ̈ܕܕܐ. Unpublished.

109 Folios 154–164 of ms. DS 28 originate from a separate codex dated to the eighth century, cf. Brock & Van Rompay, *Catalogue*, 204–205. This source was most likely a philosophical compendium. The first part of it (present fols. 154r–160r) deals with the hierarchical structure of the universe that proceeds from God above to the ranks of angels and further to other living beings.

110 Fol. 163r: ܡܡܠܠܐ ܟܝܢܝܐ.

111 Syriac: ܐܢ ܕܝܢ ܨܒܐ ܐܢܬ ܕܬܕܥ: ܕܐܝܟܢܐ ܡܬܚܝܕܝܢ ܗܠܝܢ ܐܪ̈ܒܥܐ ܐܣܛܘ̈ܟܣܐ ܕܐܡܪܢܢ ܡܢ ܠܥܠ ܥܡ ܚ̈ܕܕܐ …

112 Syriac: ܡܡܠܠܐ ܟܝܢܝܐ ܕܦܝܠܣܘܦܘܬܐ. Unpublished.

113 Wright, *Catalogue*, vol. 3, 1164–1165.

114 Ms. Alqosh, Chaldean Diocese, Syr. 61 includes a list of definitions of the term ὕλη in Syriac and Arabic, cf. Arzhanov & Kessel, "Previously Unknown Philosophical Manuscript from Alqosh", 125–126.

115 For Syriac natural philosophy in the early Islamic period, see Arzhanov & Arnzen, "Die Glossen in Ms. *Leyden Or. 583*"; Arzhanov, "Syriac Natural Philosophy".

1.5 Time and Background of the Syriac Translation

The testimony of Timothy I coming from late 781 or early 782 serves as a *terminus ante quem* for the Syriac version of the treatise *On Principles and Matter*. Thus, the translation belongs to the second period of Syriac philosophy, which is dominated by the Alexandrian philosophical tradition. What makes *PM* rather unique for this period is its focus on Platonic ideas, for, as the previous section makes apparent, Syriac philosophy between the sixth and the ninth century was predominantly Aristotelian.

The description preserved in Timothy's letter informs us that the history of *PM* was connected with the monastery Mar Mattai, which turned into one of the main intellectual centers of the West Syrian (or "Syrian Orthodox") Church and from the ninth century AD into the seat of West Syrian Maphrians. Thus, the origins of the Syriac translation of the treatise turn out to be closely connected to the history of the Syrian Orthodox Church, which from the time of its foundation expressed great interest in translations from the Greek[116].

Severus (456–538), who in 512–518 held the position of patriarch of Antioch, became one of the leading figures in the formation of the West Syrian tradition[117]. In the late fifth century, Severus received rhetorical education in Alexandria, where he came in touch with the so-called *philoponoi*, groups of Christian laymen who played an important role in the conflict between the Christian Church and the local Egyptian culture[118]. As patriarch of Antioch, Severus applied the polemic strategies of the Alexandrian *philoponoi* not only against the local "pagan" culture, but also against the Chalcedonians, i.e. the Byzantine Church that supported the dogmatic formula accepted at the Council of Chalcedon in 451.

The Syrian Orthodox Church further developed the intellectual program of Severus of Antioch based on the ideas of the *philoponoi* and actively applied the latter name to the West Syrian intellectuals[119]. In his preface to the Syriac translation of ps.-Dionysius the Areopagite, which dates to the beginning of the ninth century[120], Phocas bar Sargis[121] compared the translation activity of Sergius of Reshʿaina with that of the later generations of West Syrian scholars as follows[122]:

---

116 Cf. Tannous, "You are what you read"; Tannous, *The Making of the Medieval Middle East.*

117 Cf. Grillmeier & Hainthaler, *Christ in Christian Tradition*, vol. II/2, 21–175; Allen & Hayward, *Severus of Antioch.*

118 Cf. Watts, *City and School*, 213–219.

119 Cf. Arzhanov, *Syriac Sayings of Greek Philosophers*, 152–156.

120 Preserved in ms. BL Add. 12151 (dated to the year 804), see Wright, *Catalogue*, vol. 2, 493–497.

121 On Phocas bar Sargis, see Baumstark, *Geschichte der syrischen Literatur*, 271–272.

122 Syriac: ܡܛܠ ܕܠܐ ܗܘܐ ܦܫܝܩܬܐ ܒܟܠ܆ ܐܬܬܪܓܡܘ ܗܘܘ ܦܝܠܘܦܘܢܐ ܒܐܬܘܡܘܒܐ ܗܕܐ ܕܦܘܫܩܐ ܕܝܢ ܠܛܒܐ ܘܢܗܝܪܐ ܒܗܘ ܕܒܬܪܐ܆ ܒܗܢܐ ܕܒܪ ܡܬܬܦܫܩ ܗܘܐ ܕܒܬܪܐ܆ ܘܦܫܝܩܘܬܗ ܠܐܣܝܪܐ ܕܝܢܐ ܕܒܟܠܐ ܫܘܠܛܐ ܗܘܐ܆ ܐܝܟܢܐ ܕܦܘܫܩܐ ܘܦܬܓܡܐ܆ ܐܫܬܘܫܘ ܦܝܠܘܦܘܢܐ ܕܐܦܠܘܣܘܦܐ܆ ܘܡܫܡܫ ܐܦܝܣܩܘܦܐ ܕܐܬܪܗ܇ ܗܢܘܢ ܕܡܫܦܫܦܬܗܘܢ ܢܦܠܘܗܝ ܠܐܘܪܚܐ ܗܕܐ ܐܝܟ ܕܗܫܐ ܠܐ܆

At that age (i.e. in the time of Sergius of Reshʿaina), it was not yet customary that many people had been trained in the art of interpreting the Greek language, until the time was ripe and after several generations it brought forth other "lovers of labour" (Syr. ܪ̈ܚܡܝ ܥܡܠܐ = Gr. φιλόπονοι), like the holy and blessed Athanasius, Patriarch of Antioch, and Jacob, bishop of Edessa, who paved this way as much as possible through their abilities, having become married to both languages in some manner.

The Syriac *philoponoi* mentioned in this note, Athanasius II of Balad and Jacob of Edessa, who are praised as skilled translators from Greek into Syriac, were connected with the monastery of Qenneshre. Founded in ca. 530 by John bar Aphtonia on the Eastern bank of the Euphrates, this convent became the alma mater for a large number of scholars who were well trained in Greek philosophical literature[123]. This group included Thomas of Harkel, Paul of Edessa, Severus Sebokht, Jacob of Edessa, and others, who produced a large corpus of new translations from the Greek as well as revised editions of the earlier translations[124]. This corpus included both Aristotle's *Organon* (including Porphyry's *Isagoge*) and the writings of the Church Fathers, e.g. Basil of Caesarea, Gregory of Nazianzus, and Severus of Antioch[125].

The pedagogical activity of Severus Sebokht (d. 666/667) marked a new period of scholarly life at Qenneshre[126]. Severus Sebokht became the teacher of two renowned specialists in Greek, Athanasius of Balad (d. 687) and Jacob of Edessa (d. 708), whose friend and colleague George of the Arabs (d. 724) was also influenced by Severus' scholarly work[127]. Like most of his colleagues at Qenneshre, Severus Sebokht was well trained in Aristotelian logic, various questions of which he discussed in two of his extant letters written to his fellow-priests, Yonan[128] and Aitallaha[129]. Additionally, he

ܘܗܘܘ ܒܙܢܐ ܡܕܡ ܗ̈ܘܘ ܚܬܢܐ ܕܬܪ̈ܬܝܗܘܢ ܠܫ̈ܢܐ: (Wright, *Catalogue*, vol. 2, 494; cf. Wiessner, "Zur Handschriftenüberlieferung", 198).

123 Cf. Watt, "A Portrait of John Bar Aphtonia".

124 For the history of Qenneshre, see Tannous, *The Making of the Medieval Middle East*, 169–176; Hugonnard-Roche, "Die Schule von Keneschre".

125 Cf. Tannous, *The Making of the Medieval Middle East*, 189–192.

126 See Reinink, "Severos Sebokht".

127 Cf. Villey, "Quadrivium dans la tradition syriaque".

128 The letter was first described and summarized in Reinink, "Severus Sebokts Brief" (Reinink used ms. BL Add. 17156). The full text of the letter was published in Hugonnard-Roche, "Questions de logique au VIIe siècle" (ed. based on mss. BL Add. 17156, Berlin Petermann I 9, Cambridge Add. 2812, and Baghdad, Chaldean Monastery 171).

129 Hugonnard-Roche, "L'épître de Sévère Sebokht à Aitilaha".

was interested in natural sciences and composed a number of works in mathematics[130] and astronomy, e.g. treatises on astrolabe[131] and on the constellations[132].

Severus' interest in natural sciences is vividly expressed in his letter, which he wrote to Basil, a priest in Cyprus, who apparently had asked him about the priority of the Greeks in the astronomical sciences[133]. The title of Severus' letter appears as a programmatic answer to all who considered Syrians to be mere disciples of the Greeks[134]:

> Concerning the priority of the knowledge of the Syrians in the science of astronomy and concerning (the idea) that the knowledge of the existing things is common both for the Greeks and for the Barbarians.

In this letter, Severus Sebokht stated that there were much older civilizations than the one in Greece, and he associated Syrians with these. By so doing, the bishop of Qenneshre of the mid-seventh century seems to follow the same strategy, which was characteristic of the ʿAbbasid caliph al-Maʾmun (786–833): while supporting the Graeco-Arabic translation movement in Baghdad at the beginning of the ninth century, al-Maʾmun combined philhellenism with anti-Byzantine political bias[135]. Similarly, Severus Sebokht was eager to stress that Greek science and philosophy in reality did not belong to the Greeks — neither the ancient, nor the contemporary, i.e. the Byzantines — who became mere transmitters of universal knowledge. This argument served as a secure way of studying Greek science and philosophy that could be separated both from the contemporary Byzantine politics and from the Chalcedonian Christianity represented by the patriarchate of Constantinople.

The scholarly work of Severus Sebokht and his students resulted not only in the enlargement of the scope of the Greek philosophical and scientific literature studied at Qenneshre. It also brought about a new translation style, or "the art of interpreting the Greek language", as Phocas put it. Jacob of Edessa's letter written to George, bishop of Sarug, but addressed to the broad audience of scribes, gives us an important witness to the process of change of the philosophical terminology in the time shortly

130 Cf. Hugonnard-Roche, "La scienza siriaca"; Takahashi, "The Mathematical Sciences in Syriac".
131 Nau, "Le traité sur l'astrolabe". Cf. Villey, "Ammonius d'Alexandrie et le Traité sur l'astrolabe".
132 Nau, "Le traité sur les constellations".
133 Reich, "Ein Brief des Severus Sēḇōḵt". Partial English translation: Takahashi, "Between Greek and Arabic".
134 Syriac: ܥܠ ܩܕܡܘܬ ܝܕܥܬܐ ܕܣܘܪܝܝܐ ܕܒܝܘܠܦܢܐ ܕܐܣܛܪܘܢܘܡܝܐ ܘܕܗܝ ܕܟܠܐ ܐܝܬܘܗ̇ ܝܕܥܬܐ ܕܗܠܝܢ ܕܐܝܬܝܗܘܢ ܕܝܘܢܝܐ ܚܕܐ ܘܕܒܪܒܪܝܐ (Reich, "Ein Brief des Severus Sēḇōḵt", 479.1–3).
135 See Gutas, *Greek Thought, Arabic Culture*, 83–95.

after the death of Severus Sebokht, i.e. at the end of the seventh century[136]. Jacob suggests various examples of the new terms that were unknown to the previous generations of Syrian translators[137]:

> Both ܕܝܠܝܬܐ and ܕܝܠܢܝܘܬܐ were completely unknown a hundred years ago to the Syriac language, e.g. for Mar Ephrem (the Syrian), or for Mar Jacob (of Serug), or Mar Isaac (of Scetis), or Mar Philoxenos (of Mabbug). Neither were the words ܐܝܢܝܘܬܐ and ܐܘܣܝܐ (found) in any (books) that were translated from the Greek in those times. But instead of the word ܕܝ̈ܠܝܬܐ, they said ܫܝ̈ܢܝܬܐ, and instead of the word ܐܝܢܝܘܬܐ, ܐܝܢܐ. Instead of the word ܐܘܣܝܐ, they put either ܟܝܢܐ or ܐܝܬܘܬܐ, or, like many, they said ܐܝܬܝܐ.

Jacob of Edessa gives a number of examples of what in his time were considered to be some sort of neologisms, or at least as a creation of the last generation of scholars, whom Phocas called the "lovers of labour", i.e. the *philoponoi*, who wrote in Syriac on the topics of logic and translated Greek philosophical works. Jacob lists those terms that became products of the scholarly activity of Qenneshre, stating that "a hundred years ago", i.e. at the end of the fifth to the beginning of the sixth century, those words did not yet exist in the Syriac philosophical lexicon, neither in the work of the "classical" Syriac authors, like Ephrem the Syrian, nor in the translations from the Greek produced at that time.

This opposition made by Jacob allows us to better understand the development of the philosophical lexicon during the second period of Syriac philosophical tradition and it gives us important reference points for dating the Syriac version of *PM*. As the analysis of the text demonstrates (cf. the Syriac Glossary at the end of the book), it appears in the light of Jacob's letter as a product of the transition from pre-Qenneshre terminology to that developed by the West Syriac *philoponoi*.

Before considering the arguments for this conclusion, it should be noted that there remains no doubt that the Syriac text of *PM* is a translation from the Greek. A large number of Greek terms remains transliterated in it, e.g.:

ܐܐܪ = ἀήρ,
ܐܟܣܝܘܡܐ = ἀξίωμα,

136 Phillips, *A Letter by Mār Jacob*.

137 Syriac text: ܐܦܠܐ ܓܝܪ ܗܘ ܕܕܝܠܝܬܐ ܐܘ ܕܕܝܠܢܝܘܬܐ ܝܕܝܥ ܗܘܐ ܡܢܡ ܠܡܐܐ ܫܢܝܢ ܠܘܬ ܠܫܢܐ ܣܘܪܝܝܐ. ܘܠܐ ܡܫܬܟܚ ܠܘܬ ܡ̈ܠܦܢܐ ܣܘܪ̈ܝܝܐ ܗܟܢ: ܠܘܬ ܡܪܝ ܐܦܪܝܡ. ܐܡܪ ܐܢܐ ܐܘ ܠܘܬ ܡܪܝ ܝܥܩܘܒ. ܘܡܪܝ ܐܝܣܚܩ ܐܘ ܡܪܝ ܐܟܣܢܝܐ: ܐܘ ܒܟܬܒܐ ܡܢ ܗܠܝܢ ܕܢܦܩܘ. ܡܢ ܝܘܢܝܐ ܒܙ̈ܒܢܐ ܗܠܝܢ: ܐܘ ܐܝܢܝܘܬܐ. ܐܘ ܥܡܗ ܕܐܘܣܝܐ: ܐܠܐ ܚܠܦ ܗܝ ܕܕܝ̈ܠܝܬܐ ܐܡܪܝܢ ܗܘܘ. ܫܝ̈ܢܝܬܐ. ܚܠܦ ܕܝܢ ܗܝ ܕܐܝܢܝܘܬܐ ܐܝܢܐ. ܚܠܦ ܕܝܢ ܗܝ ܕܐܘܣܝܐ ܐܘ ܟܝܢܐ ܣܝܡܝܢ ܗܘܘ ܐܘ ܐܝܬܘܬܐ. ܐܘ ܐܝܟ ܕܣܓܝ̈ܐܐ ܐܝܬܝܐ ܐܡܪܝܢ ܗܘܘ. (Phillips, *A Letter by Mār Jacob*, ܝܘ – ܝܙ). The English translation is mine; cf. Phillips, *A Letter by Mār Jacob*, 7–8.

ܐܘܩܢܐ ܠܘܩܒܠ = ἐκμαγεῖον,
ܐܣܟܡܐ = σχῆμα,
ܗܘܠܐ = ὕλη,
ܛܘܦܣܐ = τύπος,
ܣܘܠܘ ܓܝܣܡܘܣ = συλλογισμός.

Granted that Syriac is generally characterised by a large number of Greek loanwords[138], their amount in the treatise is still quite high.

The treatise contains several expressions that reflect Greek composite words, e.g.:

ܕܡ̈ܢܝ ܕܡܘ̈ܬܐ (§10) = ὁμοιομερής,
ܩܕܡܘܬ ܝܕܥܬܐ (§26) = πρόγνωσις,
ܕܠܘܩܒܠܘܬ ܛܘܦܣܐ (§63) = ἀντίτυπον,
ܡܬܕܡܝܢܐ ܒܐܕ̈ܫܐ (§84) = ὁμοιοειδής,
ܠܝܕܘܬ ܢܦܫܐ (§87) = ψυχογονία.

Though no Greek text of the treatise is extant, the Syriac version frequently allows us to assume what Greek expressions stand behind it and thus reveals a rather literal rendering of the Greek original, which is characteristic of the Qenneshre translation style. Thus, we find a number of expressions that can easily be re-translated into Greek, e.g.:

ܗܟܢܐ ܕܝܢ ܒܗ ܒܕܡܘܬܐ ("and further in the same way") §23 = ὁμοίως δ' ἔχει καὶ...
ܘܥܠ ܐܚܪ̈ܢܝܬܐ ܒܗ ܒܕܡܘܬܐ ("and in the same way about the other things") §42 = ὡσαύτως δὲ καὶ ἐπὶ τῶν ἄλλων...
ܐܢܕܝܢ ܗܕܐ ܐܠܝܨ ܐ ܕܐܦ ... ("if this is the case, it should also be necessary that") §32 = εἰ δε τοῦτο, ἀναγκαῖον καὶ εἴη...

Some passages in the Syriac text can hardly be understood unless we try to re-translate them into the presumed Greek original form. One of the enigmatic passages occurs in §73 where the author of the treatise refers to Atticus. The text runs as follows: ܐܛܝܩܘܣ ܕܝܢ ܒܡܐܡܪܐ ܩܕܡܝܐ ܕܥܠ ܡܠܦܢܘ̈ܬܗ ܕܦܠܛܘܢ. ܗܟܢܐ ܐܡܪ ܒܦ̈ܣܩܐ ܕܒܦܣܩܘܬܐ ܠܘܬ ܚܫܒܘܢܗ ܕܦܠܛܘܢ: ܕܥܠ ܪ̈ܫܐ ܩܕ̈ܡܝܐ. A literal translation would be: "Atticus, in the first treatise on the teachings of Plato, thus briefly stated in the chapters concerning the doctrine of Plato about First Principles". However, if we assume that the expression ܒܦ̈ܣܩܐ ܕܒܦܣܩܘܬܐ goes back to Greek συντόμως καὶ κεφαλαιωδῶς, i.e. "in a concise and brief manner"[139], the text suggests a better sense.

The examples listed leave little doubt that the Syriac text is a rather literal rendering of the Greek. Such translation style was generally characteristic of the seventh

138 For the Greek loanwords in Syriac, see Butts, *Language Change*.
139 Cf. Aristotle, *Metaphysica* 988a18.

century onward, rather than the earlier period[140]. In order to date the Syriac version of *PM* more precisely, we have to compare its terminology with the early sixth century versions of the Greek texts, on the one hand, and with the versions produced in the seventh/eighth centuries by the Qenneshre scholars, on the other. The following extant Syriac translations from the Greek form the basis of the comparison[141]:

Early translations

IsagAn – Anonymous translation of Porphyry's *Isagoge* dated to the sixth century.[142]

CatAn – Anonymous translation of Aristotle's *Categories* dated to the first half of the sixth century.[144]

DeInAn – Anonymous translation of Aristotle's *De Interpretatione* dated to the second half of the sixth century.[147]

DeM – Ps.-Aristotle *De Mundo*, Syriac translation attributed to Sergius of Resh'ayna.[149]

Qenneshre translations

IsagAth – Athanasius of Balad's version of Porphyry's *Isagoge.*[143]

CatG – George of the Arab's translation of Aristotle's *Categories.*[145]

CatJ – Jacob of Edessa's translation of Aristotle's *Categories.*[146]

DeInG – George of the Arab's translation of Aristotle's *De Interpretatione.*[148]

There are a number of philosophical terms in the Syriac text of *PM*, which bring it closer to the earlier translations rather than to the philosophical lexicon characteristic of the Qenneshre translation style that is primarily associated with the work of Jacob of Edessa and George of the Arabs. See, for instance, the following terms, which we find in the Syriac version of *PM*:

---

140 Cf. Brock, "Towards a History of Syriac Translation Technique"; Brock, "Changing Fashions in Syriac Translation Technique".

141 Most of the following texts were analysied on the basis of their digital editions in the database HUNAYNNET, <https://hunaynnet.oeaw.ac.at/>, assessed on 01.10.2020.

142 Brock, "The Earliest Syriac Translation of Porphyry's Eisagoge". See also Brock, "Some Notes on the Syriac Translations of Porphyry's Eisagoge".

143 Freimann, *Die Isagoge des Porphyrius* (partial edition). For the full text of Athanasius' translation, see HUNAYNNET.

144 King, *The Earliest Syriac Translation of Aristotle's Categories.* Cf. the edition in HUNAYNNET, which in many aspects differs from King's edition.

145 Furlani, "Le Categorie e gli Ermeneutici di Aristotele".

146 Georr, *Les Catégories d'Aristote.*

147 Hoffmann, *De Hermeneuticis apud Syros Aristoteleis.*

148 Furlani, "Le Categorie e gli Ermeneutici di Aristotele".

149 De Lagarde, *Analecta Syriaca*, 134–158; McCollum, *The Syriac De Mundo.*

ܙܢܐ

IsagAn and *CatAn* use this word as a translation for ποιός. *IsagAth* and *CatJ* consequently use the term ܐܝܢܐ. In his letter to the scribes (see above), Jacob of Edessa makes clear that this was a deliberate change of the terminology accomplished by the Qenneshre scholars, from which the Syriac text of *PM*, however, remains uninfluenced.

ܝܚܝܕܐܝܬ

IsagAn thus translates ἰδίως, which in *IsagAth* is rendered as ܕܝܠܢܐܝܬ. Sergius of Resh'ayna uses this term in his translation of *DeM*.

ܕܠܩܘܒܠܐ

IsagAn, *CatAn*, and *DeM* thus translate the Greek ἐναντίος. ܕܠܩܘܒܠܐ does not appear in the Qenneshre translations (*IsagAth*, *CatJ*, and *CatG*)[150] that prefer the adjective ܣܘܩܒܠܝܐ. Cf. also ܕܠܩܘܒܠܝܘܬܐ in *CatAn* as a translation of ἐναντιότης, while *CatJ* and *CatG* have ܣܘܩܒܠܝܘܬܐ.

ܦܘܪܫܢܐ

IsagAn and *CatAn* thus translate the Greek διαφορά. This word does not appear in the later translations, where it is replaced by ܫܘܚܠܦܐ.

ܕܠܐ ܡܠܬܐ

This expression appears in *IsagAn* and *DeInAn* as a translation of the Greek ἄλογος, and it seems that it appears in *PM* with the same meaning. However, both *IsagAth* and *DeInG* use another, apparently more precise, expression ܠܐ ܡܠܝܠܐ that better renders the Greek adjective.

ܟܢܝ and ܟܘܢܝܐ

Both words appear in *CatAn* and *IsagAn* with the meaning "name" and "category". Later they were replaced by the terms ܡܬܐܡܪ ܥܠ and ܫܡܐ.

ܟܝܢܐܝܬ

The adverbial form ܟܝܢܐܝܬ appears in the early translations (*IsagAn*, *CatAn*, and *DeInAn*) in the sense "naturally"[151] or as rendering of φύσει. Later translations (*CatJ*, *CatG*, and *AnPrG*) prefer other, more literal, expressions, e.g. ܒܟܝܢܐ.

The examples listed above may serve as evidence for the early dating of the Syriac version of the treatise. They present the terminology of the treatise as preceding the scholarly activity of Jacob of Edessa and George of the Arabs.

150 The term ܕܠܩܘܒܠܝܘܬܐ appears in the last half of *CatJ* and *CatG* (after *Cat.* 11b15) as a translation of τὰ ἀντικείμενα, but this seems to be the influence of *CatAn*, cf. King, *The Earliest Syriac Translation of Aristotle's Categories*, 80–85.

151 Cf. also *CatAn* 136.32 King, where this word is added for expressing the implicit sense.

On the other hand, a number of examples bring the Syriac text of *PM* closer to the Qenneshre translations of Greek works rather than to the versions that appear earlier in the sixth century:

ܡܪܡܝܢܘܬܐ
Athanasius of Balad and later Jacob of Edessa (in *IsagAth* and *CatJ*) use this word for the translation of the Greek ἀπόφασις. The earlier translations prefer either to transliterate the Greek term or to use the word ܒܛܠ (as in *IsagAn*).

ܡܚܘܝܢܐ
This word appears in the Qenneshre translations as rendering of the Greek ἀποδεικτικός, which is usually transliterated in the earlier translations[152].

ܠܐ ܡܬܦܣܩܢܐ
This expression appears in the Qenneshre translations (*IsagAth*, *CatJ*, and *CatG*) as rendering of the Greek ἄτομος[153]. However, the same expression appears also in *CatAn* and thus it predates the Qenneshre period. At the same time, *IsagAn* consistently uses ܩܢܘܡܐ ܝܚܝܕܝܐ.

ܡܪܝܐܝܬ
IsagAth thus translates the Greek κυρίως, while *IsagAn* renders the latter with ܚܬܝܬܐܝܬ. *CatAn* translates with ܡܪܝܐܝܬ both κυρίως and οἰκείως, while *CatJ* and *CatG* make a clear distinction between the two Greek terms. The same is characteristic of the Syriac text of *PM*, cf. the next example.

ܒܝܬܝܐ
IsagAth uses this adjective for translation of the Greek οἰκεῖος, while *IsagAn* renders the latter term with ܡܚܝܢܐ. *CatJ* and *CatG* also render οἰκεῖος with ܒܝܬܝܐ, while the variant of *CatAn* is ܕܝܠܝܐ.

ܝܬܐ
This term rarely appears in the early translations. In *CatAn* and in *DeM* it renders the Greek ἑαυτοῦ, which Jacob of Edessa and George of the Arabs translated with the more traditional ܡܢܗ ܘܠܗ in their versions of the *Categories*. This term, however, appears in the anonymous scholia on *Categories* in ms. Vat. Syr. 586, where it seems to mean "(independent) existence"[154]. These scholia are based on Jacob's translation of the *Categories* and are thus not earlier than the end of the seventh century.

---

152 Cf. two Syriac versions of *Analytica Priora* 24a10–11 (περὶ ἀπόδειξιν καὶ ἐπιστήμης ἀποδεικτικῆς): ܐܦܘܕܝܩܣܝܣ ܘܝܕܥܬܐ ܐܦܘܕܝܩܛܝܩܝܬܐ (Proba) and ܡܚܘܝܢܘܬܐ ܘܝܕܥܬܐ ܡܚܘܝܢܝܬܐ (George of the Arabs).

153 *CatG* uses the transliterated form ܐܛܘ̈ܡܐ on one occasion.

154 Cf. Aydin, "The Remnant of a Questions and Answers Commentary", 78.29.

Thus, the terminology of the Syriac text of *PM* appears to be very close to the Qenneshre versions of the Greek texts. However, it differs in many ways from the translation style of Jacob of Edessa and George of the Arabs and thus maintains the terminology of the earlier translations made in the sixth century.

Based on Jacob's letter, we can assume that the second half of the seventh century witnessed a considerable reformation of the philosophical and scientific terminology that is mainly associated with the work of Jacob of Edessa and his fellow colleague George of the Arabs, in whose writings we find the new vocabulary. The Syriac version of *PM* pre-dates the terminological reform of Jacob and thus belongs to the period before the second half of the seventh century.

This period of the Qenneshre history is dominated by the scholarly activity of Severus Sebokht, whose interest in natural philosophy appears as the likely reason for producing the Syriac translation of the treatise, which could have been easily integrated into the study of logic. As was noted above, Part B of ms. DS 27 contains not only *PM*, but also a large collection of various definitions, which starts with the terms "substance", "genus", and "species", but later on turns to the topic of the "mixtures of the body", i.e. to the combination of hotness, coldness, dryness, and wetness. This topic occupies much space in the *PM* (cf. Part 4, especially §§50–55), and we see some similarities between the two works preserved in Syriac. Both of them combine questions of logic and physics (the tract *On the Division of Essence* contains a collection of scholia on Porphyry's *Isagoge*, cf. above) and probably go back to the pedagogical practice at Qenneshre.

The philosophical compendium, which contains *PM* and which now forms part B of ms. DS 27 thus turns out to be a product of the pedagogical and scholarly activity of Severus Sebokht. In its original form, a reconstruction of which was suggested above (see 1.2), it contained several letters of Severus, in which he mainly addressed questions of logic.

Severus' letter to the periodeutes Yonan includes a passage dealing with natural philosophy. In this passage, Severus answers the question of his respondent as to why Aristotle used letters of the alphabet in his explanations of logical syllogisms. The Syriac scholar suggests three explanations, the first of which runs as follows[155]:

155 English translation is mine. Syriac text: ܡܛܠ ܕܝܢ ܗ̇ܝ، ܐܫܪܬܐ ܕܡܛܠ ܡܢܐ ܠܡ ܒܐܣܛܘ̈ܟܣܐ ܗܠܝܢ ܕܐܠܦܐ ܒܝܬܐ ܪܚܒ ܐܝܟܘ، ܠܐܪ̈ܙܐ ܕܐܣ̈ܟܡܐ ܗܠܝܢ ܐܘ ܠܗܘܠܐ ܠܣܘܠܓܣܡܘܣ. ܫܪܐ ܗ̇ܝ ܥܠܬܐ ܚܕ ܗ̇ܝ، ܠܡ ܒܗܠܝܢ ܐܬ̈ܕܒ ܡܬ̈ܕܘܬܐ ܡܬܬܦܫܛܢܘܬܐ ܐܘ ܒܝܕ ܡܠ̈ܦܢܘܬܐ ܐܪܝܣܛܘܛܠܝܣ ܐܡܪ ܐܢܐ ܘ ܠܓܐܘܡܛܪܝܐ ܐܣܛܪܘܢܘܡܝܐ ܒܝܬ ܘܡܘܣܝܩܝܐ. ܗܢܝܢ ܓܝܪ ܒܝܕ ܐܣܛܘ̈ܟܣܐ ܕܐܠܦܐ ܒܝܬܐ ܡܚ̈ܘܝܢ ܬܫ̈ܡܫܬܐ ܡܛܠ ܕܒܠܬܐ ܗ̇ܝ، ܕܡ̈ܫܬܥܘܕܝܢ. ܒܗ̇، ܠܒܪ ܕܠܘ ܒܠ ܠܡ̈ܫܕܟܐ ܡ̈ܠܝܢ ܘܗ̈ܘܠܝܢܐ ܡ̈ܬܠܠ ܐܝܟ ܦܠܣܘܦܐ ܡ̈ܢܝܢܐ. ܐܠܐ ܐܝܟ ܡܬܬܦܠܣܦܘܣ ܒܠ ܡ̈ܢܝܢܐ ܘܐܣ̈ܟܡܐ ܘܪ̈ܚܒܐ ܒܝܬ ܘܡ̈ܢܚܘܬܐ ܕܗܘܠܝ. (Hugonnard-Roche, "Questions de logique au VIIe siècle", 68). Cf. ms. DS 27, fol. 103r, column 1, line 16 – column 2, line 1. This witness was not used in the Hugonnard-Roche's edition. In the quoted passage, the text of ms. DS 27 differs from other mss. only in minor details.

> Concerning another (question): For what reason (Aristotle) composed the types of the figures and of the syllogisms with the help of the letters of the alphabet? The first reason is that he was zealous in the four mathematical sciences, I mean arithmetic, geometry, astronomy, and music, which by means of the letters of the alphabet produce (visual) illustrations of the knowledge that they transmit. They speak not about the physical and material bodies, like natural philosophers, but rather like mathematicians, about number and form, and about their movements and sounds.

Severus' notion of the "natural philosophers" (Syr. ܦܝܠܘܣܘܦܐ̈ ܟܝܢܝܐ̈ that is a calque from the Greek οἱ φυσικοὶ φιλόσοφοι) is an interesting detail in his argument. This expression usually refers not just to thinkers who wrote on the philosophy of nature, but specifically to the pre-Socratics, who considered the physical elements (e.g., water or fire) to be First Principles[156]. Thus, Severus Sebokht demonstrates his knowledge of the doxographical accounts on the pre-Socratics that were important elements of the commentaries on Aristotelian works[157].

On the other hand, Severus' reference to those, who speak "about the physical and material bodies", is most likely not just a figure of speech, because Severus demonstrated solid knowledge in natural sciences, mainly in astronomy. It is also likely that the Greek text of *PM* attracted the attention of the bishop of Qenneshre, who could have been interested in producing its Syriac version for pedagogical purposes.

The attribution of the Syriac translation of *PM* to Severus Sebokht is corroborated by a number of cases where the terminology of Severus' writings turns out to be very close to the terminology of *PM*:

- In his Letter to Yonan, Severus first uses the term ܐܦܘܕܝܩܛܝܩܐ, which he explains with an alternative term ܡܚܘܝܢܐ that we also find in *PM*[158]. It is the latter term which Severus prefers to use in the rest of his letter. We can thus assume that at his time ܡܚܘܝܢܘܬܐ was not self-evident and demanded an explanation. By the time of George of the Arabs, it was already so well-known that no comment was necessary, but this was not yet the case at the time of Severus.
- In the same letter, Severus uses the term ܕܠܘܩܒܠܐ, which is characteristic of the earlier translations (and of *PM*); starting with Athanasius, the Qenneshre scholars preferred to use the adjective ܣܘܩܒܠܝܐ.

---

156 Cf. Olympiodorus, *In Arist. Meteor.* II 1 353a32 (126.14 Stüve).

157 E.g., we find references to "natural philosophers" in Sergius of Resh'ayna's long *Commentary on Categories* addressed to Theodore (cf. above).

158 Cf. the following passage from Severus' *Letter to Yonan*: ܣܘܠܘܓܝܣܡܘܣ ܐܦܘܕܝܩܛܝܩܐ̈ ܐܘܟܝܬ ܡܬܚܘܝܢܐ̈ (Hugonnard-Roche, "Questions de logique au VIIe siècle", 64.9–10).

- In his letter to Aitallaha, Severus terms human abilities, which people possess, ܟܝܢܐܝܬ, "by nature". Thus, he applies the terminology of the early translations, where his later Qenneshre colleagues would prefer to use the expression ܒܟܝܢܐ.

These examples demonstrate that Severus himself was very probably the translator of the treatise. The time of Severus appears as the transition period when traditional philosophical terminology characteristic of the earlier translations began to be replaced by new terminology characteristic of the Qenneshre translation style. The same combination of earlier terminology and Qenneshre innovations is characteristic of the Syriac text of *PM*.

Severus Sebokht could also have been interested in the Platonic teachings expressed in the treatise. In his letter on the priority of the Syrians in astronomy mentioned above, Severus refers to Plato on one occasion and even quotes a passage from the *Timaeus*[159]:

> Concerning the rather late knowledge of the Greeks, i.e. concerning their ignorance, we should listen to the Greeks themselves, I mean to Plato, who was the first and most famous philosopher among them. This is what he wrote in the treatise *Timaeus*:
> "When Solon, the wisest among the sages, had returned from Egypt, he told Critias what he had heard from an Egyptian priest who was very old. The latter told him the following: 'Oh, Solon, Solon! You Greeks will always remain children. There is no Greek who is old.' And later on he said: 'You Greeks are all young in your minds, for there you have neither any old opinion nor a teaching that would be old in time. Because writing was missing among you for many generations, you were dying voiceless'."

Severus' knowledge of the most famous Platonic dialogue is second-hand. His account turns out to be a nearly verbatim translation of the periphrasis of the *Timaeus*' passage that appears in (Ps.-)Justin Martyr's *Cohortatio ad Graecos*[160]. It is not surprising that by the seventh century Syrian intellectuals were mostly familiar with the

159 English translation is mine. Syriac text: ܡܛܠ ܕܝܢ ܡܐܚܪܘܬ ܝܘܠܦܢܐ ܐܘܟܝܬ ܠܐ ܝܕܥܬܘܬܐ ܕܝܘ̈ܢܝܐ ܢܫܡܥܘܢ ܗܟܝܠ ܡܢܗܘܢ ܕܝܘ̈ܢܝܐ. ܐܡܪ ܐܢܐ ܕܝܢ ܡܢ ܦܠܛܘܢ ܦܝܠܠܣܘܦܐ ܩܕܡܝܐ ܘܡܫܡܗܐ ܕܠܘܬܗܘܢ: ܕܗܢܐ ܡܟܬܒ ܒܛܝܡܐܘܣ ܡܐܡܪܐ. ܟܕ ܦܢܐ ܗܘܐ ܠܗ ܡܢ ܡܨܪܝܢ ܣܘܠܘܢ ܚܟܝܡ ܚܟܝ̈ܡܐ: ܐܡܪ ܠܩܪܝܛܝܐܣ. ܐܝܠܝܢ ܕܗܘ ܫܡܥ ܡܢ ܟܘܡܪܐ ܡܨܪܝܐ: ܐܝܢܐ ܕܣܒ ܛܒ ܗܘܐ. ܐܡܪ ܓܝܪ ܠܗ ܗܟܢ: ܐܘ ܣܘܠܘܢ ܣܘܠܘܢ: ܐܢܬܘܢ ܝܘ̈ܢܝܐ ܛ̈ܠܝܐ ܐܝܬܝܟܘܢ ܒܟܠ ܙܒܢ. ܗܟܢܐ ܕܝܢ ܡܘܣܦ ܠܗ: ܒܬܪܟܢ ܗܟܢ ܐܡܪ ܕܐܢܬܘܢ ܝܘ̈ܢܝܐ ܥܠܝ̈ܡܐ ܐܢܬܘܢ ܒܢܦ̈ܫܬܟܘܢ ܟܠܟܘܢ. ܐܦܠܐ ܓܝܪ ܚܕܐ ܡܣܒܪܢܘܬܐ ܥܬܝܩܬܐ ܐܝܬ ܠܟܘܢ ܬܡܢ: ܐܦܠܐ ܝܘܠܦܢܐ ܕܒܙܒܢܐ ܥܬܝܩܐ. ܐܠܐ ܠܟܘܢ ܠܫܪ̈ܒܬܐ ܣܓܝ̈ܐܬܐ: ܟܬܒܢܘܬܐ ܚܣܝܪܬܐ: ܟܕ ܡܫܬܬܩܝܢ ܗܘܝܬܘܢ ܕܠܐ ܡܠܐ. (Reich, "Ein Brief des Severus Sēḇōḵt", 480.10–17).

160 Ps.-Justin, *Cohortatio ad Graecos*, ch. 12 (39 Markovich).

Christianized image of the Athenian philosopher, which was transmitted to them by the works of the apologists[161]. Nevertheless, Severus' interest in the ideas of Plato, "the first and most famous philosopher" of the Greeks, is apparent in the quoted passage. If we take into account that *PM* mirrors his interest in natural philosophy, Severus turns out to be the most likely candidate for author of the Syriac version of this treatise, which can thus be dated to the middle of the seventh century.

In the following ca. hundred years, a copy of the Syriac translation came to the library of Mar Mattai, which after the fall of Qenneshre became the main intellectual center of the West Syrian Church. There, the treatise became known to the East Syrian Catholicos Timothy I, who was looking for it at the end of the eighth century. The treatise was still present in the library of the monastery in the 13th century when Barhebraeus used it while composing his theological compendium *Candelabra of Sanctuary*. A copy of the manuscript containing the treatise was made in the ninth century. The future Alexandrian Patriarch Abraham b. Zurʿa brought this copy to Egypt and donated it to the Dayr al-Suryan library, where it fortunately survived up until today.

161 Cf. Arzhanov, "Plato in Syriac Literature".

2 The Treatise

2.1 The Structure of the Text

The Syriac version of the treatise *On Principles and Matter* has been preserved in ms. DS 27 most likely in fragmentary form. This characteristic of the text, however, cannot be traced back to the state of the codex in which it came down to us: Part B of ms. DS 27 contains both the beginning and the end of the preserved piece, and there is no sign of lacunas that could be explained by the loss of folios (cf. 1.2, above). The description of the treatise by Timothy I (cf. 1.1, above) makes apparent that at the end of the eighth century the Catholicos was familiar with the text, which had the same volume as the one preserved in ms. DS 27.

However, Timothy's letter includes an outline of its structure, which cannot be based on the text known to us, for the latter includes no part or chapter identifiers. Timothy's description runs as follows:

> In the first *memra*, (the author of the treatise) lists the views of all the ancient philosophers and explains the Platonic Ideas and Forms. In the second *memra*, he starts to speak about Matter, species, and negation according to the Aristotelian teachings. He makes ca. 5 chapters in it, but gives no conclusion to the treatise.

Timothy speaks about two large parts (*memre*) in the treatise, the second one of which he further divides into 5 chapters. It seems that what the Catholicos defined as the first *memra* is the doxography in the beginning, while the rest of the treatise he considered as its second *memra*. This explanation seems plausible, as the remaining part of the treatise turns out to be several times longer than the first and could thus be further divided into sub-chapters.

Certain characteristics of the *PM* gave the Catholikos reason to state that the tract was written according to the "Platonic teachings" (*dogma plaṭoniqos*). Though the first part of *PM* presents a general survey of the philosophical concepts of First Principles, the rest of the treatise is focussed mainly on the views of Plato. The intention of the author to set out the Platonic "dogma" may be traced throughout the whole text, as every step in his reasoning ends with a reference to the Platonic ideas. Based on the contents of the treatise, it seems expedient to divide it into five large parts, all of which end either with an explanation of the Platonic ideas or with a reference to Plato and his philosophy.

The Syriac text as published in the present book has the following structure:

Part 1: Doxography
- §§1–2 Classification of the views of the ancient philosophers.

§§3–4	A short explanation of material principles and their relation to elements.
§§5–6	The views of Thales, including a quotation from Homer.
§7	Anaximenes, Diogenes, Hippasus, and Heraclitus.
§8	Xenophanes.
§9	Parmenides and Melissus.
§10	Anaxagoras.
§11	Leucippus and Democritus.
§12	Epicurus.
§13	Empedocles.
§14	Aristotle.
§15	The Stoics.
§16	Concluding remarks on the Pythagoreans and Plato.

Part 2: Introductory Issues

§17	Two types of the demonstrative science.
§§18–20	Knowledge of intelligible and perceptible things.
§§21–23	Bodies and their qualities.
§§24–25	Matter as receptacle of the qualities.
§26	Intellect as the active principle.
§27–28	Platonic Ideas and Forms.

Part 3: Definition of a Principle

§§29–30	A principle is simple.
§31	It is unqualified.
§32	It is eternal.
§§33–34	It is imperishable.
§35	Four elements may not be principles.
§§36–37	On the reduction of multiple principles to the prior opposition of two.
§§38–39	Three First Principles according to Plato: God, Matter, and Ideas.

Part 4: Definition of Matter

§§40–42	Platonic and Stoic terms for Matter.
§§43–45	Matter is unqualified and unspecified.
§§46–47	It may potentially receive qualities.
§§48–49	It is infinite.
§50	Matter is a subject of the four elements.
§§51–54	Common and specific characteristics of earth, water, fire, and air.
§55	Matter is the primary foundation, which is receptive of qualities.
§§56–67	Matter is neither body nor incorporeal, but body in potentiality.

Part 5: Plato's Concept of First Principles and Prime Matter

- §§68–72 Summary of Plato's views on Principles and Matter.
- §§73–83 Quotation from Atticus' commentary on the *Timaeus*, setting out the Platonic theory of First Principles.
- §§84–86 Exposition of the teachings of Plutarch and Atticus about the relation of Matter to the First Forms.
- §§87–93 Quotation from Severus' commentary on the *Timaeus*, focusing on the question of Matter and initial movement of the four elements.
- §94 Plato's concept of the constitution of the world, according to Severus.
- §95 Plotinus' support of the interpretation of Severus, different views of Boethus and Longinus.
- §§96–97 Boethus on the kind of movement in Matter.

This division into parts has been introduced into the English translation (the published Syriac text contains only paragraph numbers) by the editor to aid navigation. However, the treatise has a very clear logical structure, which its author was eager to stress. Cf. the following remarks that either conclude one of the parts or begin a new one:

> The concluding sentence of Part 1, §16: "We will speak about the principles according to the views of Plato, following what we have started (to say) above in this discourse".
>
> The concluding sentence of Part 2, §28: "And because each one of these is a prior principle of existing things, we should first say what a principle is".
>
> The opening sentence of Part 4, §40: "As these things have been defined in this way, we will first speak about Matter".
>
> The last sentence of Part 4, §67: "These things which we have gathered concerning Matter may (here) come to an end for us".
>
> The opening sentence of Part 5, §68: "Through these things that have been said clearly and very systematically, we stated the reason for Matter being necessary".

The quoted passages serve as building blocks for the structure of the text, dividing it into five main parts outlined above. These five parts, in turn, may be sub-divided into paragraphs, which usually include one argument (or a view of an ancient philosopher in the doxographical part). Thus, the division of the text into parts and paragraphs as suggested by the publisher and introduced into the edition, is based on the internal logic of the treatise, which is clearly structured as a logical exposition and has a sort of rhythm, leading from one argument to the next.

The Platonic ideas and the interpretation of the Platonic texts (first of all of the dialogue *Timaeus*) constitute the focus of the treatise. Its author proposes an outline of the views of various philosophers on the problem of First Principles, but is mainly concerned with presenting Platonic teachings. The first, doxographical part does not contain a summary of Plato's views, but ends with a note in §16 that an exposition of these views would occupy the attention of the author after an excursus into the questions of methodology that form Part 2 of the treatise. Parts 3 and 4 may be considered as definitions of First Principles and Matter from the Platonic point of view. These definitions are later summed up at the beginning of Part 5 (§§68–72) as explicitly Platonic, based on the texts of the philosopher, which, however, demand further interpretation.

A set of commentaries on the key-texts of the dialogue *Timaeus*, offered in Part 5 of the treatise, turns out to be of special interest to historians of philosophy. It contains extensive quotations from the lost commentaries on Plato's *Timaeus* of the renowned Middle Platonists Atticus and Severus, whose works were read in the school of Plotinus and thus became well known to the presumed author of the treatise, Porphyry. These quotations are supplied by a short quotation from Boethus (probably, a 2nd century Platonist) and by references to Plutarch and to Porphyry's teachers, Longinus and Plotinus.

The doxography, which forms the first part of the treatise, does not present a very original overview of philosophical ideas, as there remains little doubt that it was borrowed by the author of the treatise from other sources. However, it gives us an interesting example of a philosophical genre that is rather under-represented in Syriac literature[162], and it is worth dwelling on this part of the text before moving to its main arguments focused on First Principles and Matter.

2.2 The Doxography (Part 1, §§1–16)

PM begins with an extensive doxographical[163] section, presenting the views of philosophers on the number of First Principles and their main characteristics. This tradition goes back to Aristotle. We find a doxographical section at the beginning of his *Physics*

162 For the Syriac tradition of doxography, see Arzhanov, *Syriac Sayings of Greek Philosophers*, 127–133; Arzhanov, "Greek Philosophers in Monastic Schools".

163 The term was coined by Hermann Diels in his classical study: Diels, *Doxographi Graeci*. Jaap Mansfeldt and David Runia have made a revision of Diels' theory, see Mansfeld & Runia, *Aëtiana*, vol. 1 (cf. also vols. 2–5; *Aëtiana* V is a 4-volume new edition of the *Placita*). For the history of doxography, see Runia, "What is Doxography?".

(and in the first book of the *Metaphysics*), where the philosopher discussed the number and types of First Principles as understood by the earlier tradition, especially by the so-called "natural philosophers", i.e. thinkers prior to Socrates who focused on the philosophy of nature. In *Phys.* I.2 we read[164]:

> There must be either one principle or more than one. If one, it must be either unchangeable, the view of Parmenides and Melissus, or subject to change, the view of the physicists, of whom some make air and others water the primary principle. If there are more principles than one, they must be either limited in number – that is, there are either two, three, four, or some such definite number of them – or unlimited.

This short doxographical account was further elaborated by later commentators of the Aristotelian works. Already Aristotle's successor as the head of the Academy, Theophrastus, composed a treatise τῶν φυσικῶν δόξαι in sixteen books, according to Diogenes Laertius[165]. Theophrastus' work was accessible to a certain Aetius, who probably lived in the late first to the early second century AD. The work of Aetius was adopted by Arius Didymus (1st–3rd c. AD?) and in the second century AD by an unknown author of the treatise *Placita Philosophorum* ("Tenets of the philosophers") transmitted under the name of Plutarch. In the fifth century, the work of Aetius was used by Stobaeus, who incorporated large portions from it into his anthology[166].

The compendium of Ps.-Plutarch was known to a number of Christian authors, who included parts of it in their polemical works; e.g., Eusebius of Caesarea in the tenth book of his *Praeparatio Evangelica* gave extensive quotations from the work of Ps.-Plutarch, whose title Eusebius quoted as δόξαι φιλοσόφων περὶ ἀρχῶν[167]. (Ps.-)Justin Martyr included portions from it in the *Cohortatio ad Graecos*[168], and Clement of Alexandria used it as a source for the eighth book of his *Stromateis*, where he presented an overview of philosophical ideas[169].

---

164 Arist., *Phys.* I 2, 184b15–25: Ἀνάγκη δ' ἤτοι μίαν εἶναι τὴν ἀρχὴν ἢ πλείους, καὶ εἰ μίαν, ἤτοι ἀκίνητον, ὥς φησι Παρμενίδης καὶ Μέλισσος, ἢ κινουμένην, ὥσπερ οἱ φυσικοί, οἱ μὲν ἀέρα φάσκοντες εἶναι οἱ δ' ὕδωρ τὴν πρώτην ἀρχήν· εἰ δὲ πλείους, ἢ πεπερασμένας ἢ ἀπείρους, καὶ εἰ πεπερασμένας πλείους δὲ μιᾶς, ἢ δύο ἢ τρεῖς ἢ τέτταρας ἢ ἄλλον τινὰ ἀριθμόν. The English translation is adapted from Charlton, *Aristotle, Physics*, 1–2.

165 Diels reconstructed this treatise of Theophrastus, whom he considered to be the founder of the tradition of doxography, from the sixth century work of Simplicius; see Diels, *Doxographi Graeci*, 475–481. The fragments of Theophrastus were published anew in: Fortenbaugh, *Theophrastus of Eresus*.

166 The texts of Ps.-Plutarch, Stobaeus, and Ps.-Galen as *testimonia* for the work of Aetius were published synoptically by Hermann Diels. Cf. a new edition of all extant witnesses to Aetius' work: Mansfeld & Runia, *Aëtiana V*.

167 Eusebius, *Praeparatio Evangelica* XIV.14 (293.18 Mras & des Places).

168 See *Cohortatio ad Graecos*, ch. 3–4 (27–28 Markovich).

169 Havrda, *The So-Called Eighth 'Stromateus' by Clement of Alexandria*.

The work of Aetius was probably the most popular, but not the only, example of doxography. An independent branch of this tradition, which was not directly dependent on Aetius, has come down to us in the tenth book of the polemical work *Refutatio omnium haeresium* ascribed to Hippolytus of Rome[170]. This work is of special interest for the analysis of *PM*, as its doxographical account turns out to be particularly close to the latter[171]:

> At least some of the Greek dogmatists divided philosophy into three parts and developed their philosophies according to one of the three divisions. Some focused on what they call natural philosophy, others on ethical philosophy, and still others on dialectic. Those who preferred natural philosophy arose and discoursed as follows:
> Some say that everything was born from one, others from several things; and of those who have generated them from one, some have done so from an unqualified and others from a qualified thing; and of those who have done so from a qualified thing, some make this air, others water, others fire, others earth; and of those who have generated all from several things, some have done so from numerable things, others from things infinite in number; and of those who adopt numerables, some make them two, others four, others five, others six.

The summary of Greek natural philosophy, which we find after the words "as follows", starts with the same words that occur at the beginning of *PM*. This fact binds the two texts with each other, though the rest of the doxographical accounts in them differ in many details. It seems likely that both the *Refutatio* and *PM* made use of a common source, which started with the quoted words.

This source was used at approximately the same time as the *Refutatio*, i.e. at the end of the second to the beginning of the third century AD, by Sextus Empiricus in his

---

170 For (Ps.-)Hippolytus' *Refutatio* and its place in the tradition of *Placita*, see Osborne, *Rethinking Early Greek Philosophy*; Mansfeld, *Heresiography in Context*. For the Arabic reception of this work, see Rudolph, *Die Doxographie des Pseudo-Ammonios*.

171 (Ps.-)Hippolytus, *Refutatio omnium haeresium* X.6.1–3: οἱ μέν γε τῶν Ἑλλήνων δογματισταὶ τὴν φιλοσοφίαν τριχῇ διελόντες οὕτως ἐφιλοσόφησαν, οἱ μὲν φυσικήν, οἱ δὲ ἠθικήν, οἱ δὲ διαλεκτικὴν ⟨αὐτὴν⟩ προσαγορεύσαντες. καὶ οἱ μὲν τὴν φυσικὴν ⟨προτιμήσαντες⟩ οὗτοι γεγένηνται, οὕτως τε διηγήσαντο. Οἱ μὲν ἐξ ἑνὸς ⟨ἐγέννησαν⟩ τὰ πάντα, οἱ δὲ ἐκ πλειόνων· καὶ τῶν ἐξ ἑνὸς οἱ μὲν ἐξ ἀποίου, οἱ δὲ ἐκ [τοῦ] ποιοῦ· καὶ τῶν ἐκ ποιοῦ οἱ μὲν ἐκ πυρός, οἱ δὲ ἐξ ἀέρος, οἱ δὲ ἐξ ὕδατος, ἄλλοι δὲ ἐκ γῆς. καὶ (τ)ῶν ἐκ πλειόνων οἱ μὲν ἐξ ἀριθμητῶν, ⟨οἱ δὲ ἐξ ἀπείρων· καὶ τῶν ἐξ ἀριθμητῶν⟩ οἱ μὲν ἐκ δυ(εῖ)ν, οἱ δὲ ἐ(κ) τεσσάρων, οἱ δὲ ἐκ πέντε, οἱ δὲ ἐξ ἕξ. (380–381 Marcovich). The English translation is adapted from Litwa, *Refutation of All Heresies*, 699, 701.

tract *Against the Physicists*[172]. Sextus, who was part of the Empiricist school of medicine (hence his name), in this part of his polemical treatise was elaborating upon the topic of coming-to-be and perishing. In so doing, he did not focus primarily on Aristotelian physics, but gave an overview of the theories of ancient philosophers on First Principles, including the same taxonomy that appears in the *Refutatio* and in *PM* §1[173]:

> The investigation of coming-to-be and perishing that the Sceptics assemble against the Physicists is more or less about the Universe, given that of those who have inquired into the constitution of the all, some have generated everything from one, some from multiple things; and of those who have done so from one, some say it is something without qualities, others something with qualities, and of those who have done so from something with qualities, some say it is fire, some air, some water, and others earth; and of those who have done so from multiple things, some say it is a countable number of things, some an infinite number, and of those who have done so from a countable number, some say it is two, some four, some five, some six.

It remains a matter of debate whether the author of the *Refutatio* was familiar with the work of Sextus, or if both texts go back to a common source[174]. The latter assumption turns out to be more likely, for similar classifications of ancient philosophers according to their views on First Principles appear in a number of other authors, e.g. in Simplicius' commentary on Aristotle's *Physics*[175].

It was also included in the Alexandrian epitome of Galen's treatise *On Elements According to Hippocrates*[176]. In this work, Galen spoke about the "elements" (στοιχεῖα) both in terms of qualities (the hot, the cold, the wet, and the dry) and in terms of

---

172 The two books of *Against the Physicists* are traditionally considered Books 9 and 10 of the larger corpus that bears the title *Against the Mathematicians*, cf. Algra & Ierodiakonou, *Sextus Empiricus and Ancient Physics*, 3–7.

173 Sextus Empiricus, *Adversus Mathematicos* X, 310–318: Ἡ περὶ γενέσεως καὶ φθορᾶς ζήτησις συνίσταται τοῖς σκεπτικοῖς πρὸς τοὺς φυσικοὺς σχεδόν τι περὶ τῶν ὅλων, εἴγε τῶν σκεψαμένων περὶ τῆς τοῦ παντὸς συστάσεως οἱ μὲν ἐξ ἑνὸς ἐγέννησαν τὰ πάντα, οἱ δ' ἐκ πλειόνων, καὶ τῶν ἐξ ἑνὸς οἱ μὲν ἐξ ἀποίου, οἱ δὲ ἐκ ποιοῦ, καὶ τῶν ἐκ ποιοῦ οἱ μὲν ἐκ πυρὸς, οἱ δ' ⟨ἐξ⟩ ἀέρος, οἱ δ' ἐξ ὕδατος, ἄλλοι ἐκ γῆς, καὶ τῶν ἐκ πλειόνων οἱ μὲν ⟨ἐξ⟩ ἀριθμητῶν, οἱ δ' ἐξ ἀπείρων, καὶ τῶν ἐξ ἀριθμητῶν οἱ μὲν ἐκ δύο, οἱ δ' ἐκ τεσσάρων, οἱ δ' ἐκ πέντε, οἱ δ' ἐξ ἕξ. (366–367 Mutschmann). The English translation is adapted with some modifications from: Bett, *Sextus Empiricus*, 136–137.

174 Cf. Janáček, "Hippolytus and Sextus Empiricus"; Mansfeld, *Heresiography in Context*, 317–318; Algra & Ierodiakonou, *Sextus Empiricus and Ancient Physics*, 365–372.

175 Simplicius, *In Arist. Phys.* I 2, 184b15 (25–26 Diels). The similarity between Sextus, the *Refutatio*, and Simplicius was noticed already by Hermann Diels (Diels, *Doxographi Graeci*, 93 n. 2), who suggested that they all go back to the same source.

176 De Lacy, *Galeni De elementis ex Hippocratis*. For the Alexandrian reception of Galen's works, see Overwien, *Medizinische Lehrwerke*.

bodies (fire, air, water, and earth). He also brought the elements of human bodies into connection with the cosmic elements and understood the elements as qualities upon the background of the quality-less matter (ἡ ἄποιος ὕλη), thus adopting the Stoic terminology. The Alexandrian epitome of Galen's *On Elements* further elaborated on this point, starting the part on the elements with a doxography. This epitome has been preserved in an Arabic translation, which begins with a doxographical account of the philosophers' views on what were considered cosmic elements that understood to be principles of physical bodies[177]. It is likely that this doxography derives from the same source, which was used by both Sextus and the author of *Refutatio* in the late second century.

As Jaap Mansfeld has pointed out[178], the doxographical forms were to a large extent dependent on the school function of the texts: the classification of the views of philosophers was a practical form that could be used for pedagogical purposes[179]. The Alexandrian epitome of Galen's *On Elements* thus serves as a witness to the use of doxographies in medical training, which in Alexandria developed parallel to philosophical education (cf. the example of Sergius of Reshʿayna).

Porphyry of Tyre was one of the authors whose name was associated with the doxographical literature. Around 431, Theodoret, a Christian bishop (in ca. 423–466) of Cyrrhus, a town in North Syria (ca. 65 km north of Aleppo), composed a polemical work *On the Cure of Hellenic Diseases* (*De Graecarum affectionum curatione*)[180], in which he suggested a Christianized picture of Platonic philosophy[181]. In his work, Theodoret used a large number of sources, which also included three doxographical works[182]:

> Plutarch and Aetius taught about the tenets of the philosophers. Porphyry occupied himself with the same issue and he has attached the sayings to the biographies of each (philosopher).

177 The Arabic version of the Epitome was allegedly produced by Ḥunayn ibn Isḥaq and has been preserved in various recensions, see Walbridge, *The Alexandrian Epitomes of Galen*, vol. 1; Bos & Langermann, "An Epitome of Galen's *On The Element*".

178 Mansfeld, "Doxography and Dialectic", 3061–3062. According to Mansfeld, the active use of doxographies as separate works goes back to the skeptical school of philosophy in the third cent. BC and is connected to medical education.

179 For the pedagogical role of the doxography, see especially Hans Daiber, "Hellenistisch-kaiserzeitliche Doxographie".

180 See Scholten, *Theodoret, De Graecarum affectionum curatione.*

181 For the apologetic program of Theodoret's *Curatio*, see Siniossoglou, *Plato and Theodoret.*

182 Theodoret, *De Graecarum affectionum curatione*, §95: Πλούταρχος δὲ καὶ Ἀέτιος τὰς τῶν φιλοσόφων ἐκπαιδεύουσι δόξας· τὸν αὐτὸν δὲ καὶ ὁ Πορφύριος ἀνεδέξατο πόνον, τὸν ἑκάστου βίον ταῖς δόξαις προστεθεικώς (242, 244 Scholten). The English translation is mine.

Thus, Theodoret pointed at Porphyry as a transmitter of doxographical accounts, who was comparable to Plutarch and Aetius. Porphyry's work, which the bishop of Cyrrhus most likely had in mind, was the *Philosophical History* that contained not only biographies of philosophers, but also their sayings, which, as Theodoret notes, were attached to the biographical parts (cf. a similar structure in Diogenes Laertius' *Lives of the Philosophers*). The preserved fragments from this work[183] (the only completely preserved book of it is the *Life of Pythagoras*[184]) confirm this assumption. In his commentary on Aristotle's *Physics*, Simplicius often refers to Porphyry as his source on the views of pre-Socratics, thus corroborating Theodoret's statement[185].

Theodoret's polemical treatise serves as an important witness of the accessibility of doxographical works for Syrian scholars in the late antique and early medieval periods[186]. It also presents Porphyry as an important source of doxographical information. Especially, his *Philosophical History*, which was known probably in Greek to Theodoret in the fifth century and later was partly translated into Syriac[187], contained extensive doxographical portions. In addition, Porphyry's extant works present their author as deeply interested in the history of philosophy and doxographical accounts.

The treatise *On Principles and Matter*, which ultimately derives from Plotinus' disciple, thus serves as a further witness to Porphyry's interest in doxography. The first part of *PM* was borrowed by Porphyry from the same source, which was known to Sextus Empiricus and the author of the *Refutatio* at the end of the second to the beginning of the third century AD, but which most likely had had a long pre-history due to its use in philosophical and medical education.

---

183 See Smith, *Porphyrii Philosophi Fragmenta*, 220–247.

184 Des Places, *Porphyre. Vie de Pythagore*.

185 See, e.g., Simplicius, *In Arist. Phys.* I 4, 187a12 (149,11–18 Diels); I 4, 187a29 (163.16–20 Diels); I 4, 187b7 (165.8–10, 166.3–5 Diels); I 5, 188b30 (188.32–189.1 Diels). The main source for Simplicius was the compendium of Theophrastus. However, Simplicius refers to Porphyry as to a separate source.

186 The familiarity with Ps.-Plutarch's *Placita Philosophorum*, which was in ninth century translated into Arabic by the Christian Qusṭa ibn Luqa (see Daiber, *Aetius Arabus*), is apparent in various Syrian writers of the early Islamic period. E.g., the eighth century East Syriac author Theodore bar Koni in his *Book of Scholia* included short summaries of the philosophy of Pythagoras, Plato, Aristotle, Stoics, and Epicureans that bear a strong similarity to Aetius' work. See Addai Scher, *Theodorus Bar Kōnī Liber scholiorum II*, 292–293; Hespel & Draguet, *Theodore bar Konai*, 218. Cf. Baumstark, "Griechische Philosophen und ihre Lehren", 2–17.

187 Flügel, *Kitâb al-Fihrist*, vol. 1, 253. See 2.6, below.

2.3 Introductory Issues (Part 2, §§17–28)

As Timothy I noted in his description, the treatise that aroused his interest aimed at elucidating the "Platonic teachings" (*dogma plaṭoniqos*). The doxographical part finishes with a note that Plato's views on First Principles may be excluded from it (§16). It is apparent that they should not have been mentioned briefly among the views of other philosophers in the introduction because the whole treatise focuses on the interpretation of the Platonic notion of First Principles. The main source text was the *Timaeus*, and Part 2 appears to some extent to be a commentary on *Tim.* 27c–30a, which the author quotes several times verbatim[188].

However, before turning to the exposition of the key-passages of the *Timaeus*, which comes in the last part of the treatise, the author finds it necessary to set out some introductory issues of "the demonstrative science" (§17). In his description, Timothy I points out that what he calls "the second *memra*" is written to a large extent "according to the Aristotelian teachings" (*dogma arisṭoṭeliqos*). Indeed, the beginning of the second part of the treatise (especially §§17 and 20) focuses on Aristotle's logical categories:

> (§17) We ought to know that there are two types of the demonstrative science. One (type) is by means of prior things to demonstrate the posterior. It is characteristic of syllogisms. Those first compositions from which conclusions are drawn are prior. Another (type) is by means of posterior things to demonstrate the prior. It is characteristic of the introductory science. And now, as our discourse is about principles, prior to which nothing may be thought, we employ the initial type of the demonstrative science.
> ⟨…⟩
> (§20) The perceptible things are prior in relation to us, but are secondary in relation to nature. Further, the intelligible things are prior in relation to nature, but are secondary in relation to our perception. As those things which are prior in relation to us are posterior in relation to nature, we will start moving from the introductory argument and ascend to those things that are properly and truly called principles.

These paragraphs are based to a large extent on the *Posterior Analytics*, in which Aristotle defines two types of existing things as follows[189]:

188 In §19, *PM* quotes *Tim.* 28a1–3. In §25, a short passage from *Tim.* 30a4–5 appears.
189 Arist., *An. Post.* I 2, 71b32–72a5: πρότερα δ' ἐστὶ καὶ γνωριμώτερα διχῶς· οὐ γὰρ ταὐτὸν πρότερον τῇ φύσει καὶ πρὸς ἡμᾶς πρότερον, οὐδὲ γνωριμώτερον καὶ ἡμῖν γνωριμώτερον. λέγω δὲ πρὸς ἡμᾶς μὲν πρότερα καὶ γνωριμώτερα τὰ ἐγγύτερον τῆς αἰσθήσεως, ἁπλῶς δὲ πρότερα καὶ γνωριμώτερα τὰ πορρώτερον. ἔστι δὲ πορρωτάτω μὲν τὰ καθόλου μάλιστα, ἐγγυτάτω δὲ τὰ καθ' ἕκαστα· καὶ ἀντίκειται ταῦτ' ἀλλήλοις. The English translation is adapted from Barnes, *Aristotle. Posterior Analytics*, 3.

> Things are prior and more familiar in two ways; for it is not the same to be prior by nature and prior in relation to us, nor to be more familiar and more familiar to us. I call prior and more familiar in relation to us items which are nearer to perception, prior and more familiar *simpliciter* items which are further away. What is most universal is furthest away, and the particulars are nearest – these are opposite to each other.

Another important source for the paragraphs quoted above is the beginning of Aristotle's *Physics*. As already noted in the previous section, the first, doxographical part of the treatise finds a parallel in the second chapter of the *Physics*, where Aristotle sums up the main views of the earlier philosophers on First Principles (*Phys.* I 2, 184b15–25), a summary which was later elaborated by his successor Theophrastus and which formed the core of the tradition that became known to us from Ps.-Plutarch's *Placita Philosophorum*. The doxography on First Principles in chapter 2 of the *Physics* is preceded by the first chapter, where the philosopher sets out a definition of knowledge[190]. This chapter turns out to be another important source for the *PM*[191]:

> In all disciplines in which there is systematic knowledge of things with principles, causes, or elements, it arises from a grasp of those: we think we have knowledge of a thing when we have found its primary causes and principles, and followed it back to its elements. Clearly, then, systematic knowledge of nature must start with an attempt to settle questions about principles. The natural course is to proceed from what is clearer and more knowable to us, to what is more knowable and clear by nature; for the two are not the same. Hence we must start thus with things which are less clear by nature, but clearer to us, and move on to things which are by nature clearer and more knowable. The things which

190 For the relation between Book 1 of the *Physics* and the *Posterior Analytics*, see Horstschäfer, *'Über Prinzipien'*, 13–18.

191 Arist., *Phys.* I 1, 184a10–184b14: Ἐπειδὴ τὸ εἰδέναι καὶ τὸ ἐπίστασθαι συμβαίνει περὶ πάσας τὰς μεθόδους, ὧν εἰσὶν ἀρχαὶ ἢ αἴτια ἢ στοιχεῖα, ἐκ τοῦ ταῦτα γνωρίζειν (τότε γὰρ οἰόμεθα γιγνώσκειν ἕκαστον, ὅταν τὰ αἴτια γνωρίσωμεν τὰ πρῶτα καὶ τὰς ἀρχὰς τὰς πρώτας καὶ μέχρι τῶν στοιχείων), δῆλον ὅτι καὶ τῆς περὶ φύσεως ἐπιστήμης πειρατέον διορίσασθαι πρῶτον τὰ περὶ τὰς ἀρχάς. πέφυκε δὲ ἐκ τῶν γνωριμωτέρων ἡμῖν ἡ ὁδὸς καὶ σαφεστέρων ἐπὶ τὰ σαφέστερα τῇ φύσει καὶ γνωριμώτερα· οὐ γὰρ ταὐτὰ ἡμῖν τε γνώριμα καὶ ἁπλῶς. διόπερ ἀνάγκη τὸν τρόπον τοῦτον προάγειν ἐκ τῶν ἀσαφεστέρων μὲν τῇ φύσει ἡμῖν δὲ σαφεστέρων ἐπὶ τὰ σαφέστερα τῇ φύσει καὶ γνωριμώτερα. ἔστι δ' ἡμῖν τὸ πρῶτον δῆλα καὶ σαφῆ τὰ συγκεχυμένα μᾶλλον· ὕστερον δ' ἐκ τούτων γίγνεται γνώριμα τὰ στοιχεῖα καὶ αἱ ἀρχαὶ διαιροῦσι ταῦτα. The English translation is adapted from Charlton, *Aristotle. Physics. Books I and II*, 1.

> are in the first instance clear and plain to us are rather those which are compounded. It is only later, through an analysis of these, that we come to know elements and principles.

The second part of the treatise (§§17–28), which sets out the "introductory science", combines questions of natural philosophy with logical definitions. This combination, which becomes standard for the Neo-Platonic commentators of Aristotelian texts, is rather unusual for the previous, so-called Middle Platonic period of philosophy, which is characterised by the intention to set apart not only Aristotelian logic and Platonic cosmology, but also the teachings of the two great philosophers in general. E.g., Atticus composed a discourse addressed against "those who interpret Plato through Aristotle"[192]. Although the author of *PM* refers to Atticus as one of the authoritative interpreters of Platonic texts, he nevertheless does not share the critical bias of his predecessor. Instead, he integrates elements of Aristotle's logic and natural philosophy into his argument, not as something that potentially may contradict Plato's views, but as the "introductory science", a sort of propaedeutic with an instrumental role.

Such an attitude to Aristotelian logic as an "instrument" (an *Organon*) that leads to a better understanding of the Platonic dialogues appears already in the "Handbook of Platonism" (*Didaskalikos*) attributed to Alcinous and dated to the third century AD[193]. It became characteristic of the Alexandrian pedagogical system, especially after Ammonius, son of Hermeias. Together with the author of the *Didaskalikos* and approximately in the same period, Porphyry was eager to bring the two great philosophers into an agreement, and later Platonists (starting with his student Iamblichus) were greatly indebted to his writings[194]. *PM* reflects the philosophical position of Porphyry, who made his name both as a commentator on Platonic dialogues and as an interpreter of the Aristotelian works. This characteristic serves as another argument for ascribing the original Greek version of *PM* to Plotinus' disciple.

By "employing the initial type of the demonstrative science" (§17), the treatise suggest to "start moving from the introductory argument and ascend to those things that are properly and truly called principles" (§20). In so doing, the author turns to the four elements, or "bodies" (fire, air, water, and earth), associated with certain qualities (§§21–23). The question of where these bodies and qualities are set brings the argument to the idea of Matter as "one principle of everything" (§24). However,

192 Eusebius of Caesarea refers to this work of Atticus in *Preparatio Evangelica* XI.1.2: Πρὸς τοὺς διὰ τῶν Ἀριστοτέλους τὰ Πλάτωνος ὑπισχνουμένους (II 6.19 ff Mras = Fr. 1 des Places). George Karamanolis has agrued that the quoted words should be understood not as a title, but rather the contents of Atticus' work: Karamanolis, *Plato and Aristotle in Agreement?*, 151–152.

193 Cf. particularly ch. 5–6 of this work. See Dillon, *Alcinous*, 8–13.

194 Cf. Karamanolis, "Why did Porphyry write Aristotelian commentaries?"

the ordered state of Matter makes it apparent that there is Intellect, which brought forth the order and beauty of the material world.

In §26, the author sums up the arguments on the role of God (the Demiurge) in the following way:

> But pleasant order (τάξις) and beauty do not exist without harmony (ܠܚܡܘܬܐ = ἁρμονία). And also harmony does not exist without proportion (ܦܘܫܚܐ = ἀναλογία?). And proportion does not exist without reason (ܡܠܬܐ = λόγος). And such reason does not exist without foresight and foreknowledge (ܡܩܕܡܘܬ ܚܙܝܬܐ ܘܡܩܕܡܘܬ ܝܕܥܬܐ = ἡ πρόνοια καὶ ἡ πρόγνωσις), while the latter do not exist without intellect (ܗܘܢܐ = νοῦς). Thus, when intellect sets in motion through its actions, it imprints, adjusts, arranges, and sets in order species, qualities, and shapes.

Thus, the series of syllogisms based on the Aristotelian logic brings the author to the idea of the Maker who created all existing things with foresight. A similar summary of Plato's views on the generation of the world appears in Atticus' treatise mentioned above, *Against those who interpret Plato through Aristotle*. Eusebius of Caesarea quotes a large portion from this work as a proof of the doctrine of God's providence (πρόνοια)[195]:

> First of all, when Plato was looking into the question of the generation of the cosmos, he also had it in mind that this great and beneficial doctrine of providence needed thorough investigation. He realised that there was no need to posit an agent of creation or preservation for something that did not come into being in good order; so, to make sure he did not deprive the cosmos of providence, he did away with the idea that it was ungenerated.

The passage preserved by Eusebius presents allegedly a traditional doctrine, which the author of *PM* could have found not only by Atticus, whom he explicitly quotes in Part 5, but also by various other Platonists[196]. By turning to this doctrine at the end of the introductory part, the author lays the groundwork for the Platonist concept of three First Principles – God, Matter, and Ideas, – which he articulates at the end of

---

195 Eusebius, *Praeparatio Evangelica* XV.6.2: Πρῶτον δὴ περὶ γενέσεως κόσμου σκοπῶν καὶ τὸ τῆς προνοίας τὸ μέγα τοῦτο καὶ πολυωφελὲς δόγμα πάντα ζητεῖν ἀναγκαῖον ἡγούμενος καὶ λογισάμενος, ὅτι τῷ μὴ γενομένῳ οὔτε τινὸς ποιητοῦ οὔτε τινὸς κηδεμόνος πρὸς τὸ γενέσθαι καλῶς χρεία, ἵνα μὴ ἀποστερήσῃ τὸν κόσμον τῆς προνοίας ἀφεῖλε τὸ ἀγένητον αὐτοῦ. (359.7ff Mras & des Places = Fr. 4 des Places). The English translation is adapted from Boys-Stones, *Platonist Philosophy 80 BC to AD 250*, 202.

196 See Baltes, *Die Weltentstehung*, vol. 1, 51–53. Cf. Koch, *Pronoia und Paideusis*.

the next part (§39). However, before coming to this concept, the author finds it necessary to define what a First Principle is and in what sense Matter may be considered a principle.

2.4 Definition of First Principles and Matter (Parts 3 and 4, §§29–67)

Parts 3 and 4 of the treatise may also be characterised as introductory, for they aim at defining the First Principles, among which Matter appears as a category in its own right. In these parts, the author of the treatise shows himself to be a Platonist polemicising both against the Aristotelian concept of First Principles and against the views of the Stoics and Epicureans[197].

In §§29–34, the author suggests the following definition of a principle: it must be simple, unqualified, eternal, and imperishable. The last two categories could have caused potential discussion with Christian philosophers, who of course were eager to stress that only God is eternal, so that only God can generally be called the First Principle of all existing things, while this category could not be transmitted to other things, like Matter or Platonic Forms, which for Christian interpreters could not be considered eternal in the same sense as God[198]. It is evident, however, that this discussion is not present in *PM*, whose author, while arguing against his opponents, does not have in mind the Christian point of view.

His critique is directed against those thinkers who assume that the four elements (fire, earth, water, and air) are "the First Principles from which existing things come to be" (§35). The author of *PM* rejects this assumption with the argument that something that comes to be cannot be a principle, thus polemicising against the "natural philosophers", whose views he outlined in the doxographical part at the beginning of the treatise.

The same argument, which we find in §§29–35, appears in a compressed form in the doxography of Aetius preserved in Ps.-Plutarch's *Placita Philosophorum*[199]:

---

197 For an overview of various concepts of First Principles, see Boys-Stones, *Platonist Philosophy 80 BC to AD 250*, 83–88.

198 Cf. Karamanolis, *The Philosophy of Early Christianity*, 60–116.

199 Ps.-Plutarch, *Placita Philosophorum* I.1.2: Τίνι διαφέρει ἀρχὴ καὶ στοιχεῖα. Οἱ μὲν οὖν περὶ Ἀριστοτέλην καὶ Πλάτωνα διαφέρειν ἡγοῦνται ἀρχὴν καὶ στοιχεῖα. Θαλῆς δὲ ὁ Μιλήσιος ταὐτὸν νομίζει ἀρχὴν καὶ στοιχεῖα. πλεῖστον δὲ ὅσον διαφέρει ἀλλήλων· τὰ μὲν γὰρ στοιχεῖά ἐστι σύνθετα· τὰς δὲ ἀρχάς φαμεν εἶναι οὔτε συνθέτους οὔτε ἀποτελέσματα· οἷον στοιχεῖα μὲν καλοῦμεν γῆν ὕδωρ ἀέρα πῦρ, ἀρχὰς δὲ λέγομεν διὰ τοῦτο, ὅτι οὐκ ἔχει τι πρότερον ἐξ οὗ γεννᾶται, ἐπεὶ οὐκ ἔσται ἀρχὴ τοῦτο, ἀλλὰ ἐκεῖνο ἐξ οὗ γεγένηται. τῆς δὲ γῆς καὶ τοῦ ὕδατός ἐστί τινα πρότερα ἐξ ὧν γέγονεν, ἡ ὕλη ἄμορφος οὖσα καὶ ἀειδής, καὶ τὸ εἶδος ὃ καλοῦμεν ἐντελέχειαν, καὶ ἡ στέρησις. ἁμαρτάνει οὖν ὁ Θαλῆς στοιχεῖον καὶ ἀρχὴν λέγων τὸ ὕδωρ (275a–276a Diels). The English translation is adapted with some modifications from Boys-Stones, *Platonist Philosophy 80 BC to AD 250*, 92.

> How a principle differs from an element:
> Followers of Aristotle and Plato think that a principle is different from an element, but Thales of Miletus thinks that the same thing is a principle and an element. The greatest difference between them: elements are compounds, but we say that principles are neither compounds nor products. So, for example, we call earth, water, air, fire "elements"; but we call something a "principle" because there is nothing prior to it, out of which it is generated (if there were, it is not this thing that would be the principle, but that from which it had been generated). But there are things prior to earth and water, from which they arise: shapeless and formless matter, the form (which we call "completion"), and privation. So, Thales is wrong when he says that water is element and principle.

In Aetius (Ps.-Plutarch) we find the same line of argumentation as in *PM*, whose author thus turns out to be a follower of both Aristotle and Plato in criticizing the ideas of pre-Socratics. "Some people before Plato" (§36) stated that there were pairs of First Principles: e.g., hot and cold, love and strife, one and many. This concept becomes the next object of criticism. The opponents whom the author has in mind are apparently the Pythagoreans, about whom Simplicius writes in his commentary on Aristotle's *Physics*[200]:

> The Pythagoreans posited the contraries as secondary and elementary principles not only for physical things, but simply for all that comes after the One, which they asserted to be the principle of all things, and they subordinated (to the contraries) the two coordinated series, which are no longer properly principles.

In the next paragraphs (§§36–37), the author turns to the concept of two First Principles, which are not just opposite but related to each other as an active and a passive principle. This is the idea which Diogenes Laertius ascribes to the Stoics[201]:

200 Simplicius, *In Arist. Phys.* I 5, 188a19: οἱ Πυθαγόρειοι δὲ οὐ τῶν φυσικῶν μόνων ἀλλὰ καὶ πάντων ἁπλῶς μετὰ τὸ ἕν, ὃ πάντων ἀρχὴν ἔλεγον, ἀρχὰς δευτέρας καὶ στοιχειώδεις τὰ ἐναντία ἐτίθεσαν, αἷς καὶ τὰς δύο συστοιχίας ὑπέταττον οὐκέτι κυρίως ἀρχαῖς οὔσαις (181.7–10 Diels). The English translation is adapted from Baltussen et al., *Simplicius. On Aristotle Physics 1.5–9*, 18.

201 Diogenes Laertius VII.134: Δοκεῖ δ' αὐτοῖς ἀρχὰς εἶναι τῶν ὅλων δύο, τὸ ποιοῦν καὶ τὸ πάσχον. τὸ μὲν οὖν πάσχον εἶναι τὴν ἄποιον οὐσίαν, τὴν ὕλην, τὸ δὲ ποιοῦν τὸν ἐν αὐτῇ λόγον τὸν θεόν· τοῦτον γὰρ ἀΐδιον ὄντα διὰ πάσης αὐτῆς δημιουργεῖν ἕκαστα. ⟨...⟩ διαφέρειν δέ φασιν ἀρχὰς καὶ στοιχεῖα· τὰς μὲν γὰρ εἶναι ἀγενήτους καὶ ἀφθάρτους, τὰ δὲ στοιχεῖα κατὰ τὴν ἐκπύρωσιν φθείρεσθαι. ἀλλὰ καὶ σωμάτα εἶναι τὰς ἀρχὰς καὶ ἀμόρφους, τὰ δὲ μεμορφῶσθαι. (552 Dorandi). The English translation is adapted with some modifications from Hicks, *Diogenes Laertius*, 239. Cf. Gourinat, "The Stoics on Matter and Prime Matter".

> They (i.e. Stoics) suppose that there are two principles of the universe, the active principle and the passive. The passive principle, then, is unqualified substance, i.e. Matter, whereas the active is the reason inherent in this substance, i.e. God. For he is everlasting and is the artificer of each several thing throughout the whole extent of Matter. ⟨…⟩ There is a difference, according to them, between principles and elements; the former being without generation or destruction, whereas the elements are destroyed when all things are resolved into fire. Moreover, the principles are incorporeal and without form, while the elements have been endowed with form.

In accordance with the Stoic philosophy, §38 identifies the active principle with God and the passive one with Matter. The author, however, does not say explicitly that he thus defends the Stoic ideas. Apparently, he considered this concept as Platonic. In fact, Simplicius writes that the doctrine of the two principles, God and Matter, was attributed to Plato already by Theophrastus, whom he quotes as follows[202]:

> (Plato) wished to make the principles two in number, one underlying (things) as Matter – and this he calls "receptive of all things"; the other being cause and source of movement, and this he attaches to the power of God and of the Good.

The notion of a principle that is a "source of movement" will be discussed by Atticus, who thus considered it possible to speak of four principles (see below). But it is interesting to note that *PM* easily combines various notions, some of which were considered purely Platonic, and others as Stoic. In the next paragraph (§39), the author states that there are in fact three principles of the existing things: God, Matter, and First Ideas. This conclusion breaks somewhat abruptly the whole line of reasoning in Part 3, bringing up the traditional Middle Platonic triad of First Principles[203].

Having thus defined the First Principles, the author shifts the focus of the discussion to Prime Matter as one of them. This topic occupies the central position in the rest of the treatise, first as a theoretical question in Part 4 and further in relation to Plato's dialogue *Timaeus* in Part 5.

Part 4 begins in §40–41 with the definition of the term "matter". Although the idea of Matter was present already in the philosophy of the Pythagoreans and that of

202 Simplicius, *In Arist. Phys.* I 2, 184b15: ἐν ᾗ δύο τὰς ἀρχὰς βούλεται ποιεῖν τὸ μὲν ὑποκείμενον ὡς ὕλην ὃ προσαγορεύει πανδεχές, τὸ δὲ ὡς αἴτιον καὶ κινοῦν ὃ περιάπτει τῇ τοῦ θεοῦ καὶ τῇ τοῦ ἀγαθοῦ δυνάμει. (26.11–13 Diels). The English translation is adapted from Fortenbaugh, *Theophrastus of Eresus*, vol. 1, 423 (Fr. 230).

203 H. Dörrie notes that the notion that God, Ideas, and Matter form the triad of First Principles is "Kernsatz des Mittelplatonismus" (Dörrie, *Platonica Minora*, 342 n. 16). It appears in multiple authors, cf., e.g., Apuleius, *On Plato and his Doctrine* I.5 (92 Moreschini); Ps.-Plutarch, *Placita Philosophorum* I.3 (287–288 Diels); Alcinous, *Didaskalikos*, ch. 9 (20 Whittaker [= 162.29–42 Heinsius]).

Socrates, it received original expression by Plato. Plato, however, never used the word ὕλη, which after Aristotle became a standard term for Matter. Rather, Plato preferred descriptive expressions, like the "mother that is receptive to every being", and the like (§41)[204]. We find a similar reflection on Plato's definition of Matter in the *Didaskalikos*, a work dated to the third century AD[205]:

> Plato calls this a "mould", "all-receiver", "nurse", "mother", and "space", and a substratum "tangible by non-sensation" and graspable (only) "by a bastard reasoning". He declares that it has the characteristic of receiving the whole realm of generation by performing the role of a nurse in sustaining it, and receiving all the forms, while of itself remaining without shape, or quality, or form, but it can be moulded and imprinted with such impressions like a mould and shaped by these, having no shape or quality of its own. For nothing would be readily adapted to (receiving) a variety of imprints and shapes unless it were itself devoid of qualities and without participation in those forms which it must itself receive.

Plato's idea of Matter as being "without shape, quality, and form" (ἄμορφόν ἄποιον καὶ ἀνείδεον) is accepted and analyzed in detail in §§44–49, which thus prove to express the same understanding of Platonic teachings as the *Didaskalikos*.

In §§42–43, the treatise addresses the views of the Stoics, which appear to be closest to those of Plato. However, the author finds it necessary to rule out the Stoic definition of Matter as quality; rather, it may potentially receive qualities. In the course of the argument, the author goes back to the question of the relation between Matter and the four elements and presents Matter as the primary foundation that makes possible the transformation of the four elements into each other (§§50–55).

Here we find the image of the wax and brass that change their form, but maintain their essence, which both Plato and Aristotle employ[206]. A similar summary of Plato's notion of Matter (and a similar example) is found in Alcinous' *Didaskalikos*, which again demonstrates a close parallel to the *PM*[207]:

---

204 Cf. Plato, *Tim.* 49a6 (πάσης γενέσεως ὑποδοχή) and 51a5 (μήτηρ καὶ ὑποδοχή).

205 Alcinous, *Didaskalikos* 8.2: Ταύτην τοίνυν ἐκμαγεῖόν τε καὶ πανδεχὲς καὶ τιθήνην καὶ μητέρα καὶ χώραν ὀνομάζει καὶ ὑποκείμενον ἁπτόν τε μετ' ἀναισθησίας καὶ νόθῳ λογισμῷ ληπτόν· ἰδιότητα δ' ἔχειν τοιαύτην, ὥστε πᾶσαν γένεσιν ὑποδέχεσθαι τιθήνης λόγον ἐπέχουσαν τῷ φέρειν αὐτὰς καὶ ἀναδέχεσθαι μὲν αὐτὴν πάντα τὰ εἴδη, αὐτὴν δὲ καθ' αὑτὴν ἄμορφόν τε ὑπάρχειν καὶ ἄποιον καὶ ἀνείδεον, ἀναματτομένην δὲ τὰ τοιαῦτα καὶ ἐκτυπουμένην καθάπερ ἐκμαγεῖον καὶ σχηματιζομένην ὑπὸ τούτων, μηδὲν ἴδιον σχῆμα ἔχουσαν μηδὲ ποιότητα. Οὐ γὰρ γένοιτ' ἄν τι εὖ παρεσκευασμένον πρὸς ποικίλας ἐκτυπώσεις καὶ μορφάς, εἰ μὴ ἄποιον αὐτὸ ὑπάρχοι καὶ ἀμέτοχον ἐκείνων τῶν εἰδῶν, ἃ δεῖ αὐτὸ δέξασθαι· (19, 21 Whittaker [= 162.29–42 Heinsius]). The English translation is adapted from Dillon, *Alcinous*, 15.

206 Cf. Plato, *Tim.* 50a and Aristotle, *Metaph.* Z 8, 1033a–1033b.

207 Alcinous, *Didaskalikos* 8.3: Προσήκει δὴ καὶ τῇ πανδεχεῖ ὕλῃ, εἰ μέλλει κατὰ πᾶν δέχεσθαι τὰ εἴδη, τῷ μηδεμίαν αὐτῶν φύσιν ἔχειν ὑποκεῖσθαι, ἀλλ' ἄποιόν τε εἶναι καὶ ἀνείδεον πρὸς ὑποδοχὴν

> It is likewise proper to all-receptive Matter, if it is to receive the forms thoroughly, not to have subsistent in itself any of their nature, but to be without quality or form in order to be the receptacle of the forms. And being such, it will be neither body nor incorporeal, but potentially body, just as we understood the bronze to be potentially a statue, because once it has received the form it will be a statue.

Alcinous' observation that, according to Plato, Matter is "neither body nor incorporeal, but potentially body" forms the contents of the rest of Part 4 of the treatise. Its author, who expresses general sympathy with some Stoic views while rejecting others, in this case seems to devote much energy to refuting the Stoic concept that Matter is corporeal[208]. In §63, the author applies the characteristic Stoic terminology, which presented Matter as three-dimensional and "having resistance" (Syr. ܕܠܘܩܒܠܝܘܬ ܛܘܦܣܐ = Gr. ἀντίτυπον). These ideas were rejected by Porphyry's teacher Plotinus, but were later restored and refined by the Neo-Platonists (first of all, by Philoponus)[209].

A series of arguments demonstrates that Matter is not a body. But neither can it be incorporeal, for in this case it may not become a body. Thus, the author reaches the conclusion that Matter is neither body, nor incorporeal, but rather is potentially body.

These characteristics of Matter in §41 derive from Plato's texts and they appear in the Middle Platonists' exposition of Platonic teachings. Compare, for example, Apuleius' summary in his treatise "On Plato and his Doctrine"[210]:

τῶν εἰδῶν· τοιαύτη δ' οὖσα οὔτε σῶμα ἂν εἴη οὔτε ἀσώματον, δυνάμει δὲ σῶμα, ὡς καὶ τὸν χαλκὸν ὑπακούομεν δυνάμει ἀνδριάντα, διότι τὸ εἶδος δεξάμενος ἀνδριὰς ἔσται. (20 Whittaker [= 163.4–10 Heinsius]). The English translation is adapted from Dillon, *Alcinous*, 15–16.

208 Cf. Ps.-Plutarch, *Placita Philosophorum* I.9.7: Οἱ Στωικοὶ σῶμα τὴν ὕλην ἀποφαίνονται – "Stoics declare matter to be body" (308b.14–15 Diels) = Stobaeus, *Eclogae* I.11.5 (I 133.16 Wachsmuth).

209 For the history of the notion of three-dimensionality, see De Haas, *John Philoponus' New Definition of Prime Matter*.

210 Apuleius, *De Platone et eius dogmate* I.5: *Materiam vero improcreabilem incorruptamque commemorat, non ignem neque aquam nec aliud de principiis et absolutis elementis esse, sed ex omnibus primam, figurarum capacem fictionique subiectam, adhuc rudem et figurationis qualitate viduatam deus artifex conformat universa⟨m⟩. Infinitam vero idcirco quod ei sit interminata magnitudo. Nam quod infinitum est indistinctam magnitudinis habet finem atque ideo, cum viduata sit fine, infinibilis rectc videri potest. Sed neque corpoream nec sane incorpoream concedit esse. Ideo autem non putat corpus, quod omne corpus specie qualicumque non careat; sine corpore vero esse non potest dicere, quod nihil incorporale corpus exhibeat, sed vi et ratione sibi eam videri corpoream, atque ideo nec ⟨t⟩actu solo ncque tamen sola opinione cogitationis intellegi. Namque corpora propter insignem evidentiam sui simili iudicio cognosci, sed quae substanciam non habent corporum, ea cogitationibus videri. Unde adulterata opinione ambiguam materiae huius intellegi qualitatem.* (92.15–93.17 Moreschini). The English translation is adapted from Boys-Stones, *Platonist Philosophy 80 BC to AD 250*, 93–94.

> Ungenerated, imperishable matter is, he (i.e. Plato) notes, neither fire, nor water, nor any other of the primary, composite elements. What the creator moulds into a universe is prime matter – matter which underlies everything, which can take on shapes, and is subject to moulding, but which is yet unformed and unqualified by shape. Matter is infinite, because its size is indeterminate. (What is infinite has no definite boundary to its size, and since matter is devoid of boundaries, it rightly seems boundless.) Plato does not allow that matter is corporeal – or, indeed, incorporeal. He does not think it a body because all bodies have some sort of definition; but on the other hand, matter cannot be said truly to lack body, because nothing incorporeal produces body. Plato thinks, then, that it is potentially and theoretically corporeal. As such, it cannot be understood by touch alone, nor by reasoned judgement alone. Bodies, in line with the particular kind of clarity they have, are understood by a corresponding form of judgement; things that do not have corporeal substance are perceived in thought. The ambiguous nature of matter means that it is grasped by "illegitimate reasoning".

The reference to "illegitimate reasoning" is a quotation from *Tim.* 52b2, where Plato notes that Matter may only be understood λογισμῷ νόθῳ, a notion that *PM* stresses several times (see §§41, 70).

At the beginning of Part 5 (§§68–73), the author sums up Plato's view of First Principles and Matter, which he elaborated in the form of coherent logical argument in the previous two parts: According to Plato, Matter is an ungenerated principle, it is unqualified, and body in potentiality. It is receptive to everything and thus may receive qualities, forms, and measures. It is unlimited and has neither beginning nor end.

As the previous exposition demonstrated, *PM* presents the traditional Middle Platonist system of philosophy concerning First Principles and Matter. It is not surprising that in the next section the treatise goes into further details, by quoting several authoritative Middle Platonists, whose arguments the author of the treatise critically analyses.

2.5 Various Interpretations of Plato's *Timaeus* (Part 5, §§73–97)

Part 5 contains quotations from the earlier philosophers, and these quotations turn out to be of great interest for the history of philosophy. They add not only new evidence for the views of Boethus, Plutarch, Atticus, and Severus, but allow a better understanding of the relation between Porphyry, the disciple of Plotinus and the presumed author of the treatise, and the previous generations of Plato's commentators.

2.5.1 Atticus

In §§73–83, we encounter a large quotation from the second century head of the Athenian Academy, Atticus[211]. It derives from his "first treatise on Plato's teachings" (ܡܐܡܪܐ ܩܕܡܝܐ ܕܥܠ ܝܘ̈ܠܦܢܘܗܝ, ܕܦܠܛܘܢ). This reference allows us to assume that the quoted work was a general overview of Platonic philosophy. It is interesting to note that the Syriac text can be interpreted in such a way that the quotation from Atticus begins with words which could be considered a sub-title: ܥܠ ܪ̈ܫܐ ܩܕ̈ܡܝܐ – "On First Principles". Thus, it is possible that the quoted discourse dealt with central issues of Platonic philosophy, presented in several books.

However, no such treatise of Atticus is attested by other authors[212]. Much of what we know about this philosopher derives from Eusebius of Caesarea's *Praeparatio Evangelica*[213], who refers to Atticus' work written against those who try to interpret Plato through Aristotle[214]. This polemical discourse[215] was directed against the Peripatetics, and the quotations from it preserved by Eusebius deal with general questions (like the division of philosophy), but mostly focus on ethical issues. It is possible that the "treatise on Plato's teachings" mentioned in the Syriac text may be the same work of Atticus which was known to Eusebius; however, the latter seems to be mostly focused on the questions of ethics.

It is much more likely that the work in question is Atticus' commentary on the *Timaeus*, which served as a reference work for Proclus in his commentary on this Platonic dialogue. Additional evidence about Atticus' philosophy comes from Simplicius' commentary on the *Categories*, from Philoponus' *De Aeternitate mundi*, and from some other authors who, like Proclus, most likely had no access to the full works of the philosopher, but mainly derived their information from Porphyry[216].

In the preserved sources, the views of Atticus are often associated with those of Plutarch, so that the two philosophers appear like some sort of twins[217], and the same

---

211 For Atticus, see Dillon, *Middle Platonists*, 247–258; Baltes, "Zur Philosophie des Platonikers Attikos"; Moreschini, "Attico: Una figura singolare del medioplatonismo"; Whittaker, "Atticus"; Karamanolis, *Plato and Aristotle in Agreement?*, 150–190.

212 The extant fragments of Atticus' works have been published in Des Places, *Atticus. Fragments.*

213 Fragments 1–9 by Édouard des Places (des Places, *Atticus. Fragments*, 38–69).

214 Πρὸς τοὺς διὰ τῶν Ἀριστοτέλους τὰ Πλάτωνος ὑπισχνουμένους (Eusebius, *Praeparatio Evangelica* XI.1.2, 6.19 Mras & des Places). G. Boys-Stones interprets this title as "Against those who undertake to reconstruct Plato's doctrines through Aristotle", see Boys-Stones, *Platonist Philosophy 80 BC to AD 250*, *passim*.

215 On the possible historical setting of this polemic, see Dillon, *Middle Platonists*, 249–250.

216 Cf. Baltes, *Die Weltentstehung*, vol. 1, 45.

217 An expression of M. Baltes: "...Plutarch und Attikos, die wie ein Zwillingspaar bis in die Spätantike hinein als *die* Vertreter einer zeitlichen Genese der Welt im *Timaios* gelten" (Baltes, *Die Weltentstehung*, vol. 1, 65).

association is characteristic of *PM*. They are usually mentioned together as the partisans to the idea that the world had a temporal beginning. In *Tim.* 28b, Plato referred to the world as "generated" (γενητόν), a notion which was understood in different ways by his commentators. According to various witnesses, Plutarch and Atticus interpreted Plato's text so that the world had a beginning in time[218]. Later Platonists (Taurus, Severus, Plotinus, and Porphyry) revised this view, but kept their interest in the ideas of Plutarch and Atticus, who seem to have maintained some influence upon the next generations of Platonic commentators. See, e.g., the following notion of Proclus in his commentary on the *Timaeus*[219]:

> Followers of Plutarch of Chaeronea and Atticus persistently cite these words (i.e. *Tim.* 28b) as showing that there was a temporal beginning to the genesis of the cosmos; and they say that unordered matter had prior existence, prior to creation, and that the maleficent soul which was responsible for its chaotic movement also had prior existence. For where does movement come from if not soul?

From Proclus' words it becomes clear that both Plutarch and Atticus interpreted Plato's text as asserting that Matter was ungenerated[220] and that its unordered state was due to Soul. The quotation from Atticus attested in *PM* does not dwell on various meanings of the word γενητόν in *Tim.* 28b, but focusses on the same aspect of Plato's cosmology, which Proclus mentions in relation to Plutarch and Atticus, i.e. the relation of Matter to Soul.

In speaking about First Principles according to Platonic philosophy, Atticus states that they are four in number: God, Forms, Matter, and Soul (§73). Another way of presenting this question would be to combine God and Forms under the category "active cause", and Matter and Soul under the category "passive cause", thus reducing the number of principles to two (§74).

A similar outline of Atticus' concept of First Principles appears in Proclus' commentary on the *Timaeus*, who explicitly refers to Porphyry as his source. According to

218 See Baltes, *Die Weltentstehung*, vol. 1, 28–69.

219 Proclus, *In Tim.*: Οἱ μὲν οὖν περὶ Πλούταρχον τὸν Χαιρωνέα καὶ Ἀττικὸν λιπαρῶς ἀντέχονται τούτων τῶν ῥημάτων ὡς τὴν ἀπὸ χρόνου τῷ κόσμῳ γένεσιν αὐτοῖς μαρτυρούντων καὶ δὴ καί φασι προεῖναι μὲν τὴν ἀκόσμητον ὕλην πρὸ τῆς γενέσεως, προεῖναι δὲ καὶ τὴν κακεργέτιν ψυχὴν τὴν τοῦτο κινοῦσαν τὸ πλημμελές· πόθεν γὰρ ἡ κίνησις ἦν ἢ ἀπὸ ψυχῆς; (I 381.26–382.3 Diehl = Fr. 23 des Places). The English translation is adapted from Boys-Stones, *Platonist Philosophy 80 BC to AD 250*, 121.

220 Cf. Proclus, *In Tim.*: περὶ δὲ τῆς ὕλης αὐτῆς ζητήσειεν ἄν τις, εἴτε ἀγένητός ἐστιν ἀπ' αἰτίας, ὥς φασιν οἱ περὶ Πλούταρχον καὶ Ἀττικόν, εἴτε γενητή, καὶ ἐκ ποίας αἰτίας (I 384.2–5 Diehl = Fr. 24 des Places) – "Concerning Matter itself, one might ask whether it is created by no cause, as followers of Plutarch and Atticus say, or whether it is created and [if so] by what cause" (Boys-Stones, *Platonist Philosophy 80 BC to AD 250*, 117).

Proclus, Porphyry not only transmitted Atticus' views, but also critically assessed them[221]:

> So, let's come to grips briefly with Porphyry's pious thoughts on these things. He first attacks those followers of Atticus who champion a plurality of mutually conjoined principles – the Creator and the Forms – and who also say that Matter is moved by an ungenerated Soul, an irrational and maleficent one, moved "without measure, without order"; and that Matter exists before the perceptible chronologically, the irrational before reason, and disorder before order.

Proclus' summary of Porphyry's "pious thoughts" concerning Atticus find close parallels in the quotation from the latter preserved in *PM* §§73–83. Here, Atticus argues against those who do not recognize Soul as one of the First Principles in Platonic philosophy. By so doing, he refers to the famous passage in Plato's *Timaeus*[222]:

> Desiring, then, that all things should be good and, so far as might be, nothing imperfect, the God took over all that is visible – not at rest, but in discordant and unordered motion – and brought it from disorder into order.

Atticus interpreted these words to mean that Matter, which the Demiurge took over, was "neither unmovable nor unqualified" (§75). As, according to Plato ("Plato demonstrates everywhere"), Soul is a source of all movability, it is clear that Soul should be counted among the First Principles (§76). Introducing the category of Soul allows Atticus to maintain the traditional Platonic notion of Matter as unqualified and incorporeal, but potentially and theoretically corporeal (*contra* Stoic notion that it is a body, see above). For it is due to the activity of Soul that Matter receives not only movability, but also qualities, as Atticus further explains in §82.

In §76, he argues: "If one agrees to call both of them 'matter', because Soul and what is properly called Matter were unseparated from each other, then it is clear that

221 Proclus, *In Tim.*: Φέρε δὴ οὖν καὶ ὅσα ὁ φιλόσοφος Πορφύριος ἐν τούτοις ἱεροπρεπῆ νοήματα παραδέδωκε, συντόμως περιλάβωμεν. πρῶτον μὲν οὖν ἀποτείνεται πρὸς τοὺς περὶ Ἀττικὸν πολλὰς ὑποτιθεμένους ἀρχὰς συναπτούσας ἀλλήλοις τὸν δημιουργὸν καὶ τὰς ἰδέας, οἳ καὶ τὴν ὕλην ὑπὸ ἀγενήτου φασὶ κινουμένην ψυχῆς, ἀλόγου δὲ καὶ κακεργέτιδος, πλημμελῶς καὶ ἀτάκτως φέρεσθαι, ⟨καὶ⟩ προϋφιστᾶσι κατὰ χρόνον τὴν μὲν ὕλην τοῦ αἰσθητοῦ, τὴν δὲ ἀλογίαν τοῦ λόγου, τὴν δὲ ἀταξίαν τῆς τάξεως. (I 391.4–12 Diehl = Fr. 26 des Places = Fr. 51 Sodano). The English translation is adapted with some modifications from Boys-Stones, *Platonist Philosophy 80 BC to AD 250*, 121. Cf. Michalewski, "Atticus et le nombre des principes".

222 Plato, *Tim.* 30a2–5: βουληθεὶς γὰρ ὁ θεὸς ἀγαθὰ μὲν πάντα, φλαῦρον δὲ μηδὲν εἶναι κατὰ δύναμιν, οὕτω δὴ πᾶν ὅσον ἦν ὁρατὸν παραλαβὼν οὐχ ἡσυχίαν ἄγον ἀλλὰ κινούμενον πλημμελῶς καὶ ἀτάκτως, εἰς τάξιν αὐτὸ ἤγαγεν ἐκ τῆς ἀταξίας. The English translation is adapted from Cornford, *Plato's Cosmology*, 33.

it is right to speak in this way about three Principles". It becomes clear from Atticus' words that the notion of Soul as one of the principles plays a rather instrumental role, which allows him to maintain the classical Platonic idea of Matter as incorporeal and unqualified without destroying the traditional triad of Principles.

In the paragraphs that follow the quotation (§§84–86), the author of the treatise, i.e. Porphyry, stresses that Plutarch and Atticus agree in stating that Soul exists from eternity and that it is eternally associated with Matter. In §86, the author criticizes the views of the two philosophers. In so doing, he suggests differentiating between the generation of the world and the generation of primary bodies, an argument which John Philoponus and Proclus explicitly ascribe to Porphyry (for details, see 2.6, below). This paragraph of the Syriac text leaves little doubt that its Greek prototype derives from Plotinus' disciple, who not only polemicised against the views of Plutarch and Atticus, but also carefully transmitted them in his writings.

It is worth noting that the view of Plutarch and Atticus that the world had a temporal beginning was naturally close to the Christian authors who were eager to refer to them, arguing against those philosophers who defended the eternity of the world. Thus, the Christian polemicist Aeneas, who lived in Gaza in the late fifth to the beginning of the sixth century, refers to Atticus in his polemical treatise *Theophrastus* in the following way[223]:

> The great Atticus, Plato's lover, expounding his beloved's views, said somewhere that he was seeking the nature and order of the universe, and, being such as it is, it was not ungenerated or eternal, but created by one greater in power and more perfect, the oldest God, the intelligible God: for, being visible, tangible and in every way corporeal it was impossible for it to be ungenerated. How can we not admit that things whose being needs the help of something else to ensure their existence have come into being and are preserved by their maker? He calls Aristotle ridiculous, because he admits on the one hand that this world is visible, tangible and corporeal, but contends strongly that it is ungenerated and indestructible.

223 Aeneus of Gaza, *Theophrastus*: Ὁ δὲ πολὺς Ἀττικός, ὁ τοῦ Πλάτωνος ἐραστής, τὰ τῷ ἐρωμένῳ δοκοῦντα διεξιών, ἔφη που τοῦ κόσμου τὴν φύσιν καὶ τάξιν ἐπιζητεῖν, τοιοῦτον δ' αὐτὸν ὄντα οὐκ ἀγέννητον οὐδ' ἀΐδιον εἶναι, ἀλλ' ὑπὸ τοῦ μείζονος τὴν δύναμιν καὶ τελειοτέρου, Θεοῦ τοῦ πρεσβυτάτου καὶ νοητοῦ γεγονέναι· ὁρατὸν γὰρ ὄντα καὶ ἁπτὸν καὶ πάντη σωματοειδῆ, ἀμήχανον ἦν ἀγένητον εἶναι· ὧν γὰρ ἡ οὐσία βοηθείας δεῖται τῆς παρ' ἑτέρου πρὸς τὸ εἶναι. Πῶς ταῦτα μὴ ὁμολογοῦμεν γεγονέναι τε καὶ ὑπὸ τοῦ ποιήσαντος διασῴζεσθαι; Τὸν δὲ Ἀριστοτέλη καὶ γελοῖον ἀποκαλεῖ, ὁμολογοῦντα μὲν τόδε τὸ πᾶν ὁρατὸν εἶναι καὶ ἁπτὸν καὶ σωματοειδές, ἀγένητον δὲ καὶ ἄφθαρτον εἶναι φιλονεικοῦντα. (46.16–47.2 Colonna). English translation is adapted from Gertz et al., *Aeneas of Gaza. Theophrastus*, 40–41.

The ideas of Atticus (and Plutarch) were praised by the later contemporary of Aeneas, John Philoponus, who shared the same apologetic bias and opposed the views of Atticus to those of Proclus in *Contra Proclum*[224]. It is thus not unlikely that the name of Atticus, who came for the Christian readers to be associated with the idea of the temporal beginning of the world, served as the basis for transmitting *PM* until the time when it became known to the Syriac Hellenophiles of the monastersy of Qenneshre.

2.5.2 Severus

In criticizing the views of Plutarch and Atticus, the author of the treatise turns to the authority of another Platonist, Severus. Not much is known of this philosopher, who was probably active in Athens in the second century[225]. Proclus mentions his name several times in his commentary on the *Timaeus*, and his knowledge of Severus' views most probably derives from Porphyry. The latter became familiar with them during his study with Plotinus, who, according to Porphyry's biography of his teacher, read Severus' works, together with those of Atticus, with his students[226]. In his account, Porphyry puts the name of Severus as the first in the line of the authoritative writings read by Plotinus, and this may be interpreted as a chronological arrangement, which thus sets Severus before Atticus, though we have no further evidence for that.

Severus is credited with a commentary on Plato's *Timaeus*[227] and a treatise *On the Soul*[228]. Proclus puts Severus in line with Plutarch and Atticus[229], however he notes that Severus' interpretation of Plato's account of the generation of the world differed in certain details from the views of Plutarch and Atticus. This notion is corroborated by the witness of *PM*, whose author contrasted Severus' views with the the interpretation of the two other commentators. According to Proclus, Severus maintained the

---

224 Fragments 38a–39 by des Places.
225 For Severus, see Dillon, *Middle Platonists*, 262–264; Goulet, "Severus". The extant fragments from Severus' works were edited by Adriano Gioè: Gioè, "Il medioplatonico Severo". See also Gioè, *Filosofi Medioplatonici*, 377–433.
226 See Porphyry, *Vita Plotini* 14.10–12: Ἐν δὲ ταῖς συνουσίαις ἀνεγινώσκετο μὲν αὐτῷ τὰ ὑπομνήματα, εἴτε Σεβήρου εἴη, εἴτε Κρονίου ἢ Νουμηνίου ἢ Γαίου ἢ Ἀττικοῦ (19.10–12 Henry & Schwyzer).
227 Cf. Proclus, *In Tim.*, I 204.17–18 Diehl = Test. 3 (422 Gioè).
228 Cf. Eusebius, *Preparatio Evangelica* XIII.17.1–7 (239.9–240.16 Mras & des Places) = Fr. 1 (428–429 Gioè).
229 Proclus, *In Tim.*: εἰ παρ' ἑαυτῶν μὲν λυτά ἐστι, κατὰ δὲ τὴν βούλησιν ἄλυτα τοῦ πατρός, ὥσπερ εἰώθασι λέγειν Σευῆρος Ἀττικὸς Πλούταρχος, πρὸς οὓς καὶ οἱ ἀπὸ τοῦ Περιπάτου πολλὰ διὰ πολλῶν ἀντειρήκασι, πόθεν ἔχει τοῦτο τὸ παρ' ἑαυτῶν λυτόν; (III 212.8–9 Diehl = Test. 8 [424 Gioè]) – "If things are dissoluble in themselves, but indissoluble by the will of the father, as Severus, Atticus and Plutarch used to say (to many and various objections from members of the Peripatos), how do they come to be dissoluble in themselves?" (Boys-Stones, *Platonist Philosophy 80 BC to AD 250*, 201).

temporal beginning of the world, though he suggested further points for understanding the Platonic text[230]:

> After this view, we should examine Severus, who says that the cosmos simpliciter is sempiternal, but that this present cosmos, moving in the way that is, was generated. For there are two cycles, as the Eleatic Stranger showed: the one which the universe presently follows, and its opposite. So the cosmos is generated and had a beginning insofar as it is revolving in this cycle; simpliciter, though, it is not generated.

The quotation from Severus that appears in §§88–93 derives most certainly from his lost commentary on the *Timaeus*. Unfortunately, similar to the case of Atticus, the reference to the work of Severus is probably corrupt. It runs as follows: ܒܡܐܡܪܐ ܩܕܡܝܐ ܕܗܠܝܢ ܕܥܒܕ ܦܠܛܘܢ ܠܘܬ ܛܝܡܬܐܘܣ – “in the first treatise concerning those things, which Plato did for Timotheos”. The proper name at the end is a corruption of ܛܝܡܐܘܣ, the form which was probably not familiar to the copyist of ms. DS 27, but which has been preserved correctly in Barhebraeus’ text[231].

The passage quoted in *PM* deals with that part of the Platonic dialogue which runs “from the beginning of the passage on nature until that one which is called ‘generation of Soul’”, i.e. *Tim.* 31c–36d. If we take into account Proclus’ remark[232] that Severus left the introductory part of the dialogue out of his commentary, it seems probable that Severus’ work did not embrace the whole text of the *Timaeus*, and that one part of it (the first book?) was focused on Plato’s cosmology and the World Soul.

In the passage quoted in *PM*, Severus defends an understanding of the Platonic text to the effect that the four natural bodies (i.e. elements) existed prior to the creation of the world and Matter and that they were initially moving in an unordered manner. This last characteristic of the state of the four elements before the introduction of order by the Demiurge turns out to be Severus’ prime concern in the quoted passage. The philosopher suggests several philological observations that aim at clarifying the term ἄτακτος, “unordered”, by Plato. Severus interprets the privative prefix “un-” (ἀ-) not as something contrary but rather “that which is intermediate to the extremes”, i.e. what has not yet acquired the ability which it may possess. Thus, a bunch of plants

---

230 Proclus, *In Tim.*: μετὰ δὲ ταύτην τὴν δόξαν ἐπισκεψώμεθα Σευῆρον, ὅς φησιν ἁπλῶς μὲν ἀίδιον εἶναι τὸν κόσμον, τοῦτον δὲ τὸν νῦν ὄντα καὶ οὕτως κινούμενον γενητόν· ἀνακυκλήσεις γὰρ εἶναι διττάς, ὡς ἔδειξεν ὁ Ἐλεάτης ξένος, τὴν μὲν ἣν νυνὶ περιπορεύεται τὸ πᾶν, τὴν δὲ ἐναντίαν· γενητὸς οὖν ὁ κόσμος καὶ ἀπ’ ἀρχῆς ἤρξατό τινος ὁ ταύτην τὴν ἀνακύκλησιν ἀνακυκλούμενος, ἁπλῶς δὲ οὐ γενητός. (I 289.6–13 Diehl = Test. 6 [423 Gioè]). The English translation is adapted from Boys-Stones, *Platonist Philosophy 80 BC to AD 250*, 201.

231 See Bakoš, *Le candélabre du sanctuaire*, 546.11.

232 Proclus, *In Tim.*, I 224.17 Diehl.

which has not yet been planted in a particular order may be called "unordered" because they have not yet acquired the state of order which will be established after they have been planted (§92). This analogy, according to Severus, serves as an explanation of the state of the four primary bodies.

It turns out that Severus' method was much more philological than philosophical. Plotinus, who, according to §95, agreed with Severus' treatment of this passage, ascribed the same philological tendency to Longinus, another Middle Platonist who *PM* refers to.

2.5.3 Longinus and Boethus

The figure of Longinus[233] appears only briefly in *PM*, but nevertheless, it plays a special role for its author, who calls Longinus (together with Plotinus) his teacher. These references make evident that the Syriac text ultimately derives from Porphyry (see the next section). In *Vita Plotini*, Porphyry writes that, when Plotinus had two of Longinus' treatises read to him, he remarked: "Longinus is a philologist, no philosopher at all"[234]. Similarly, Proclus calls him ὁ κριτικός, who dealt with the Platonic text primarily from the philological perspective[235].

This characteristic which Plotinus attributed to Longinus, according to Porphyry's account, was addressed to a contemporary and to another teacher of the latter. Porphyry maintained a close connection with his former tutor and kept up a correspondence with him[236]. In *Vita Plotini*, Porphyry quotes one of these letters, in which Longinus expresses great interest in Plotinus' writings and asked his former disciple to send him better copies of them[237]. Porphyry further characterizes Longinus as κριτικώτατος[238], which reminds us of Proclus' notion, and quotes a polemical treatise of Longinus against Plotinus and his disciple Amelius that bore the title Περὶ τέλους.

233 For Longinus and his legacy, see Brisson & Patillon, "Longinus Platonicus Philosophus et Philologus"; Männlein-Robert, *Longin, Philologe und Philosoph*.

234 Porphyry, *Vita Plotini* 14.18–20: Ἀναγνωσθέντος δὲ αὐτῷ τοῦ τε «Περὶ ἀρχῶν» Λογγίνου καὶ τοῦ «Φιλαρχαίου», «φιλόλογος μέν», ἔφη, «ὁ Λογγῖνος, φιλόσοφος δὲ οὐδαμῶς» (19–20 Henry & Schwyzer).

235 Proclus, *In Tim.*: Λογγῖνος μὲν ὁ κριτικός, ἐφιστὰς τῇ ῥήσει ταύτῃ φιλολόγως ... (I 14.7–8 Diehl).

236 For the relation of Longinus to his disciple, see Männlein-Robert, *Longin, Philologe und Philosoph*, 90–91.

237 Porphyry, *Vita Plotini* 19 (25–26 Henry & Schwyzer).

238 Porphyry, *Vita Plotini* 20.1–5: Ταῦτα ἐπιπλέον παρατέθεικα τοῦ καθ' ἡμᾶς κριτικωτάτου γενομένου καὶ τὰ τῶν ἄλλων σχεδὸν πάντα τῶν καθ' αὐτὸν διελέγξαντος δεικνὺς οἵα γέγονεν ἡ περὶ Πλωτίνου κρίσις. (26 Henry & Schwyzer) – "I have cited these remarks at length to illustrate how Plotinus was judged by the foremost critic of our time, one who was rigorous in his strictures on almost all his other contemporaries" (Edwards, *Neoplatonic Saints*, 35).

Porphyry's account of Plotinus' teaching practice includes references to Longinus' two treatises, Περὶ ἀρχῶν and Φιλαρχαίος. Proclus' references to Longinus in his commentary on the *Timaeus* make probable that Longinus had composed a commentary of his own on this Platonic dialogue[239], one which was known to Porphyry and in this way was transmitted to Proclus. Thus, while referring to the views of Longinus, the author of *PM* could have had in mind some of the written treatises of this philosopher, or he could have based his words on first-hand knowledge.

Proclus writes that Porphyry was eager not only to quote his teacher, but also to criticize his views, e.g. in the question of the relation of First Forms to Demiurge, in which Longinus' ideas differed from those of his disciple. Proclus notes[240]:

> Among the ancients, some made the Demiurge himself contain the paradigms of wholes, as Plotinus; others thought that the paradigm was not the Demiurge, but something prior to him or posterior to him – prior to him, like Porphyry; posterior to him, like Longinus.

§95 of *PM* not only opposes the positions of Porphyry's teachers, Plotinus and Longinus, but also claims that the latter derived his views from the earlier philosopher Boethus[241], who comes as the last authority in *PM*. Longinus' interest in Boethus' writings was probably the reason Porphyry was well acquainted with them and even found it necessary to compose a treatise Περὶ ψυχῆς πρὸς Βόηθον, which according to the Suda contained five books, i.e. was a voluminous work[242]. It was known to Eusebius, who included large quotations from it in the *Praeparatio Evangelica*[243]. The object of Porphyry's polemic in this treatise might have been the Peripatetic Boethus of Sidon (2nd century BC)[244]. However, it is also possible that both in the treatise *On*

---

239 Cf. Männlein-Robert, *Longin, Philologe und Philosoph*, 36–38.

240 Proclus, *In Tim.*: ἐπεὶ γὰρ τῶν παλαιῶν οἳ μὲν αὐτὸν τὸν δημιουργὸν ἐποίησαν ἔχοντα τὰ παραδείγματα τῶν ὅλων, ὡς Πλωτῖνος, οἳ δὲ οὐκ αὐτόν, ἀλλ' ἤτοι πρὸ αὐτοῦ τὸ παράδειγμα, ἢ μετ' αὐτόν, πρὸ αὐτοῦ μὲν ὡς ὁ Πορφύριος, μετ' αὐτὸν δὲ ὡς ὁ Λογγῖνος (I 322.20–24 Diehl). The English translation is adapted from Boys-Stones, *Platonist Philosophy 80 BC to AD 250*, 178.

241 For various philosophers bearing this name, see Wissowa, *Paulys Real-Encyclopädie*, vol. 5, 601–607; Goulet, *Dictionnaire*, vol. 2, 122–132 (B42–49).

242 Περὶ ψυχῆς πρὸς Βόηθον ε′ (Suda 2098, IV 178.20 Adler). See Dillon, "Boéthos". Wilhelm Kutsch published a fragment from a treatise *On the Soul* preserved in Arabic as a work of Porphyry: Kutsch, "Ein arabisches Bruchstück". It is unlikely that this fragment derives from the Περὶ ψυχῆς πρὸς Βόηθον; rather, it stands in the tradition of the so-called "Theology of Aristotle".

243 Eusebius, *Preparatio Evangelica* XI.27–28; XIV.10.3; XV.10–11; XV.15–16 (II 62.25–65.18, 287.1–7, 373.23–375.4, 380.18–381.7 Mras & des Places = Fr. 242–250 Smith).

244 See Gottschalk, "Boethus' Psychology and the Neoplatonists"; Trabattoni, "Boéthos de Sidon et l'immortalité de l'âme".

the Soul and in the *PM* Porphyry was addressing the Platonic lexicographer bearing the same name, who apparently lived in the second century AD[245].

The preserved fragments from Περὶ ψυχῆς πρὸς Βόηθον focus mainly on the question of the immortality of the soul, considered in connection with Plato's *Phaedo*[246]. The short quotation from Boethus in *PM* does not deal directly with Soul, but the absence of this topic from the quoted passage may be interpreted as a deliberate tactic of Boethus. In §§96–97, namely, Boethus states that Matter must possess some sort of movability of its own. Given that this statement appears after the long quotation from Atticus, who believed that Soul is the source of any movability, including that of Matter, while quoting Boethus Porphyry was purporting to give a counter-argument.

In one of the quotations preserved by Eusebius, Porphyry accuses some unnamed opponents of assigning the properties of physical bodies to Soul[247]:

> But to liken the soul to weight or (any other) simple and unmoved qualities of bodies, is the notion of someone, who willingly or unwillingly, has completely failed to understand the dignity of the soul and has not seen that the body of the animal has become alive because of the presence of the soul.

Though Porphyry's critique as recorded by Eusebius is anonymous, the last paragraphs of *PM* make apparent that it could be Boethus and those who shared his ideas whom Plotinus' disciple could have had in mind[248]. The argument, which becomes the object of criticism by Porphyry, appears in *PM* §96, where Boethus turns to the image of a stone, which may be thrown up, but eventually always falls down. These parallels make it quite likely that the philosopher whom Porphyry addressed in his polemical treatise *On the Soul*, and the one whose words appear at the end of *PM*, was the same person.

245 See Dyck, "Notes"; Auffret, "La doctrine de l'âme".
246 According to Gottschalk ("Boethus' Psychology and the Neoplatonists", 253), it could be Alexander of Aphrodisias, whom Porphyry had in mind.
247 Eusebius, *Preparatio Evangelica* XV.11.2: Τὸ δὲ βαρύτητι ἀπεικάζειν τὴν ψυχὴν ἢ ποιότησι μονοειδέσι καὶ ἀκινήτοις σωματικαῖς, καθ' ἃς ἢ κινεῖται ἢ ποιόν ἐστι τὸ ὑποκείμενον, ἐκπεπτωκότος ἦν τέλεον ἢ ἑκόντος ἢ ἄκοντος τῆς ψυχικῆς ἀξίας καὶ οὐδαμῶς καθεωρακότος ὡς παρουσίᾳ μὲν τῆς ψυχῆς ζωτικὸν γέγονε τὸ τοῦ ζῴου σῶμα (374.9–12 Mras & des Places = Fr. 248 Smith). The English translation is adapted from Gottschalk, "Boethus' Psychology and the Neoplatonists", 250.
248 See Gottschalk, "Boethus' Psychology and the Neoplatonists", 244–245.

2.6 Porphyry as the Author of the Treatise

The last part of the treatise gives us evidence for the historical and educational background of the author of the Greek text that underlies the Syriac translation. The treatise contains references to or quotations from philosophers belonging to the second or early third century Athenian philosophical school. In §95, the author refers to two philosophers of the third century, Longinus and Plotinus, both of whom he calls his teachers. Provided these references are taken literally, we may assume that the author of the Greek work, whose Syriac version we now possess, was Porphyry of Tyre (ca. 232/233–301/305 AD), who studied philosophy first with Longinus in Athens and later with Plotinus in Rome[249].

This attribution is corroborated by the testimony of Barhebraeus. In his epitome, Barhebraeus omitted the long quotations from Atticus, Severus and Boethus (the Maphrian points out that this omission was deliberate, see the passage below), which we find in the extended version of the treatise preserved in ms. DS 27. After these quotations, the author of *PM* simply refers to Plotinus and Longinus as his teachers. Barhebraeus, who had access to the version of the text that lies behind the copy of ms. DS 27, made these references explicit and transformed the expression "my teacher" into "the teacher of Porphyry":

PM §§94–95	Barhebraeus, *Cand.*, *Base* 2[250]
With these (arguments) Severus precisely explained this passage. ⟨...⟩ Our teacher Plotinus also shared this view, when he interpreted the *Timaeus*. Boethus, instead, who was followed by our teacher Longinus, thought that these words of Plato refer to Matter...	Severus, then, whom Plotinus followed, and Boethus, who was followed by Longinus, the teacher of Porphyry, have said a lot concerning the aim of the teachings of Plato. But we omit their (words) in order not to make our exposition too long.

Barhebraeus' version allows an assumption that the text was originally translated into Syriac as a work of Porphyry, whose name later became lost together with the beginning and/or the end of the work. This assumption conflicts, however, with a much earlier testimony of Timothy I. Timothy's reference, dated to 781/782, makes

249 For the state of the art of the study of Porphyry and his legacy, see Karamanolis & Sheppard, *Studies on Porphyry*. See also Hadot, *Porphyre et Victorinus*; Smith, *Porphyry's Place in the Neoplatonic Tradition*; Deuse, *Untersuchungen*; Chase, "Porphyry".

250 Syriac text: ܠܣܐܘܝܪܘܣ ܕܝܢ ܗܘ ܕܠܗ ܢܩܦ ܦܠܘܛܝܢܘܣ ܘܠܒܘܐܬܘܣ ܗܘ ܕܠܗ ܢܩܦ ܠܘܢܓܝܢܘܣ ܡܠܦܢܗ ܕܦܘܪܦܘܪܝܘܣ ܣ̈ܘܓܐܐ ܐܡܝܪ̈ܢ܂ ܥܠ ܢܝܫܐ ܗܘ ܕܝ̈ܘܠܦܢܘܗܝ ܕܦܠܛܘܢ܂ ܘܕܠܐ ܬܐܪܝܟ ܡܠܬܐ ܫܒܩܝܢ ܐܢ̈ܝܢ. (Bakoš, *Le candélabre du sanctuaire*, 547.3–4 = Çiçek, *Mnorath Kudshe*, 48.35–49.6). The English translation is mine, cf. Gottheil, "A Synopsis of Greek Philosophy", 254.

clear that an abridged version of the treatise which lacked the name of the author already existed by the end of the eighth century, and it was this version which was used as the source text for the copy of Part B of ms. DS 27. Barhebraeus' addition of Porphyry's name to those of his teachers may be the result of a marginal gloss, which the Maphrian found in the codex he used, and which he introduced into the main text. However, if this really was the case, it is hard to imagine that a Syriac scholar in the early medieval time had an independent source of information on Porphyry's biography, including the names of his teachers. It is much more likely that Porphyry's name was initially present in the Syriac version of the treatise. Thus, it remains unclear whether it was at some point intentionally omitted by Syriac scribes, or whether it just dropped off by mistake.

Though Porphyry as an author of the polemical tract *Contra Christianos* may have been known to some learned Syrians as an opponent to Christianity[251], his name was primarily associated with the famous *Introduction to Aristotle's Categories*, which became a standard schoolbook for the study of logic and was transmitted as part of Aristotle's *Organon*[252]. The ninth century ms. Vat. Syr. 158 has preserved for us a collection of logical works that most likely reflect the curriculum at the monastery of Qenneshre[253]. It begins with Athanasius of Balad's Syriac version of Porphyry's *Isagoge*, which is prefaced by a short treatise with the title: "A history that explains for what reason Porphyry has written this *Isagoge*, which follows below, to Chrysaorius, and how it was written"[254]. A marginal note (written by the same hand) informs us that "originally, this Porphyry was a believer (i.e. a Christan), but finally perverted to paganism"[255]. Further commentaries on the "History" appear later on in the codex[256]. They contain not only notes on the life of Porphyry, but also an excursus into the question of the origins of the four mathematical sciences. This excursus has been

251 See Becker, *Porphyrios. Contra Christianos*. Cf. Altheim & Stiehl, "New Fragments of Greek Philosophers".

252 Two Syriac translation of the *Isagoge* have come down to us. The early anonymous translation: Brock, "The Earliest Syriac Translation of Porphyry's Eisagoge". Partial edition of the version of Athanasius of Balad: Freimann, *Die Isagoge des Porphyrius*. The full edition of the Athanasius' version was prepared by the present author for the database HUNAYNNET, <https://hunaynnet.oeaw.ac.at/>, assessed on 01.10.20. For the Syriac versions of *Isagoge*, see Brock, "Some Notes on the Syriac Translations of Porphyry's Eisagoge"; Hugonnard-Roche, "Les traductions syriaques de l'*Isagoge*"; Hugonnard-Roche, "Porphyre de Tyr, Isagogè: Traduction syriaque".

253 For the codex, see Assemanus & Assemanus, *Bibliothecae Apostolicae Vaticanae codicum manuscriptorum catalogus*, I/3, 304–307.

254 Ms. Vat. Syr. 158, fol. 1v: ܬܫܥܝܬܐ ܕܡܘܕܥܐ ܕܡܛܠ ܐܝܕܐ ܥܠܬܐ ܟܬܒ ܦܘܪܦܘܪܝܘܣ ܐܝܣܓܘܓܐ ܠܗ ܠܗ ܗܕܐ ܕܡܢ ܠܬܚܬ ܠܘܬ ܟܪܘܣܐܘܪܝܘܣ ܘܐܝܟܢܐ ܐܬܟܬܒܬ.

255 Ms. Vat. Syr. 158, fol. 1v, right margin: ܗܘ ܦܘܪܦܘܪܝܘܣ ܡܗܝܡܢܐ ܗܘܐ ܡܢ ܩܕܝܡ. ܠܚܪܬܐ ܐܬܚܢܦ.

256 Ms. Vat. Syr. 158, fols. 129r–131r. The Syriac text of the scholia was partially edited with a German translation in Baumstark, *Aristoteles bei den Syrern*, ܝܒ [12] – ܝܗ [15] (Syriac); 177–181 (German).

transmitted as a separate treatise in a number of Syriac manuscripts, providing Syrian readers with a short introduction in the quadrivium[257]. The Syriac scholia to the *Isagoge* serve as evidence of the role of this text in Syriac education, and present its author as an authority, not only in logic, but also in the history of sciences.

Porphyry's lost work *Philosophos historia* must also have been known to Syrian scholars, as it left traces in Theodore Bar Koni's *Book of Scholia*[258]. The parables that were included by Porphyry in the *Life of Pythagoras*, the only extant part of his *Philosophos historia*, were transmitted in Syriac in various forms as part of the corpus of sayings of Pythagoras[259].

The tenth-century Baghdad bookseller Ibn al-Nadim wrote in his *Catalogue* (*Fihrist*) that he was aware of a number of translations of Porphyry's works into Syriac[260]. Thus, he reported that he had seen a Syriac version of the fourth part of Porphyry's *Book of Histories of the Philosophers* (i.e. of his *Philosophos historia*), which was probably devoted to the life and teachings of Plato[261]. Additionally, Ibn al-Nadim testifies to the existence of the Syriac version of Porphyry's otherwise unknown *Book of the Elements* that contained only one part[262]. Thus, the name and the writings of Porphyry must have been familiar to the learned Syrians not only due to the famous *Isagoge*, but also due to his treatises on the history of philosophy and on physics.

This evidence makes it rather unlikely that Porphyry's name was intentionally deleted from the title of the treatise due to a negative attitude towards him. Rather, it must have fallen victim to the loss of the introductory part of the text and of its title that had taken place already at the initial stage of transmission. This fact is attested as early as the end of the eighth century by the letter of Timothy I, who clearly stated in his description that in his time the treatise had no title, so that he had to quote it by the opening lines, which remained the same in ms. DS 27.

In establishing the lost title of the Greek work which underlines *PM*, we are confined to the internal witness of the Syriac version. A possible hint appears in §17, where the author thus defines the contents of his work:

257 Mss. Berlin, Petermann I 9 (Sachau 88), fols. 180r–v; Cambridge Add. 2812, fol. 107r; Alqosh, Chaldean Diocese, Syr. 61, fol. 242r–v. See Sachau, *Verzeichniss der syrischen Handschriften*, vol. 1, 331; Wright, *A Catalogue of the Syriac Manuscripts Preserved in the Library of the University of Cambridge*, vol. 1, 640–641; Arzhanov & Kessel, "A Previously Unknown Philosophical Manuscript from Alqosh".

258 Cf. Baumstark, "Griechische Philosophen und ihre Lehren".

259 For the corpus of sayings of Pythagoras and the Pythagoreans in Syriac, see Arzhanov, *Syriac Sayings of Greek Philosophers*, 84–90.

260 Flügel, *Kitâb al-Fihrist*, vol. 1, 253 (فرفوريوس). The account of Ibn al-Nadim was borrowed by al-Qifṭi in the *Ta'rīḫ al-Ḥukamā'* (Lippert, *Ibn al-Qifṭī*, 256–257) and by Barhebraeus in the *Ta'rīḫ muḫtaṣar al-duwal* (Ṣāliḥānī, *Abū l-Faraǧ Ġrīġūriyūs Ibn al-'Ibrī*, 132–133).

261 كتاب اخبار الفلاسفة ورأيت منه المكالة الرابعة سريانى – "The Book of the Histories of the Philosophers. I have seen its fourth part in Syriac".

262 كتاب الاسطقسات مقالة سريانى – "The Book of the Elements. One Part. In Syriac".

> As our discourse is about principles, prior to which nothing may be thought, we employ the initial type of the demonstrative science.

Based on this passage, we may assume that the original title of Porphyry's work may have been Περὶ ἀρχῶν. The lexicon of Suda provides us with a notion that Porphyry indeed composed a treatise with this title and that it included two books or parts[263]. Proclus thus refers to this work in his *Platonic Theology*[264]:

> But, after him (i.e. Plotinus), Porphyry in his treatise *On Principles*, demonstrates by many and beautiful arguments that Intellect is eternal, but that, at the same time, it contains in itself ⟨something prior to the eternal⟩, through which it is conjoined with the One (for the One is above all eternity). For the eternal has a second, or rather third order in it (i.e. in Intellect).

This passage presents Porphyry as a true disciple of Plotinus and contains a summary of the text, which may also reflect Proclus' interpretation of Porphyry's thought[265]. This witness does not match the contents of the piece preserved in ms. DS 27. This might be explained by an assumption that the Syriac version of *PM* is only a fragment of a larger treatise that originally contained two books. However, another assumption seems to be more likely, namely, that *PM* goes back to a discourse which was focused not on the Plotinus' teachings primarily, but rather on the Platonic notion of Matter, which forms the larger part of the content of *PM*.

It is interesting to note that the next title listed by the Suda in the list of Porphyry's writings is the treatise Περὶ ὕλης, which contained six books or parts[266]. An extensive quotation from this work appears in Simplicius' commentary on Aristotle's *Physics*[267]:

---

263 Περὶ ἀρχῶν β′ (Suda 2098, IV 178.19 Adler). Cf. Dörrie & Baltes, *Der Platonismus im 2. und 3. Jahrhundert nach Christus: Bausteine 73–100*, 282–285.

264 Proclus, *Theol. Plat.* I.11: Πορφύριος δὲ αὖ μετὰ τοῦτον ἐν τῇ Περὶ ἀρχῶν πραγματείᾳ τὸν νοῦν εἶναι μὲν αἰώνιον ἐν πολλοῖς καὶ καλοῖς ἀποδείκνυσι λόγοις, ἔχειν δὲ ὅμως ἐν ἑαυτῷ καὶ προαιώνιόν ⟨τι· καὶ τὸ μὲν προαιώνιον⟩ τοῦ νοῦ τῷ ἑνὶ συνάπτειν (ἐκεῖνο γὰρ ἦν ἐπέκεινα παντὸς αἰῶνος) τὸ δὲ αἰώνιον δευτέραν ἔχειν, μᾶλλον δὲ τρίτην ἐν ἐκείνῳ τάξιν· (51.4–11 Saffrey & Westerink = Fr. 232 Smith). For the English translation, cf. Taylor, *Proclus' Theology of Plato*, 79.

265 Cf. Smith, *Porphyry's Place in the Neoplatonic Tradition*, 112, n. 2; Rist, "Mysticism and Transcendence in Later Neoplatonism". Hadot found parallels to the summary of Porphyry's views in an anonymous commentary on the *Parmenides* (ed. in Kroll, "Ein neuplatonischer Parmenidescommentar"), which he attributed to Porphyry: Hadot, "Fragments d'un commentaire de Porphyre sur le Parmenide".

266 Περὶ ὕλης ς′ (Suda 2098, IV 178.19 Adler).

267 Simplicius, *In Arist. Phys.* I 7, 191a7: καὶ ταῦτα δὲ ὁ Πορφύριος ἐν τῷ δευτέρῳ Περὶ ὕλης τὰ τοῦ Μοδεράτου παρατιθέμενος γέγραφεν ὅτι "βουληθεὶς ὁ ἑνιαῖος λόγος, ὥς πού φησιν ὁ Πλάτων, τὴν γένεσιν ἀφ' ἑαυτοῦ τῶν ὄντων συστήσασθαι, κατὰ στέρησιν αὑτοῦ ἐχώρησε τὴν ποσότητα πάντων αὐτὴν στερήσας τῶν αὑτοῦ λόγων καὶ εἰδῶν. τοῦτο δὲ ποσότητα ἐκάλεσεν ἄμορφον καὶ ἀδιαίρετον

> Porphyry, who sets out these views of Moderatus in the second book of *On Matter*, has written that "As Plato says somewhere, the unified *logos*, wanting to bring about the coming to be of things from itself, found room for the quantity of all things by privation of itself, depriving quantity of its own *logoi* and forms. He called this thing formless, indivisible, and shapeless quantity, but (said it is) receptive of form, shape, division, quality, everything of this kind. He says that Plato seems to have predicated many words of this quantity, 'omnirecipient' and 'formless' and 'invisible', and said it shares in a most perplexing way in the intelligible and is barely graspable by a bastard reasoning and all sorts of things like this. He says that this quantity and this form, which is understood by privation of the unified logos which embraces all the *logoi* of existing things in itself, are paradigms of the matter of bodies, which itself, he said, was also called quantity by the Pythagoreans and Plato, not quantity as form but quantity which is derived from privation and loosening and extending and spreading out (and exists) because of deviation from being, for which reason matter is also thought to be evil since it flees away from the good. And it is apprehended by it (the good) and is not allowed to escape determination, its extension receiving the *logos* of eidetic magnitude and being determined by it, its spreading-out being given form by numerical discrimination."

This exposition taken from Porphyry's Περὶ ὕλης brings forth a number of ideas that Porphyry, like most other Platonists, would express while speaking about the Platonic notion of Matter. *PM* contains the same characteristics of Matter based on the *Timaeus*, which are listed in the quotation above. This quotation, however, does not provide us with much information about Porphyry's own opinion, for it informs us about the views of Moderatus of Gades, who stated that Plato's "receptacle", i.e. Matter, was bad and was a source of evil in the world. This idea was taken as early as Aristotle, who considered Plato's receptacle maleficent[268], and was later adopted by

καὶ ἀσχημάτιστον, ἐπιδεχομένην μέντοι μορφὴν σχῆμα διαίρεσιν ποιότητα πᾶν τὸ τοιοῦτον. ἐπὶ ταύτης ἔοικε, φησί, τῆς ποσότητος ὁ Πλάτων τὰ πλείω ὀνόματα κατηγορῆσαι "πανδεχῆ" καὶ ἀνείδεον λέγων καὶ "ἀόρατον" καὶ "ἀπορώτατα τοῦ νοητοῦ μετειληφέναι" αὐτὴν καὶ "λογισμῷ νόθῳ μόλις ληπτήν" καὶ πᾶν τὸ τούτοις ἐμφερές. αὕτη δὲ ἡ ποσότης, φησί, καὶ τοῦτο τὸ εἶδος τὸ κατὰ στέρησιν τοῦ ἑνιαίου λόγου νοούμενον τοῦ πάντας τοὺς λόγους τῶν ὄντων ἐν ἑαυτῷ περιειληφότος παραδείγματά ἐστι τῆς τῶν σωμάτων ὕλης, ἣν καὶ αὐτὴν ποσὸν καὶ τοὺς Πυθαγορείους καὶ τὸν Πλάτωνα καλεῖν ἔλεγεν, οὐ τὸ ὡς εἶδος ποσόν, ἀλλὰ τὸ κατὰ στέρησιν καὶ παράλυσιν καὶ ἔκτασιν καὶ διασπασμὸν καὶ διὰ τὴν ἀπὸ τοῦ ὄντος παράλλαξιν, δι ἃ καὶ κακὸν δοκεῖ ἡ ὕλη ὡς τὸ ἀγαθὸν ἀποφεύγουσα. καὶ κατα λαμβάνεται ὑπ' αὐτοῦ καὶ ἐξελθεῖν τῶν ὅρων οὐ συγχωρεῖται, τῆς μὲν ἐκτάσεως τὸν τοῦ εἰδητικοῦ μεγέθους λόγον ἐπιδεχομένης καὶ τούτῳ ὁριζομένης, τοῦ δὲ διασπασμοῦ τῇ ἀριθμητικῇ διακρίσει εἰδοποιουμένου". (231.5–24 Diels = Fr. 236 Smith). The English translation is adapted with some modifications from Baltussen et al., *Simplicius. On Aristotle Physics 1.5–9*, 113.

268 Arist. *Phys.* I 9, 192a15 (κακοποιόν).

Moderatus and a number of Platonists, among others by Porphyry's teacher Plotinus[269]. However, having referred to the views of Moderatus, Porphyry has not explicitly supported them. His interest in them turns out to be rather that of a historian of philosophy than of a promoter of particular views.

The interpretation of Porphyry's philosophy at present faces the fact that much of his written heritage is lost. This is particularly sad in the case of his commentary on Plato's *Timaeus*, which must have been a rather voluminous work[270]. This commentary became a source of knowledge about other philosophers for later generations of scholars. Philoponus points out[271] that Proclus took the greatest part of his commentary on the *Timaeus* from Porphyry's work with the same title[272]. This is particularly apparent in Proclus's analysis of *Tim.* 30a3–6, where he explicitly stated that the whole passage was based on Porphyry's work, which was paraphrased in a concise manner[273]. This part of Proclus' commentary starts with an exposition of the ideas of Plutarch and Atticus on the temporal beginning of the cosmos and ends with a summary of Porphyry's (originally very detailed[274]) refutation of the views of his predecessors. Proclus' summary, which was partly quoted above (see 2.5.1), contains the same arguments, which we find in the concluding, fifth, part of *PM*. But in contrast to Proclus, the preserved Syriac version contains not summaries of the views of earlier philosophers, but direct quotations from their works.

It is not always possible to determine the attitude of Porphyry to the arguments of other philosophers, which he carefully transmitted. Porphyry's method in elaborating philosophical topics apparently included an extensive presentation of the views of other philosophers, among which he was not eager to take part quickly. Instead, he pondered and proved various interpretations, some of which he himself was ready to adopt and some to refute[275]. This method resulted in the active use of doxographical sources, and we find this also in *PM*, which includes a taxonomy of the

269 See O'Brien, "Plotinus on Matter and Evil".

270 Though the full text of the commentary has not come down to us, a large number of quotations from it have been preserved by other late ancient and early medieval authors. They were collected in Sodano, *Porphyrii In Platonis Timaeum Commentariorum Fragmenta*. Additional fragment: 172 Smith.

271 Philoponus, *Contra Proclum* VI.2 (126.10–16 Rabe).

272 Cf. Baltes, *Die Weltentstehung*, vol. 1, ix: "Man kann sagen, dass die Geschichte der Frage nach der Weltentstehung bis zu Proklos hin durch Porphyrios bestimmt ist". David Runia and Michael Share stress that particularly Book 2 of Proclus' commentary is based on Porphyry's work: "By means of his commentary Porphyry placed the interpretation of the *Timaeus* on a new footing and it is only a slight exaggeration to say that Proclus is indebted to it on almost every page" (Runia & Share, *Proclus. Commentary on Plato's Timaeus*, vol. 2, 10).

273 Proclus, *In Tim.*: Φέρε δὴ οὖν καὶ ὅσα ὁ φιλόσοφος Πορφύριος ἐν τούτοις ἱεροπρεπῆ νοήματα παραδέδωκε, συντόμως περιλάβωμεν (I 391.4–6 Diehl).

274 Proclus sums up four chapters (κεφάλαια) of Porphyry's work that were dedicated specifically to the ideas of Plutarch and Atticus (see Proclus, *In Tim.* I 393.14, 393.31, 395.10 Diehl).

275 Cf. Baltes, *Die Weltentstehung*, vol. 1, 163f, 201f.

views of natural philosophers on First Principles in Part 1[276] and a series of quotations from the Middle Platonists in Part 5.

The references to Longinus and to Plotinus at the end of the treatise (§95) reveal the educational background of its author and point clearly to Porphyry, who first studied with Longinus in Athens and later in Rome with Plotinus. The author's training explains also the appearance of the names of Atticus, Severus and Boethus. As we read in Porphyry's *Life of Plotinus*, his teacher used to read the works of Atticus and Severus together with his pupils[277]. Porphyry's interest in Boethus' philosophy, a quotation from whom comes at the end of the Syriac text (§§96–97), was great enough that, according to the Suda, he composed a treatise *On the Soul* addressed to Boethus and comprising five books[278]. Thus, the *PM* preserved in Syriac translation turns out to be a further witness not only to the Middle Platonist commentaries on Plato's *Timaeus*, but also to the role of Porphyry in the transmission of these texts.

The second and third parts of the treatise focused on introductory issues (§§17–39) reveal to us a masterful teacher of logical questions, whom we know from the *Introduction* to Aristotle's *Categories*, the famous *Isagoge* (in §58, we read about "the first genera of categories" that constitute natural bodies: substance, quantity, qualification, etc.). In the second part of *PM* (§§17–28), the author appeares as a Platonist, who expresses Platonic philosophy by means of Aristotle's logic and natural philosophy. The tendency to combine both traditions was characteristic of the Neo-Platonic period, starting with Porphyry, who was interested in both Plato and Aristotle and wrote a book on the agreement between the two philosophers[279].

According to Simplicius, Porphyry believed that it was not the task of a scientist to inquire into the question of the First Principles of natural bodies, for they are already given to him. Thus, neither a geometer nor a doctor search for their respective first principles, but take them for granted. Rather, it is the task of those who "have been elevated above" the science of nature[280]. This statement, if it really reflects Porphyry' view, would corroborate the contents of the Syriac text, where Platonic philosophy stands above Aristotelian, while the latter is treated as an instrument.

---

276 In the tradition of Neopythagoreanism, Porphyry was interested in the figure of Pythagoras. His idea was to present the similarity between Platonic and Pythagorean philosophy. The same idea possibly underlies the final passage of the first, introductory, part of the treatise (§16). There, the author expresses his intention to discuss Pythagoras' views on First Principles, not together with other philosophers, but to deal with both philosophers separately later.

277 See 2.5.2 and 2.5.3, above.

278 See 2.5.3, above.

279 See Karamanolis, *Plato and Aristotle in Agreement?*, 243.

280 Simplicius, *In Arist. Phys.* I 1, 184a10: ὁ δὲ Πορφύριος οὐδὲ φυσικοῦ φησιν εἶναι τὸ ζητεῖν, εἰ εἰσὶν ἀρχαὶ τῶν φυσικῶν, ἀλλὰ τοῦ ἀναβεβηκότος· ὁ γὰρ φυσικὸς ὡς δεδομέναις χρῆται. ἔτι δὲ μᾶλλον φαίη ἂν τὸ τίνες αἱ ἀρχαὶ τοῦ ἀναβεβηκότος εἶναι ζητεῖν. οὐδὲ γὰρ ὁ γεωμέτρης ἢ ὁ ἰατρὸς τὰς ἑαυτοῦ ἀρχὰς ἀποδείκνυσιν, ἀλλ' ὡς οὔσαις καὶ τοιαῖσδε οὔσαις χρῆται. (9.11–15 Diels).

In the discussion on the generation of the world, Porphyry stated that Plato talked about the world as generated (γεννητός) for the sake of exposition (διδασκαλίας χάριν)[281]. This notion makes Porphyry's interpretation of Plato's γεννητός a complex issue which could be understood in various ways by different authors[282]. This question is not explicitly discussed in *PM*, though it plays a decisive role in the interpretation of Prime Matter[283], the issue that stands at the core of the treatise.

Part 4, which deals with the definition of Matter as one of the principles, contains an extensive discussion of the question whether Matter is incorporeal (§§56–67). This portion of the treatise provides more material for the comparison between *PM* and the preserved texts of Porphyry[284]. In his *Sententiae*, Porphyry defines Matter as "incorporeal (because it is other than bodies), lifeless (because it is neither Intellect, nor Soul, nor living by itself), formless, irrational, infinite, impotent"[285]. The same definitions appear in *PM* §§40–67. They do not necessarily point to Porphyry as the author, for they reflect traditional Platonic teachings. However, what makes it very likely that it was Plotinus' disciple who composed the text is the combination of Platonic ideas with Aristotelian methods of expounding them, a tendency which was not apparent before Porphyry.

The exposition of the notion of Prime Matter in *PM* ends with the conclusion that Matter is neither a body, nor incorporeal, but is potentially body, which reflects a standard Middle Platonist interpretation of Plato's texts (see above). In so doing, the author of *PM* suggests a series of arguments as to why Matter is not a body, which in §63 specifically addresses the Stoic understanding of Matter as three-dimensional and having resistance (ἀντιτυπία).

Porphyry's arguments in these paragraphs derive to a large extent from the discourse *On Matter* of his teacher Plotinus (*Enneads* II.4)[286], who vigorously criticized Stoic materialism. Plotinus' exposition of the topic of Matter and his anti-Stoic arguments served as a source for Simplicius, who, in his commentary on Aristotle's

281 Cf. Proclus, *In Tim.* 28bc (I 382.12–383.22 Diehl); Philoponus, *Contra Proclum* XIV.3 (546.5–547.19 Rabe = Fr. 48–50 Sodano). Cf. Baltes, *Die Weltentstehung*, vol. 1, 148–150.

282 For a detailed analysis of Porphyry's views, see Baltes, *Die Weltentstehung*, vol. 1, 136–163. Cf. Verrycken, "Porphyry In Timaeum Fr. XXXVII".

283 Philoponus, *Contra Proclum* VI.2 (126–127 Rabe): Porphyry differentiates between God, who is Father and thus begets the world, and Creator, who takes the pre-existing Matter.

284 For Porphyry's notion of Matter, see Smith, "The Significance of 'Physics' in Porphyry".

285 *Sent.* 20: Τῆς ὕλης τὰ ἴδια κατὰ τοὺς ἀρχαίους τάδε· ἀσώματος — ἑτέρα γὰρ σωμάτων —, ἄζωος — οὔτε γὰρ νοῦς οὔτε ψυχὴ οὐ ζῶν καθ' ἑαυτό —, ἀνείδεος, ἄλογος, ἄπειρος, δύναμος (10–20 Lamberz). See also *Sent.* 42 (53–54 Lamberz), where Porphyry makes a distinction between two kinds of incorporeals. For Porphyry's idea of incorporeals, see Karamanolis, *Plato and Aristotle in Agreement?*, 308–313; Chiaradonna, "Porphyry's views on the immanent incorporeals".

286 Περὶ ὕλης: Plotinus, *Enn.* II.4 (I 184–201 Henry & Schwyzer). Cf. De Haas, *John Philoponus' New Definition of Prime Matter*, 100–112.

Physics, exposed them in a series of logical syllogisms, stating that Matter is not a body. The exposition of Simplicius turns out to be particularly close to the *PM*:

Simplicius, In Arist. Phys.[287]

So you might also syllogise it the following ways: In itself matter has neither magnitude nor shape nor number; but body in itself does have magnitude and shape and number; therefore matter is not body. Matter is not a composite of matter and form; but body is a composite of matter and form.

⟨...⟩

Furthermore, body is composed of genus and differentiae, since it is a three-dimensional substance. However, such a thing is a form, but it is not matter. Furthermore, body is logically opposed to incorporeal qualities, but matter is related in the same way to all things. Furthermore, body is determined by three dimensions, but matter is completely indeterminate.

PM §§56, 57, 62, 63

It follows from this that we should consider whether Matter is embodied or not embodied. I state, namely, that it is not simply embodied, and neither is it unembodied, but rather it is potentially a body and something embodied. For that which is properly called body is composed of matter and quality. Therefore, it is not a body. Further, there is no body which is not qualified. But Matter by its own definition has no quality. Therefore, it is not a body. Further, similarly, every body has limits and boundaries. But Matter by its definition has no limits and boundaries. Therefore, it is not a body.

⟨...⟩

Further, Matter is something simple and not composite. A body is not simple, but composite. Therefore, it is not a body. Further, if Matter were a body, it would have the definition of a body, that is, it would have three dimensions, or it could be divided three-dimensionally, and have resistance. But Matter does not have these, otherwise it too would be quantified and qualified, but all this does not belong to the account of its essence. Therefore, it is not a body.

287 Simplicius, *In Arist. Phys.* I 7, 191a7: ὥστε καὶ συλλογίσαιο ἂν οὕτως· ἡ ὕλη οὔτε μέγεθος ἔχει οὔτε σχῆμα οὔτε ἀριθμὸν καθ’ αὑτήν· τὸ σῶμα μέγεθος ἔχει καὶ σχῆμα καὶ ἀριθμὸν καθ’ αὑτό· ἡ ὕλη ἄρα οὐκ ἔστι σῶμα. ἡ ὕλη οὐκ ἔστι σύνθετος ἐξ ὕλης καὶ εἴδους· τὸ σῶμα σύνθετόν ἐστιν ἐξ ὕλης καὶ εἴδους. ⟨...⟩ ἔτι δὲ τὸ σῶμα ἐκ γένους καὶ διαφορῶν συνέστηκεν· οὐσία γάρ ἐστι τριχῇ διαστατή. τὸ δὲ τοιοῦτον εἶδός ἐστιν, ἀλλ’ οὐχὶ ὕλη. ἔτι δὲ τὸ σῶμα πρὸς τὰς ἀσωμάτους ποιότητας ἀντιδιῄρηται, ἡ δὲ ὕλη ὁμοίως ἔχει πρὸς πάντα. ἔτι δὲ τὸ σῶμα τρισὶν ὥρισται διαστάσεσιν, ἡ δὲ ὕλη παντελῶς ἐστιν ἀόριστος. (229.16–230.14 Diels). The English translation is adapted with some modifications from Baltussen et al., *Simplicius. On Aristotle Physics 1.5–9*, 111–112.

Simplicius points to Plotinus as the source of this series of syllogisms that aim to demonstrate that Prime Matter is not body. A similar logical exposition appears in John Philoponus' *De Aeternitate mundi contra Proclum*[288], and we can thus assume that both authors derived it from the same source, in which Plotinus' treatise *On Matter* had been transformed into a set of logical syllogisms. Porphyry, who was a disciple of Plotinus and who had heard those lectures of his master, which turned into part II.4 of the *Enneads*, would be a likely author of such an exposition of Plotinus' thoughts on Matter. It is thus possible that Simplicius borrowed his syllogisms not from the *Enneads*, but from Porphyry, whose treatise Περὶ ὕλης he quotes immediately after the set of syllogisms about Prime Matter. The quoted passage from Porphyry's Περὶ ὕλης contains the presentation of the views of the Pythagorean Moderatus (see above). Given Porphyry's method of presentation, it is very likely that he has also included the arguments of his teacher Plotinus in his work, which were similar to those found in *PM*, and that this text became Simplicius' source.

A further parallel between the Syriac treatise and Porphyry appears in §86, where the author suggests making a distinction between the constitution of the world and the constitution of bodies. The author of *PM* argues that the category of Matter belongs to the constitution of bodies, while the category of First Principles belongs to the constitution of the world, and that without differentiating between these two things, one may fall into the mistake of misunderstanding the words of Plato as referring to the world and apply them to bodies. In §86, we read a summary of this argument:

> One thing is the constitution of the world, and another is that of the bodies. For the constitution of the world as world has primary bodies as principles, while that of bodies as bodies has matter, form, and shapes.

Proclus makes the same distinction between the constitution of the world and the constitution of the primary bodies in his commentary on *Tim.* 30a, i.e. in that part which presents a summary of Porphyry's ideas (see above)[289]. Proclus' testimony is corroborated by Philoponus. In the *De Aeternitate mundi contra Proclum*, the Alexandrian philosopher has preserved the following two extensive quotations from Porphyry's commentary on the *Timaeus*[290]:

288 Cf. De Haas, *John Philoponus' New Definition of Prime Matter*, 109–112.

289 Proclus, *In Tim.* II [Tim. 30A]: τί δή ποτε οὖν ὑπέθετο τὴν ἀταξίαν; ἢ ἵνα θεωρήσωμεν, ὅπως ἄλλη μὲν ἡ τῶν σωμάτων γένεσις, ἄλλη δὲ ἡ γενομένων αὐτῶν τάξις, ὑποθετέον ὄντα μὲν αὐτά, κινούμενα δὲ ἀτάκτως· αὐτὰ γὰρ τάττειν τὰ σώματα ἀδύνατον (I 394.25–29 Diehl).

290 Philoponus, *Contra Proclum* VI.14: ὅτι δὲ τοῦτό ἐστιν ἀληθές, μάρτυς καὶ αὐτὸς ὁ Πορφύριος· καίτοι γὰρ εἰπὼν γενητὸν λέγεσθαι τὸν κόσμον ὡς σύνθετον ἐξ ὕλης καὶ εἴδους προελθὼν καὶ ἐξηγούμενος τὸ 'παραλαβὼν ὁ θεὸς ὅσον ἦν ὁρατὸν οὐχ ἡσυχίαν ἄγον ἀλλὰ πλημμελῶς καὶ ἀτάκτως κινούμενον' φησὶν ἐπὶ λέξεως ταῦτα 'οὐκ ἔστιν ταὐτὸν κόσμου ποίησις καὶ σώματος ὑπόστασις οὐδὲ

> Porphyry himself is a witness that this is true. Although he has previously stated that the world is said to be generated in that it is composed of matter and form, later, when commenting on the words "the god, taking over all that was visible, not at rest but moving in a discordant and disorderly manner", he, to quote his exact words, writes this:
> "The making of the world and the creation of body are not the same thing, nor are the beginnings of body and of the world the same. For the world to come to be, both bodies and God must exist, for bodies to exist, there must be matter, God, and supervening [form] (one lot so that the matter may become body, and another to give order to the things that have become body). All of these always come into existence at once and not separately over time, but instruction necessarily separates them so as to be able to explain that which comes to be accurately. The beginnings of body are God, who is the begetter, matter, and the shapes that [Plato] will tell us about later, the things from which bodies are composed being begotten of God; those of the world are bodies, which already exist through the agency of God, and God, who gives them order."
> And a bit later:
> "It should be taken as evidence that the framing of body and that of the world are not in Plato's view the same thing and that at this point [the creator] takes over not matter but bodies that have been produced from matter, that he says that what is taken over is visible — and what could visible things be other than bodies? Matter in his view is invisible and formless, being apprehended only with difficulty by [a kind of] spurious reasoning – and that he goes on to show the generation of bodies even though he has [already] shown the framing of the world in this passage. After the generation of the world he returns to the generation of body."

The last sentence, in the first fragment quoted by Philoponus, stresses that primary bodies "already exist through the agency of God" before God "gives them order", the

---

αἱ αὐταὶ ἀρχαὶ σώματός τε καὶ κόσμου, ἀλλ' ἵνα μὲν κόσμος γένηται, δεῖ σώματα εἶναι καὶ θεὸν εἶναι, ἵνα δὲ σώματα, δεῖ ὕλην εἶναι καὶ θεὸν καὶ τὸ ἐπιγινόμενον ἄλλο μέν, ἵνα σωματωθῇ ὕλη, ἄλλο δέ, ἵνα τὰ σωματωθέντα ταχθῇ. ταῦτα δὲ ἀεὶ ἅμα γίνεται πάντα καὶ οὐ χρόνῳ διηρ τημένα, ἀλλ' ἥ γε διδασκαλία ἀναγκαίως διαιρεῖ, ἵνα διδάσκῃ ἀκριβῶς τὸ γιγνόμενον· σώματος μὲν γὰρ ἀρχαὶ θεὸς μὲν γεννῶν, ὕλη δὲ καὶ τὰ σχήματα, ἃ προϊὼν ἡμᾶς διδάξει, ὡς ἐξ ὧν συνέστηκεν τὰ σώματα γεννηθέντων ἀπὸ θεοῦ, κόσμου δὲ τὰ ἤδη ὑποστάντα σώματα ὑπὸ θεοῦ καὶ θεὸς ὁ ταῦτα τάσσων'· καὶ μετ' ὀλίγα 'τεκμήριον δὲ τοῦ τε μὴ ταὐτὸν εἶναι κατὰ Πλάτωνα σώματος σύστασιν καὶ κόσμου καὶ ὅτι νῦν μὴ τὴν ὕλην παραλαμβάνει ἀλλὰ τὰ ἐξ ὕλης ἀποτελεσθέντα σώματα ἐκεῖνο γινέσθω τὸ ὁρατὰ λέγειν εἶναι τὰ παραληφθέντα (τὰ δὲ ὁρατὰ τί ἂν εἴη ἢ σώματα; ἡ δὲ ὕλη ἀειδὴς καὶ ἄμορφος κατ' αὐτὸν καὶ μόγις νόθῳ λογισμῷ λαμβανομένη) καὶ τὸ προελθόντα σωμάτων γένεσιν δεικνύναι καίτοι ἐνταῦθα κόσμου ἐπιδείξαντα σύστασιν· ἀλλ' ἀπὸ τῆς τοῦ κόσμου γενέσεως ἀνατρέχει ἐπὶ τὴν τοῦ σώματος γένεσιν'. (164.12–165.16 Rabe = Fr. 47 and 49 Sodano). The English translation is adapted from Share, *Philoponus. Against Proclus*, 39–40.

statement that forms the content of the last paragraphs of *PM* with the reference to the authority of Severus.

In the twelfth century, Philoponus' treatise probably served as a source for the exposition of Porphyry's notion of Prime Matter for the Arabic philosopher Ibn Rushd (Averroes), who in his epitome of Aristotle's *Metaphysics* suggests the following summary of this issue[291]:

> Some (philosophers) made the three dimensions the first thing installed in formless prime matter and the principles of a thing whereby matter receives form. Furthermore, they maintained that the term "body" signifies most properly this meaning (of informed matter), since "substance" signifies this only *qua* (abstract) root morpheme because substances are (that which is) not in a substrate. This is what Porphyry taught, who claimed that this is the doctrine of previous philosophers such as Plato and others.

The account of Ibn Rushd, which is second-hand, does not bring us additional information on Porphyry's notion of Prime Matter. However, it sums up the main points which we find in *PM* and testifies to knowledge of Porphyry's philosophy among the Arabic scholars of early medieval times[292].

Based on the preserved evidence concerning Porphyry's writings and due to the apparent loss of the beginning of the Syriac translation, we cannot state with certainty what the original title of the Greek work he composed was. It is likely that Plotinus' disciple wrote several works concerning First Principles and Matter that are now lost in Greek, one of which has been preserved in Syriac translation. The title proposed for the present edition, *On Principles and Matter*, is based first of all on the internal evidence; it should be taken as a description of the contents of the published text rather than the actual title of Porphyry's lost work.

The *terminus post quem* for the composition of the Greek text of *PM* may be 263 AD. In that year, Porphyry moved from Athens to Rome, where he started to take classes with Plotinus. It was only after that date that Porphyry was able to call himself a disciple of both Longinus and Plotinus, a self-characterisation which the author of

291 Arabic text: فنقول ان قوما جعلوا اول شيء يحل في الهيولى الاولى الغير مصورة الابعاد الثلاثة وانها اول شي يتصور بها الهيولى وراوا ان اسم الجسم ادل على هذا المعنى اذ كانت الجواهر انها تدل عليها بالمثل الاولى من اجل انها ليست في موضوع وهذا القول قول فرفريوس وزعم انه قول الفلاسفة المتقدمة افلاطن وغيره (Rodríguez, *Averroes. Compendio de Metafísica*, 76.6–11). The English translation is adapted from Arnzen, *Averroes on Aristotle's Metaphysics*, 89–90. Cf. the translation of David Wasserstein in Smith, *Porphyrii Philosophi Fragmenta*, 541 (Fr. 464).

292 Another account of Porphyry's notion of Prime Matter, which is most likely based on second-hand knowledge, has been preserved by al-Shahrastani, see Cureton, *Kitāb al-milal wa-l-niḥal*, 345–346. An English translation of this fragment by David Wasserstein is included in Smith, *Porphyrii Philosophi Fragmenta*, 541–542 (Fr. 465).

the Syriac text makes. The form of the treatise, which is composed as some kind of propedeutic, makes it rather likely that it appeared at a later time, namely in the last decades of the third century, when Porphyry took over the school of Plotinus after his death in 270. If the latter assumption is correct, then the date of the composition of the Greek treatise lies between 270 and 301/305.

The reference to Porphyry's works by Proclus and the quotations by Philoponus and Simplicius make it probable that the treatise was read both in Athenian and in Alexandrian philosophical circles in the fifth-sixth centuries. Later on, it became known not only to the Alexandrian *philoponoi*, but also to the Syrian scholars, who labelled themselves with the same title and considered themselves the heirs of the Alexandrian Christian apologists. The alleged references to Porphyry by the Arabic philosophers demonstrate that Porphyry's works and ideas made the journey "from Alexandria to Baghdad"[293] which was characteristic of a large amount of scholarly and philosophical literature in the late ancient and early medieval periods.

293 See Meyerhof, "Von Alexandrien nach Bagdad".

3 Conclusion

The Syriac text published in the present book has had a long transmission history before it came to light at the beginning of the 21st century. The main stages of this history may be outlined as follows:

end of the 2nd to the beginning of the 3rd c.	The doxographical source, which was known to Sextus Empiricus, to the author of the *Refutatio* (ascribed to Hippolytus of Rome), and to Porphyry, probably appeared at this period, although an earlier dating is also possible. At this time, the Middle Platonists Atticus and Severus wrote their commentaries on Plato's *Timaeus*.
between 270 and 301/305	Porphyry of Tyre composed the Greek version of *PM*, which integrated both the doxographical source and the Middle Platonist commentaries.
middle of the 7th c.	The Greek text of the treatise was translated into Syriac in the Syrian Orthodox monastery Qenneshre. It is most likely that Severus Sebokht (d. 666/667) was responsible for the translation.
mid-7th to mid-8th c.	A copy of the Syriac version came to the library of the monastery Mar Mattai, where it was preserved until the 13th century, when Barhebraeus consulted it.
781/782	The East Syrian Catholicos Timothy I described the contents of the Syriac version of the treatise, which at that time was in the library of Mar Mattai.
late 9th c.	A copy of the codex described by Timothy was produced. This copy later became Part B of ms. DS 27.
ca. 975	The copy of the codex from Mar Mattai (Part B of ms. DS 27) reached the Egyptian monastery Dayr al-Suryan as part of the collection of manuscripts brought to Egypt by the Coptic partriarch Abraham b. Zurʿa.
1266/1267	Syrian Orthodox Maphrian Barhebraeus composed an epitome of the treatise, which he integrated into his theological compendium *Candelabra of Sanctuary*.

1951	Murad Kamil wrote a first description of the codex, containing *PM*, for his unpublished Arabic catalogue.
2014	A detailed description of ms. DS 27 and its contents appeared in the catalogue of S. Brock and L. Van Rompay.

Thus, the treatise *On Principles and Matter* has had a long history of nearly two thousand years before it may now be published in the present volume, and it seems proper to apply to it the well-known proverb: *habent sua fata libelli* – "Books have their own fate". These words derive from a treatise of the third-century Roman grammarian Terentianus Maurus, and the full version of the sentence containing them reads: *pro captu lectoris habent sua fata libelli* – "Books have their fate depending on the mental capacity of the reader"[294].

A similar idea came to mind of an unknown scribe in the monastery Dayr al-Suryan, who wrote in the margin of a Syriac codex[295]:

> We books are many, but there is no one who reads us!
> Oh, what a great pity that we remain unused!

It was due to the learned monks of Dayr al-Suryan that the Syriac version of Porphyry's work has been preserved until our days and can now be published in the present volume. Hopefully, this plea, written in the margin of an old Syriac codex, which has now reached us from a long historical remove, will be proven false by the readers of this edition.

---

294 Terentianus Maurus, *De Syllabis*, v. 1286 (363 Keil).

295 Ms. BL Add. 12170, f. 135r: ܣܓܝ ܟܬܒ̈ܐ ܩܪ̈ܝܝܐ ܐܝܬܝܢ. ܘܠܝܬ ܐܢܫ ܕܩܪܐ ܠܢ. ܗܐ ܣܓܝ ܪܒܐ ܟܪܝܘܬܐ. ܕܦܫܝܢ ܒܛ̈ܝܠܐ. (cf. Wright, *Catalogue*, vol. 2, 460–461).

Porphyry
On Principles and Matter

Syriac Text and English Translation

https://doi.org/10.1515/9783110747027-002

Abbreviations and signs used in the edition

cod.	*codex* Dayr al-Suryan 27, Part B (9th cent.)
Barhebr.	Barhebraeus, *Candelabra of Sanctuary* (ed. Bakoš)
add.	*addidit* "added (in the ms.)"
corr.	*correxit* "(a scribe) corrected"
fort. leg.	*fortasse legendum* "perhaps one should read"
in marg.	*in margine* "in the margin (of the ms.)"
om.	*omisit* "(ms.) omits"
parum cl.	*parum clare* "not clear enough (in the ms.)"
scr.	*scripsi* "I (i.e. the editor) have written"
supra lin.	*supra lineam* "above the line (in the ms.)"
§	paragraph division introduced by the editor
⟨...⟩	material supplied by the editor
[...]	material secluded by the editor
(...)	additions in the English translation

f. 114v

§1 ܐܝܠܝܢ ܓܒܪܘ ܒܥܘܩܒܐ ܥܠ ܙܘܥܐ ܟܝܢܝܐ. ܐܝܬ ܡܢܗܘܢ ܕܐܡܪܘ ܕܚܕ ܗܘ ܙܘܥܐ ܡܕܡܝܐ. ܘܐܝܬ ܡܢܗܘܢ ܕܐܡܪܘ. ܕܦܠܝܓܐ ܐܢܘܢ ܙܘܥܐ ܕܒ̈ܝ ܒܗܘܬܐ ܟܝܢܝܬܐ. ܘܗܠܝܢ ܕܐܡܪܘ ܕܚܕ ܗܘ. ܡܢܗܘܢ ܠܐ ܡܬܬܙܝܥܢܐ ܐܡܪܘ ܕܐܝܬܘܗܝ, ܘܡܢܗܘܢ ܡܬܬܙܝܥܢܐ. ܘܗܠܝܢ ܬܘܒ ܕܐܡܪܘ ܕܦܠܝܓܐ ܐܢܘܢ ܙܘܥܐ ܟܝܢܝܐ. ܡܢܗܘܢ ܡܣܝܟܐ ܐܡܪܘ ܕܐܝܬܝܗܘܢ: ܘܡܢܗܘܢ ܠܐ ܡܣܝܟܐ ܣܟܐ ܐܢܘܢ. ܘܗܠܝܢ ܬܘܒ ܕܣܟܐ ܐܢܘܢ ܡܣܝܟܐ. ܡܢܗܘܢ ܬܪܝܢ ܐܡܪܘ ܕܐܝܬܝܗܘܢ. ܘܡܢܗܘܢ ܬܠܬܐ ܘܡܢܗܘܢ ܐܪܒܥܐ ܐܡܪܘ ܕܐܝܬܝܗܘܢ.

§2 ܡܢ ܦܘܠܓܐ ܕܝܢ ܗܢܐ. ܘܠܐ ܚܕܐ ܡܢ ܗܪܣܝܣ ܦܠܛܐ. ܐܠܐ ܡܢ ܐܝܟܢܐ ܡܫܟܚܐ ܗܝ, | ܬܫܥܝܬ ܦܘܠܓܐ ܗ̇ܘ ܕܐܡܪ ܕܚܕ ܗܘ ܙܘܥܐ. ܐܘ ܬܫܥܝܬ ܗ̇ܘ ܕܦܐܡ ܕܦܠܝܓܐ ܐܢܘܢ. ܘܐܢ ܚܕ ܗܘ. ܡܫܟܚ ܗܘ ܬܫܥܝܬ ܦܘܠܓܐ ܕܐܡܪ. ܐܘ ܡܬܬܙܝܥܢܐ ܗܘ ܐܘ ܠܐ ܡܬܬܙܝܥܢܐ ܗܘ. ܘܐܢ ܦܠܝܓܐ ܡܫܟܚ ܗܘ ܒܡܢܝܢܐ ܕܐܢ ܡܣܝܟܐ ܐܘ ܠܐ ܡܣܝܟܐ.

col. b

§3 ܦܠܝܓܐ ܕܝܢ ܡܢ ܦܝܠܘܣܘܦܐ ܡܕ̈ܢܚܝܐ ܕܚܒܒܘ ܥܠ ܟܝܢܐ. ܙ̈ܘܥܐ ܗ̈ܘܠܝܐ ܐܡܪܘ ܕܐܝܬܝܗܘܢ. ܕܗܠܝܢ ܕܐܝܬܝܗܘܢ. ܗ̇ܘ ܠܡ ܕܝܢ ܕܡܢܗ ܐܝܬܘܗܝ, ܒܠܚܘܕܝܗ. ܘܡܢܗ ܡܬܡܛܝܐ ܗ̣ܘܐ ܒܠܚܘܕܝܗ. ܘܠܗ ܬܘܒ ܡܬܚܫܒ ܐܣܝܪܬ: ܒܪ ܗ̣ܘ ܒܟܝܢܗ ܕܠܐ ܫܘܚܠܦ: ܡܫܬܢܐ ܕܝܢ ܒܓܕ̈ܫܘܗܝ,

§4 ܠܗܢܐ ܐܣܛܘܟܣܐ ܘܙܘܥܐ ܐܡܪܝܢ ܕܐܝܬܘܗܝ, ܕܗܠܝܢ ܕܐܝܬܝܗܘܢ. ܘܡܛܠ ܕܙܘܥܐ ܗܘ. ܠܐ ܗ̇ܘܐ <ܘܠܐ> ܡܬܚܫܒ. ܐܠܐ ܒܠܥܕ ܢܛܪ ܒܐܝܬܘܬܗ. ܕܠܐ ܫܘܚܠܦ. ܡܛܠ ܟܠܗ ܕܐܝܬ ܓܕ̈ܫܐ ܕܒܗ. ܐܝܟܢܐ ܕܝܢ ܕܗܘܪܡܝܣ ܠܐ ܐܡܪܝܢ ܦܝܠܘܣܘܦܘܬܐ ܕܗ̣ܘܐ ܡܢ ܕܢܗܘܐ ܚܘܪܐ ܐܘ ܐܘܟܡܐ: ܘܠܐ ܬܘܒ ܕܐܬܚܫܒ ܡܢ ܕܢܬ ܟܠ ܡܢ ܗܠܝܢ: ܡܛܠ ܕܢܛܪ ܘܐܟܡ ܗ̣ܘ ܢܬܗ ܗܘܪܡܝܣ ܒܥ̈ܩܠܬܐ ܕܐܝܟ ܗܠܝܢ. ܗܟܢܐ ܐܝܬ ܠܡܐܡܪ ܐܦ ܥܠ ܙܘܥܬܐ ܗܘܠܢܝܬܐ.

§5 ܠܘ. ܕܝܢ ܚܕܐ ܗ̇ܝ, ܒܪ ܗ̇ܝ, ܐܡܪܘܗ̇ ܒܐܕܫܐ ܘܒܡܢܝܢܐ ܠܙܘܥܬܐ ܗܕܐ: ܗܠܝܢ ܕܚܒܒܘ ܡܕܡܝܐܝܬ ܥܠ ܟܝܢܐ. ܐܠܐ ܬܐܠܝܣ ܗ̇ܘ ܕܗ̣ܘ ܡܕܡܝܐܝܬ ܗ̣ܘܐ ܡܚܘܝܢܐ ܕܦܝܠܘܣܘܦܘܬܐ ܗܕܐ. ܟ̈ܝܢܐ ܐܡܪ ܕܐܝܬܝܗܘܢ ܙ̈ܘܥܬܐ ܡܕܡܝܬܐ

1 ܓܒܪܘ scr.: ܓܒܪ cod. 18 ܘܠܐ] om. cod. 21 ܐܘܟܡܐ scr.: ܐܘܣܡܐ cod.

(1. Doxography)

§1 Among those who did research on natural principles, some said that the first principle is one, and some said that the principles of natural things are many. And among those who said that (the first principle) is one, some said that it is motionless and some that it is in motion. And further, among those who said that the natural principles are many, some said that they were finite and some stated that they were infinite. And further, among those who stated that they were finite, some said that they were two, some that they were three, some that they were four.

§2 Now, not a single philosophical school (αἵρεσις) escapes from this division. But necessarily, it may either be classified under the category that states that there is one principle, or under that one which states that there are many. And if there is one, it may be classified either under the category that says that it is in motion or that it is motionless. And if there are many, it may be classified as follows: they are either finite or infinite.

§3 For many ancient philosophers who did research on nature supposed that there were material (ὑλικός) principles of existing things. Namely, that there is something out of which everything exists, from which everything originally came to be, and into which (everything) also will finally perish, while it remains unchangeable in its nature but changes in its accidents.

§4 About such a thing we say that it is an element (στοιχεῖον) and a principle of existing things. And because it is a principle, it neither comes to be, ⟨nor⟩ perishes, but always remains unchangeable in its essence, while it may change in its accidents. For as in the case of Socrates we do not say simply that he comes to be when he becomes white or black[1], neither that he perishes when he is deprived of these (colours), because the essence of Socrates is preserved and exists through such changes; in the same way we ought to speak about the material principle.

§5 However, it was not in one and the same way that those who originally did research on nature spoke about this principle concerning its kind and number. But Thales, who was the original inventor of this philosophy, said that water was the first principle, from which everything came into existence,

1 Ms. has "substance", which is probably a scribal mistake.

ܕܒܗܿ ܟܠ ܗ̇ܘܐ. ܡܢ ܗ̇ܝ ܕܒܢܝܐ ܕܡܫܒܚܘܬܐ ܕܠܥܠܡܝܢ ܦܪܢܘܣܬܐ ܗ̇ܝ. ܘܗ̇ܝ ܬܘܒ ܫܡܫܘܬܐ ܡܢ ܗܕܐ ܗܘܝܐ. ܗ̇ܘ ܓܝܪ ܕܒܗ ܗ̇ܘܝܢ ܟܠ ܕܗܘܝܢ. ܗ̇ܘ ܗܘ ܐܠܗܘܬܗ̇ ܪܫܝܬܐ ܘܡܕܒܪܢܘܬܐ ܕܟܠ.

§6 f. 104r ܡܫܬܟܚܢ ܠܗ | ܕܝܢ ܕܗ̇ܝ ܗܕܐ ܐܣܒܪܘ ܐܦ ܐܢܫܝܢ ܡܢ ܦܝ̈ܠܣܘܦܐ ܕܡܠܠܘ ܥܠ ܐܠܗܐ. ܠܗܘܡܝܪܘܣ ܓܝܪ ܕܗ̇ܘ ܡܟܐ: ܘܠܦܠܛܘܢ ܕܗ̇ܝ ܗ̇ܝ ܦܪܢܘܣܬܐ: ܐܒܘܗ̇ ܕܗܘܝܐ ܩܪܘ. ܘܡܥܠܝ ܡܢ ܟܠܗܘܢ ܐܠܗ̈ܐ ܠܚ̈ܬܝܐ ܐܡܪܘ. ܗܕܐ ܗ̇ܝ ܡܟܝܠ ܬܘܕܝܬܐ ܘܡܕܒܪܢܘܬܐ ܕܟܠ ܪܫܝܬܐ ܗܘܠܢܝܬܐ: ܕܬܐܠܝܣ ܗ̇ܘܐ ܠܗ̇ ܡܥܪܢܐ ܐܝܟ ܕܐܡܪܝܢ.

§7 ܐܢܟܣܝܡܢܣ ܕܝܢ ܘܡܢ ܕܡܢܗܘܢ, ܕܝܢ ܓܢܣܐ ܠܐܐܪ ܣܡܘ ܕܐܠܗܘܬܗ̇, ܪܫܝܬܐ ܘܡܕܒܪܢܘܬܐ. ܘܗܦܣܘܣ ܕܝܢ ܘܗܪܩܠܝܛܘܣ ܠܢܘܪܐ. ܟܠ ܚܕ ܚܕ ܡܢ ܗܠܝܢ ܓܝܪ ܪܫܝܬܐ ܗܘܠܢܝܬܐ ܘܡܬܬܙܝܥܢܝܬܐ ܘܚܕܐ ܣܡܘ.

§8 ܚܕܐ ܕܝܢ ܘܠܐ ܡܬܬܙܝܥܢܝܬܐ. ܒܗܘܦܣܛܣܝܣ. ܗܕܐ ܓܝܪ ܡܟܝܠ ܠܟܠ ܗܘܝܐ ܘܫܘܠܡܐ ܘܡܢ ܠܟܠ ܡܬܬܙܝܥܢܘܬܐ. ܘܚܕ ܐܡܪ ܕܐܠܗܘܬܗ̇ ܠܟܠܗܘܢ. ܘܠܒܪ ܡܢ ܟܠ ܫܘ ܓܢܣܐ ܗܘ ܕܐܠܗܘܬܗ̇.

§9 ܗܟܢܐ ܓܝܪ ܐܡܪ ܦܐܪܡܢܝܕܝܣ ܘܡܠܝܣܘܣ. ܚܕ ܪܫܝܬܐ ܠܐ ܡܬܬܙܝܥܢܝܬܐ ܐܡܪܘ. ܗ̇ܘ ܡܟܐ ܕܐܠܗܘܬܗ̇ ܚܕ. ܐܠܐ ܕܟܐ ܠܗ ܦܐܪܡܢܝܕܝܣ. ܕܚܕ ܐܡܪ ܕܐܠܗܘܬܗ̇. ܗ̇ܘ ܡܟܐ ܕܐܠܗܘܬܗ̇. ܒܪ ܒܡܠܬܐ ܢܣܒ ܠܗ ܕܐܠܗܘܬܗ̇ ܚܕ ܘܠܐ ܒܡܢܝܢܐ. ܡܠܝܣܘܣ ܕܝܢ ܒܡܢܝܢܐ ܘܒܣܘܟܠܐ ܗܘ ܚܕ. ܘܒܪ ܓܒܗ. ܗ̇ܘ ܡܢ ܡܣܝܟܐ ܐܡܪܗ̇. ܗܟܢܐ ܕܝܢ ܠܐ ܡܣܝܟܐ.

§10 ܐܢܟܣܓܘܪܣ ܕܝܢ. ܠܪ̈ܫܝܬܐ ܠܐ ܡܣܝܟܬܐ ܗܘ. ܒܪ ܡܢ ܟܠ ܪ̈ܫܝܬܐ ܕܬܩܢ ܡܬܩܢܬܐ. ܘܠܗܠܝܢ ܒܪ ܟܝܠܐ ܘܡܬܦܪܫ: ܘܡܟܕ ܕܐܬܩܢܘ ܐܣܝܪܝܬܐ ܠܗܘܢ ܫܕܪܐ. ܗܟܢܐ ܡܥܠܠܐ ܗ̇ܘܝܐ ܘܣܘܟܠܐ ܡܢ ܗܠܝܢ ܕܬܬܣܠܠܝ. ܘܡܬܦܪܫ. col. b ܘܓܠܬܐ ܒܥܘܕܬܐ ܕܗܘܝܐ ܠܗܘܢܐ | ܗܘ ܕܐܠܗܘܬܗ̇. ܠܐ ܕܝܢ ܡܥܒܪ ܠܗ̇ܘܢ ܗܢܐ. ܐܠܐ ܐܝܟ ܡܢ ܕܠܒܪ ܠܗܕܐ. ܬܘܒ ܠܗܘܢ ܪܫܝܬܐ ܗܘܠܢܝܬܐ ܟܠܗ̇.

§11 ܠܘܩܝܦܘܣ ܕܝܢ ܐܦ ܗ̇ܘ. ܠܐ ܡܣܝܟܬܐ ܐܡܪ ܕܐܠܗܘܬܗܘܢ ܪܫܝܬܐ. ܘܕܝܠܝܢ ܥܡ ܓܢܣܐ ܘܗܘܝܐ ܐܡܪܝܢܐ. ܬܘܒ ܕܝܢ ܐܡܪ. ܕܠܝܬ ܡܟܝܠ ܕܬܬܪܐ

10 ܘܗܦܣܘܣ scr.: ܘܗܦܦܣ cod. | ܘܗܪܩܠܝܛܘܣ scr.: ܘܗܪܩܝܛܘܣ cod. 12 ܒܗܘܦܣܛܣܝܣ scr.: ܒܗܘܦܘܣܛܣܝܣ cod. 20 ܐܢܟܣܓܘܪܣ scr.: ܐܢܟܣܐܓܐܪܣ cod.

in that he saw that wetness gave nourishment for everything and that heat also came into existence from it. Thus, because everything that comes to be originates from it, it is the first principle of everything.

§6 It seems to me that this is also what some of the poets meant who spoke about the gods. For they called Oceanus, that is the sea, and Tethys, that is moisture, "the parents of everything that existed"[2] and they said that of all gods water should be honored first of all. Thus, this is the first doctrine about a material principle. As we said, its author was Thales.

§7 Anaximenes, then, and before him Diogenes, stated that the first principle is air, whereas Hippasus and Heraclitus (declared) that it is fire. Each one of them stated that the material principle is in motion and one.

§8 That it is one and motionless (was stated by) Xenophanes. For he rejected any generation and corruption and any motion at all. He said that everything is one and stated it to exist apart from any change.

§9 This is (also) what Parmenides and Melissus said. They said that the principle is one and motionless, and that what exists is one. But it seems to me that Parmenides says that what exists is one, while he considers it to be one in reason and not in number; whereas Melissus states that it is one in number and in matter. Therefore, the former said that it is finite, while the latter that it is infinite.

§10 Anaxagoras states that principles are infinite, while he introduces things with like parts (i.e. ὁμοιομέρειαι) as principles. And while he mingles and separates them, he makes other things concomitant with each other. This is how generation and corruption occur to those things which are mixed and divided. He stated that the active cause of generation is intellect. However, he did not remain in this (opinion), but, like someone who vacillates on this issue, he turned back again towards material principles.

§11 Leucippus, too, says that principles are infinite and that they have change and continuous generation. Further, he said that something that exists is not

2 Homer, *Iliad* XIV.246 (52 West).

ܐܝܬܘܗܝ، ܐܘ ܠܐ ܐܝܬܘܗܝ. ܠܗܢܐ ܒܪ ܢܦܩ ܕܘܡܩܪܛܝܣ. ܐܡܪ ܐܦ ܗܘ ܕܠܐ ܣ̈ܘܟܠܐ ܐܝܠܝܢ ܪ̈ܫܐ. ܒܪ ܒܓܘܫܡܐ ܚܕ ܐܡܪ ܕܐܝܬܘܗܝ. ܒܐܦ̈ܝܡܐ ܕܝܢ ܘܒܐܕ̈ܥܐ ܦܪܝܫܝ. ܐܘ ܒܪ ܠܡܘܒܠܘܬܐ.

§12 ܠܗܠܝܢ ܕܝܢ ܕܗܟܐ ܕܥܠܡ ܘܐܦ ܐܦܝܩܘܪܘܣ: ܐܦ ܗܘ ܚܢܪ ܠܐ <ܡܣ̈ܩܒܠܐ> ܐܡܪ ܕܐܝܬܝܗܘܢ ܪ̈ܫܐ ܘܠܐ ܡܬܦܣܩܢܐ. ܡܬܬܪܝܨܝܢ ܕܝܢ ܗܠܝܢ ܒܦܣܝܣܘܬܐ ܠܐ ܡܣܬܟܠܬܐ. ܘܐܝܬ ܠܗܘܢ ܐܣ̈ܟܡܐ ܘܡܫܘܚ̈ܬܐ ܘܝܘܩܪܐ. ܘܡܬܪܡ ܠܗܬ ܕܠܐ ܡܢܘܢ ܡܢ ܛܠܐ. ܘܗܠܝܢ ܒܪ ܡܬܚܒܪܝܢ ܘܕܒܩܝܢ ܒܚܕ̈ܕܐ ܡܥܒܕܝܢ ܠܗ ܠܥܠܡܐ ܘܠܗܠܝܢ ܕܒܗ.

§13 ܐܡܦܕܘܩܠܝܣ ܕܝܢ ܡܣܩܒܠܐ ܐܡܪ ܕܐܝܬܝܗܘܢ ܪ̈ܫܐ. ܐܪ̈ܒܥܐ ܐܡܪ ܕܐܝܬܝܗܘܢ ܒܡܢܝܢܐ ܕܗܠܝܢ ܕܐܝܬܝܗܘܢ. ܐܪܥܐ ܘܡ̈ܝܐ ܘܢܘܪܐ ܘܐܐܪ. ܘܕܗܠܝܢ ܗܘܐ ܫܘܠܛܢܐ ܘܦܘܪܫܢܐ ܒ̈ܢܝܗܘܢ ܣ̈ܢܝܗܘܢ. ܘܠܫܘܠܛܢܐ ܕܐܝܬܘܗܝ، ܗܘܝܐ ܦܪܐ ܪܚܡܘܬܐ. ܘܠܦܘܪܫܢܐ ܕܐܝܬܘܗܝ، ܣܢܝܐܬܐ ܕܒܗܬܐ. ܐܪ̈ܒܥܐ ܡܕܡ ܐܝܬܝܗܘܢ ܪ̈ܫܐ ܐܝܟ ܙܒܢܗ ܕܗܘܝܐ.

§14 ܐܪܣܛܛܠܝܣ ܕܝܢ ܗܘܠܐ ܘܐܕܫܐ ܘܓܠܝܘܬܐ ܐܡܪ ܕܐܝܬܝܗܘܢ ܪ̈ܫܐ ܕܓܘ̈ܫܡܐ ܟ̈ܝܢܝܐ ܐܣܛ̈ܘܟܣܐ ܕܝܢ ܘܐܕ̈ܫܐ ܦܪܝܫܝ.

§15 ܗܠܝܢ ܕܝܢ ܕܡܢ ܐܣܛܘܐ. ܐܠܗܐ ܘܗܘܠܐ ܐܡܪܘ ܕܐܝܬܝܗܘܢ ܪ̈ܫܐ. ܒܪ ܕܐܘܣܝܐ ܠܐ ܡܬܚܫܚܝܢ ܘܦܪܝܫܝܢ ܠܗ ܠܗܘ ܡܐ ܕܥܒܕ ܡܢ ܗܘ ܡܐ ܕܚܐܫ.
f. 104v ܚܝܠܐ ܕܝܢ ܐܡܪܝܢ ܕܦܪܝܫ. ܘܗܘ ܡܐ ܕܥܒܕ ܡܢ ܗܘ ܡܐ ܕܚܐܫ. | [ܚܝܠܐ ܕܝܢ ܐܡܪܝܢ ܕܦܪܝܫ.] ܘܗܘ ܡܐ ܕܥܒܕ ܐܝܬܘܗܝ، ܐܠܗܐ. ܗܘ ܕܝܢ ܕܚܐܫ ܗܘܠܐ.

§16 ܟܠ ܙܒܢܐ ܕܝܢ ܕܒܥܬ ܦܝܠܘ ܓܢܘܣ ܐܡܪܝܢ. ܡܐ ܕܝܢ ܕܟܠ ܗܘ ܕܦܠܛܘܢ ܢܐܡܪ. ܐܡܪܝܢ ܕܝܢ ܟܠ ܙܒܢܐ ܐܝܟ ܙܒܢܗ ܕܦܠܛܘܢ. ܡܐ ܕܡܢ ܕܟܠ ܢܦܪܐ ܒܗ ܒܟܠܬܐ.

§17 ܘܕܡ ܕܝܢ ܠܡܕܒܪ. ܕܬܪܝܢ ܐܝܠܝܢ ܐܕ̈ܫܐ ܕܡܠܦܢܘܬܐ ܡܫܝܚܝܬܐ. ܘܚܕ ܡܢ ܟܕ ܩܕܡܝܬܐ ܡܫܝܚܐ ܠܗܠܝܢ ܐܚܪ̈ܢܝܬܐ. ܗܕܐ ܕܐܝܬܘܗܝ ܕܠܝܬܐ

1 ܐܝܬܘܗܝ، ܐܘ ܠܐ ܐܝܬܘܗܝ،] add. in marg.: ܐܝܬܘܗܝ، ܗܕܐ ܠܦ̈ܪܕܐ ܠܐ ܡܬܦܣܩܢܐ ܠܗ ܠܐ ܐܝܬܘܗܝ، ܕܝܢ ܠܡܦܣܩܘܬܐ 4 ܡܣ̈ܩܒܠܐ] corr. in marg., Barhebr. 12 ܗܘܝܐ scr.: ܗܘܐ cod. 13 ܡܕܡ scr.: ܡܪܡ cod. 22 ܕܡܢ] add. supra lin.

more than something that does not exist[3]. This was supported by Democritus. He, too, said that principles are infinite, declaring that they are one in genus (γένος) but different in shapes (σχήματα), forms (εἴδη), or in opposition.

§12 Epicurus also seems to have agreed with them. He, too, said that the principles are in⟨finite⟩[4] and indivisible, that they are moving in the infinite void, that they have size, shape, and weight, and further that they are similar to something without parts. When they interweave with and adhere to one another, they complete the world and what is in it.

§13 Empedocles said that the principles are finite. He said that there are four roots of existing things – earth, water, fire, and air – and that combination and separation of them come about part by part. Combination, that is coming-to-be, he called "love", and separation, that is corruption, (he called) "victory"[5]. Thus, according to this doctrine of his, there are four principles.

§14 Aristotle said that the principles of physical bodies are matter (ὕλη), form (εἶδος), and privation, while shapes (σχήματα) and forms (εἴδη) are different.

§15 Those from the Stoa said that the principles are God and Matter, while they neither define in substance (οὐσία) nor differentiate that which is active from that which is passive. But they say that that which is active differs from that which is passive in potentiality. [But they say that they differ in potentiality.][6] What is active is God. What is passive is Matter.

§16 The views of the Pythagoreans we will discuss when we speak about those of Plato. Thus, we will speak about the principles according to the views of Plato, following what we have started (to say) above in this discourse.

(2. Introductory Issues)

§17 We ought to know that there are two types of the demonstrative science. One (type) by means of prior things demonstrates the posterior. It is character-

---

3 A commentary in the left margin of the ms.: "By 'exists' he meant atoms, i.e. the indivisible, and by 'does not exist' the void."

4 The word "finite" is added in the margin of the ms. and it occurs in the main text of the version of Barhebraeus (Bakoš, *Le candélabre*, 544.8).

5 Syriac has ܙܟܘܬܐ corresponding to Gr. νῖκος (a late ancient variant of νίκη), "victory", instead of νεῖκος, "strife". The same error occurs in the version of Barhebraeus (Bakoš, *Le candélabre*, 545.2) and it may be based either on a variant in the Greek text or, more likely, on a misunderstanding by the Syriac translator.

6 These words appear twice in the manuscript, first at the end of fol. 104r and then at the beginning of fol. 104v. This is most likely a dittography.

ܕܣܘܠܢ ܒܫܡܝܐ. ܙܥܒܒܐ ܕܝܢ ܗܘܘܢ ܩ̈ܕܡܝܐ ܕܡܒܣܘܢ ܗܘܐ ܒܡܘܫܐ. ܩ̈ܕܡܝܐ ܐܢܘܢ. ܐܚܪ̈ܢܐ ܕܝܢ ܕܒܬܪ ܐܚܪ̈ܬܐ ܒܫܡܐ ܗܠܝܢ ܩ̈ܕܡܝܬܐ. ܘܗܕܐ ܕܐܝܬܝܗ ܗܝ ܕܡܠܟܘܬܐ ܗ̇ܝ ܦܘܪܫܬܐ. ܘܡܫܟܚܐ ܕܝܢ ܕܡܛܠ ܕܟܠ ܙܒܢܐ ܐܝܬܝܗ̇ ܡܠܬܐ. ܕܡܬܚܫܒܢ ܘܠܐ ܡܕܡ ܡܬܦܪܫܐ. ܡܬܚܫܒܝܢ ܚܝ ܒܐܕܫܐ ܗܘ ܦܘܪܫܐ ܕܡܠܘܫܬܐ ܡܫܘܚܠܦܬܐ.

§18 ܐܡܪܝܢ ܗܟܝܠ ܕܡܬܬܘܕܝܐ ܡܢ ܟܠܗܘܢ ܝܘܢܝܐ. ܘܡܢ ܦܛܠܡܘܣܐ ܘܡܢ ܐܝܟ ܕܠܗ ܦܛܠܡܘܣܐ ܐܢܘܢ. ܕܐܡܪܬ ܠܝ ܬ̈ ܫܥܐ ܘܐܡܪܬ ܠܝ ܐܦ ܡܕܒܪܐ. ܘܗܠܝܢ ܦܘܫܟܝܢ ܐܢܘܢ ܡܢ ܕܪ̈ܓܐ. ܘܐܢܘܢ ܗܕܐ ܦܘܪܫܐ. ܐܠܐ ܐܝܟ ܕܐܦ ܡܫܘ̈ܚܬܗܘܢ ܢܗܘܘܢ ܦܘܫܟ ܡܢ ܕܪܓܐ. ܐܝܟܐ ܒܝܢ ܕܫܠܐ ܦܘܫܟ ܡܢ ܕܪܓܐ. ܐܦ ܡܫܘ̈ܚܬܗܘܢ ܦܘܫܟ ܡܢ ܕܪܓܐ. ܡܫܘܚܬܐ ܕܝܢ ܕ̈ܙ ܫܥܐ ܐܝܬܝܗ ܬ ܒܫܘܥܬܐ. ܕܡܕܒܪܐ ܕܝܢ ܒܘܟܘܬܐ.

§19 ܐܠܐ ܐ ܕܢܗܘܘܢ ܐܝܬܝܗܘܢ ܡܬܬܪܡܢܝܬܐ ܘܡܬܪ̈ ܒܫܘܠܬܐ: ܐܝܢ ܗܘ ܕܐܡܪܢܐ ܐܝܬܝܗܘܢ ܗܠܝܢ ܕܠܘܬ ܡܕܡ ܐܝܟ ܘܡܬܪ̈ܚܝܬܐ. ܡܢܗܝܢ ܡܬܚܙܝܢ ܠܐܢܫܐ ܒܗ ܡܠܬܐ. ܡܢܗܝܢ ܕܝܢ ܡܬܬ̈ܚܙܝܢܬܐ ܐܝܟ ܗܠܝܢ ܕܡܢܝܢ

col. b | ܠܗܘܢ ܐܦ ܡܛܠ ܒܫܘܠܬܐ. ܘܡܬܚܙܝܢ ܒܡܬܒܪܢܬܐ ܒܗ ܬ ܒܫܥܬܐ ܕܠܐ ܡܠܬܐ. ܘܡܬܚܙܝܢ ܡܬܬܚܙܝܢܬܐ. ܘܗܝܢ ܗܢ ܐܡܪܝܢܢ ܐܝܬܝܗܘܢ ܘܠܐ ܩܢܝܢ ܗܘܝܐ. ܗܢܝܢ ܕܝܢ ܕܠܐ ܐܝܬܝܗܘܢ ܐܡܪܝܢܢ ܘܗܘܝܐ ܩܢܝܢ.

§20 ܘܗܠܝܢ ܡܛܠ ܒܫܘܠܬܐ ܐܝܟ ܕܠܘܬ ܩ̈ܕܡܝܬܐ ܐܝܢ. ܐܝܟ ܕܠܘܬ ܒܢܝܐ ܕܝܢ ܬܪ̈ܝܢܘܬܐ. ܬܘܒ ܕܝܢ ܗܠܝܢ ܡܬܬܪ̈ܝܡܬܐ. ܐܝܟ ܕܠܘܬ ܒܢܝܐ ܩ̈ܕܡܝܬܐ. ܐܝܟ ܕܠܘܬ ܬ ܒܫܘܠܢ ܕܝܢ ܬܪ̈ܝܢܘܬܐ. ܒܪ ܕܝܢ ܗܠܝܢ ܩ̈ܕܡܝܬܐ ܕܠܘܬܗܝܢ: ܐܚܪ̈ܝܬܐ ܕܝܢ ܠܘܬ ܒܢܝܐ. ܡܥܢܝܢ ܠܡܕܪܐ ܒܡܠܬܐ ܦܘܪܫܬܐ. ܠܘܬ ܗܠܝܢ ܕܡܕܢܚܐ ܘܦܪ̈ܫܢ ܡܬܦܪܫܝܢ ܬ̈ܫܥܐ ܦܠܓܝܢ.

§21 ܐܝܬܝܗܘܢ ܕܝܢ ܩ̈ܕܡܝܬܐ ܐܝܟ ܕܠܘܬ. ܒܠܘܢ ܡܛܠ ܒܫܘܠܬܐ. ܕܐܝܟ ܐܡܪ. ܢܦܪܐ ܘܡܫܚܐ ܘܐܪܙ ܘܐܪܒܐ. ܡܬܚܙܝܢ ܠܝ ܢܛܪ ܙ̈ܒܒܐ ܘܡܫܘܚ ܒܟܐ ܕܡܢ ܗܠܝܢ ܗܘܘ. ܬܘܒ ܕܝܢ ܢܛܪ ܡܬܚܙܝܢ ܠܝ ܡܢ ܗܠܝܢ ܦ̈ܠܓܝܢ. ܘܡܦܠܓܝܢ ܬܘܒ. ܐܝܬ ܗܘ ܡܕܡ ܡܫܟܚܢܐ ܘܡܕܡ ܡܥܢܝܐ. ܘܡܕܡ ܡܬܚܫܒܢܐ ܘܡܕܡ ܡܬܠܒܒܢܐ.

6 ܕܡܬܬܘܕܝܐ scr.: ܕܡܬܬܬܘܕܝܐ cod.

istic of syllogisms. Those first compositions from which conclusions are drawn are prior. Another (type) by means of posterior things demonstrates the prior. It is characteristic of the introductory science. And now, as our discourse is about principles, prior to which nothing may be thought, we employ the initial type of the demonstrative science.

§18 Now, we say that it is acknowledged by everyone, both by philosophers and by those who are not philosophers, that we have senses and that we also have intellect, and that they differ from each other. And if this is true, their activities also necessarily differ from each other. For just as the faculties differ from each other, likewise their activities differ from each other. So, the activity of senses is sensation and that of intellect is thinking.

§19 There are necessarily intelligible things and perceptible things. If things exist completely in relation to something and are intelligible, they "can be apprehended by thought with the support of a reasoned account"[7]. And those things that are presumed and are also called perceptible, they are apprehended "by belief supported by unreasoned sensation"[8], and they are called believed. The former exist permanently and are not subject to generation, while the latter do not exist permanently and are subject to generation.

§20 The perceptible things are prior in relation to us, but are secondary in relation to nature. Further, the intelligible things are prior in relation to nature, but are secondary in relation to our perception. As those things which are prior in relation to us are posterior in relation to nature, we will start moving from the introductory argument and ascend to those things that are properly and truly called principles.

§21 Thus, those things that are prior in relation to us are all perceptible ones, like fire, water, air, and earth. Those things that are composed and mixed from them are close to us. And even closer to us than those things are bodies. And inside bodies there is something hot, and something hard, something that can be seen, and something that can be grasped.

7 Plato, *Tim.* 28a1–2.
8 Plato, *Tim.* 28a2–3.

§22 ܐܠܐ ܚܕܝܐ ܗܿ، ܕܠܝܬ ܡܕܡ ܡܬܠܒܒܢܐ ܘܡܥܝܩܐ ܠܒܪ ܡܢ ܐܪܥܐ. ܘܠܐ ܬܗܘܐ ܡܬܚܙܝܢܐ ܫܘܚܠܦܐ ܕܠܐ ܢܘܪܐ. ܡܕܡ ܐܝܬ ܗܘ ܒܗ ܘܡܕܡ ܐܪܒܥܐ. ܘܡܕܡ ܢܘܪܐ. ܐܝܬ ܗܘ ܒܗ ܕܝܢ ܐܦ ܪܘܚܐ ܡܕܡ ܕܫܚܝܢ ܒܥܘ̈ܠܐ. ܘܒܢܝܐ ܪܦܝܐ ܕܫܚܝܢ ܒܗܘܢܐ. ܘܡܕܡܐ ܕܠܐ ܒܢܝܐ ܪܦܝܐ ܠܒܪ ܡܢ ܓ̈ܫܡܐ. ܘܠܐ ܪܘܚܐ ܡܕܡ ܠܒܪ ܡܢ ܐܐܪ ܐܝܬ. ܡܕܡ ܐܝܬ ܗܘ ܒܗ ܘܡܚܝܠܬܐ ܡܕܡ ܡܢ ܓ̈ܫܡܐ. ܘܡܚܝܠܬܐ ܬܗܘܐ ܕܐܐܪ.

§23 ܡܛܠ ܕܝܢ ܕܐܝܬܝܗܘܢ ܒܢ ܗܠܝܢ ܕܐܝܬܝܗܘܢ ܟ̈ܝܢܘܬܐ. ܐܝܟܢܐ ܕܐܦ ܗܠܝܢ ܕܕܝܠܗܘܢ ܐܢ̈ܫܝܢ ܟ̈ܝܢܘܬܐ ܐܝܬܝܗܘܢ ܒܢ. ܗܢܘ ܕܝܢ ܕܠܐ ܐܝܬ ܗܘ ܡܕܡ ܒܚܠܡܘܗܝ ܒܫܘ̈ܚܠܦܐ ܕܗܠܝܢ. ܢܘܪܐ ܘܡ̈ܝܐ ܘܐܐܪ. ܘܐܪܥܐ ܠܗܘܢ ܬܗܘܐ | ܠܗܠܝܢ ܒܫܘ̈ܚܠܦܐ ܡܫܠܡܢ ܠܐܪ̈ܥܐ ܘܠܢܚܬܘܬܐ. ܠܢܘܪܐ ܕܝܢ ܠܫܡܝܡܘܬܐ f. 105r ܘܚܡܝܡܘܬܐ ܘܠܥܠܝܘܬܐ. ܘܒܗ ܗܠܝܢ ܬܗܘܐ ܠܐܣܛܘܟܣܗ ܘܦܘܚܡܗ ܕܝܢ ܕܗܕܐ. ܘܠܐܪܥܐ ܬܗܘܐ ܡܫܠܡܢ ܠܝܒܝܫܘܬܗ ܘܠܩܪܝܪܘܬܗ. ܘܒܗ ܗܠܝܢ ܬܗܘܐ. ܘܠܩܘܡܗ ܘܠܡܦܪܪܘܬܗ. ܘܡܟܝܟܘܬܗ ܘܐܣܛܘܟܣܗ. ܗܟܢܐ ܕܝܢ ܒܗ ܒܕܡܘܬܐ. ܘܠܒܫܘ̈ܚܠܦܐ ܬܗܘܐ ܗܢܘܢ ܬܪ̈ܝܢ ܕܒܟܝ ܟܠܬܐ ܐܐܪ ܐܚ̈ܪܢܐ ܘܡ̈ܝܐ. ܡܦܪܫܝܢ ܘܡܬܚܠܦܝܢ ܠܗܘܢ ܒܪܝܫܐ. ܠܢܝܚܘܬܗܘܢ ܫܟܝܚܬܐ ܘܠܐܣܛܘ̈ܟܣܝܗܘܢ ܦܫ̈ܝܛܐ.

§24 ܘܒܬܪ ܗܠܝܢ ܡܬܡܠܝܢ. ܕܢܚܙܐ ܗܘ ܡܢܐ ܕܒܗ ܡܬܚܙܝܢ ܗܠܝܢ ܕܪ̈ܝܫܐ ܘܐܪ̈ܥܐ ܕܡܫܟܚܝܢ ܘܐܝܬܝܗܘܢ. ܡܫܟܚܝܢ ܕܝܢ ܕܐܝܬܝܗܘܢ، ܗܘ ܡܢܐ ܕܒܗ ܡܫܟܚܝܢ ܗܠܝܢ. ܗ̇ܘ ܡܢܐ ܕܢܦܩ ܕܢܗܘܐ ܠܗܠܝܢ ܕܚܕܝܢ ܘܠܓܡܝܢ ܠܘܬ ܠܗܘܢ ܡܫܡܫܐ. ܠܗ ܕܝܢ ܠܗܢܐ ܡܕܡ ܕܒܗ ܓܫܝܫܝܢ ܐܪ̈ܥܐ ܘܢܝܚܘܬܐ ܘܒܗ ܦܩܚܝܢ. ܗ̇ܘܠܐ ܦܪܝܫ. ܐܫܬܟܚܬ ܠܝ ܡܕܡ ܒܪ ܡܬܠܦܘܬܐ ܗܕܐ ܫܘܪܝܬܐ. ܫܪܝܐ ܪܫܝܡܬܐ ܕܟܠ ܕܡܬܦܪܫܐ ܗܘܠܝܬܐ ܘܗܘܠܐ.

§25 ܡܛܠ ܕܝܢ ܕܢܦܫܐ ܗܿ، ܠܡܠܦܘܬܐ ܗܕܐ ܫܘܪܝܬܐ ܗ̇ܝ، ܡܪܒܝܢܬܐ. ܘܠܗ̇، ܡܪܒܝܢܬܐ ܘܡܫܠܡܢܬܐ ܗܕܐ ܡܬܩܦܢܘܬܐ. ܕܐܡ ܠܡܕܒܪ. ܒܪ ܠܗܠܝܢ ܒܪ̈ܢܫܐ ܐܢܫܝܢ ܡܢ ܗܘܠܐ. ܬܗܘܐ ܡܩܦܝܢ ܠܗ̇ ܘܡܪܒܝܢ ܒܠܥܗ̇. ܠܐܕ̈ܫܐ ܘܠܐܩ̈ܢܘܡܐ ܘܠܝܕ̈ܝܥܬܐ. ܘܬܗܘܐ ܠܗܘܢ ܠܗܠܝܢ ܡܩܦܝܢ ܘܐܡܪܝܢ. ܕܠܘ ܒܠܒܝܠܘܬ ܘܠܐ ܡܬܝܕܥܢܘܬ ܐܝܬܝܗܘܢ ܒܗܘܠܐ. ܐܠܐ ܒܡ ܫܘܦܪܐ ܡܕܡ ܘܝܕܥܬܐ ܦܐܝܐ.

§22 But it is known that there is nothing tangible and hard without earth, and also there is nothing visible (and) hot without fire. Therefore, there is something of earth and something of fire in us. There is also something of spirit in us that is contained in the arteries, and a wet nature contained in the veins. And it is evident that there is no wet nature without water and nothing like spirit appears unless there is air. Therefore, there is some part of water and also a part of air in us.

§23 And because those things which are parts are in us, it is also necessary that those parts which are in them are in us. That is, the whole, therefore, is present in all bodies here, fire, water, air, and earth. Further, these bodies are divided into forms (εἴδη) and qualities. Fire (is divided) into heat, brightness, and lightness, and together with them into its shape (σχῆμα) and aggregation. Further, we divide earth into its dryness and its coldness, and with them also into its stability, its firmness, its fixedness, and its shape. And in the same way, we also divide and differentiate in mind those two bodies that are in the middle, I mean air and water, making a distinction between their proper qualities and their distinct shapes.

§24 After this, we investigate what it is, in which these qualities and forms (εἴδη) appear to subsist and exist. For we discover that there is something in which they are set, something that is established in order to receive them, while they do not have a basis for their existence in themselves. This thing, in which forms and qualities are imprinted and where they are set, we call "matter" (ὕλη). Thus, by means of this introductory science it became apparent to us that there is one principle of everything which is called "material" and "matter".

§25 But because the introductory science is followed by the complex one, which supplements a negative statement by a positive one, it is necessary to know that there are things which we exclude intellectually from Matter but then attach to it, and we supply it with forms, shapes, and qualities. To these things we further attach (other ones) and say that they are not "in a discordant and disorderly state"[9] in Matter, but rather have some beauty and pleasant order.

9 Plato, *Tim.* 30a4–5.

§26 ܛܟܣܐ ܕܝܢ ܦܐܝܐ ܘܡܫܘܦܪܐ. ܠܘ ܟܠܗ̇ ܠܫܘܡܬܐ ܐܝܬܘܗ̇ܝ. ܘܠܫܘܡܬܐ ܬܘܒ (col. b) | ܠܐ ܐܝܬܝܗ̇ ܒܟܠܗ ܡܢ ܦܘܫܚܐ. ܘܦܘܫܚܐ ܠܐ ܐܝܬܘܗܝ ܒܟܠܗ ܡܢ ܡܠܬܐ. ܘܡܠܬܐ ܕܐܝܟ ܗܕܐ. ܠܐ ܐܝܬܝܗ̇ ܕܠܐ ܩܕܡܘܬ ܫܥܬܐ ܘܩܕܡܘܬ ܫܒܬܐ. ܗܠܝܢ ܕܝܢ ܠܐ ܐܝܬܝܗܝܢ ܒܟܠܗ ܡܢ ܗܘܢܐ. ܗܘܢܐ ܡܕܝܢ ܒܪ ܒܗܠܝܢ ܡܬܒ̈ܪܝܢܘܬܗ ܐܬܬܐܝܕ. ܠܗܠܝܢ ܐܕ̈ܫܐ ܘܙܢ̈ܝܬܐ ܘܐܣ̈ܟܡܐ ܛܟܣ ܘܠܒܫ ܘܛܟܣ ܡܢ̈ ܟܠ.

§27 ܐܫܬܡܥܬ ܡܕܝܢ ܒܡܠܦܢܘܬܐ ܗ̇ܝ ܡܪܟܒܢܝܬܐ ܘܡܦܣܩܢܝܬܐ. ܐܦ ܙܥܘܪܬܐ ܒܒܘܕܬܐ. ܕܐܝܬܘܗܝ ܗܘܢܐ. ܡܛܠ ܕܝܢ ܕܗܘܢܐ ܛܟܣ ܡܢ̈ ܟܠ ܘܐܝܟܢ ܠܗܠܝܢ ܒܡ̈ܬܒܪܝܢܘܬܗ. ܡܬܒ̈ܪܝܢܘܬܗ ܕܝܢ ܕܗܘܢܐ ܬ̈ܪܝܢܐ ܐܝܬܝܗ̈ܝܢ. ܠܬ̈ܪܝܢܐ ܕܝܢ ܗܠܝܢ ܦܐܪ̈ܝ ܨܦܪܐ ܘܪܡܫܐ ܘܬܫ̈ܒܚܬܐ ܡܙܡܪܢܐ ܕܒ̈ܝ ܒܝܬܐ. ܕܒ̈ܗܘܢ ܘܒܕ̈ܡܘܬܗܘܢ ܘܐܟܘܬܗܘܢ ܐܬܬܐܝܕ ܘܐܦ̈ ܛܟܣ ܝ̈ ܩܘܬܐ.

§28 ܐܫܬܡܥܬ ܠܝ ܬܘܒ ܐܦ ܙܥܘܪܬܐ ܕܬܠܬ. ܕܒܕ̈ܡܘܬܗ ܗ̇ܘ̈ܝܢ ܝ̈ ܩܘܬܐ. ܡܕܝܢ ܒܡܠܦܢܘܬܐ ܗ̇ܝ ܥܢܘܝܬܐ. ܐܫܬܡܥܬ ܠܝ ܗܘܠܐ. ܘܒܗ̇ ܡܪܟܒܢܝܬܐ ܟܠܬܐ ܒܒܘܕܬܐ. ܒܡܬܒ̈ܪܝܢܘܬܗ ܕܝܢ ܕܗܕܐ. ܐܫܬܡܥ ܠܝ ܙܥܘܪܬܐ ܘܫܘܪܐ ܕܒܕܡܘܬܗ ܐܬܬܦܘ ܒ̈ܢܝܐ. ܡܛܠ ܕܝܢ ܕܟܠ ܚܕ ܡܢ ܗܠܝܢ ܐܝܬܘܗܝ ܙܥܘܪܐ ܡܕܡܝܐ ܕܗ̈ܘܝܐ. ܢܐܡܪ ܡܕܡܟܝܢܘܬ ܕܡܕܡܐ ܐܝܬܘܗܝ ܙܥܘܪܐ.

§29 ܙܥܘܪܐ ܐܝܬܘܗܝ. ܗܟܢܐ ܡܕܡܝܢܐ ܕܗܠܝܢ ܕܒܠܬܗ. ܕܡܕܡܐ ܡܕܡܝܢܐ ܗܘܘ. ܘܡܛܠ ܗܟܢ ܕܟܠ ܙ̈ܥܘܪܐ ܒܗܕܐ ܕܙܥܘܪܐ ܩܕܡ ܟܠ ܐܝܬܘܗܝ. ܢܦܩܐ ܠܗ ܕܝܢ ܠܙܥܘܪܐ ܐܦ ܗܕܐ. ܕܦܫܝܛܐ ܘܕܠܐ ܠܐ ܢܗܘܐ ܐܝܬܘܗܝ ܘܡܬܬܘܡܐܝܬ ܬܘܒ.

§30 ܐܢ ܕܝܢ ܠܐ ܐܝܬܘܗܝ ܦܫܝܛܐ. ܡܕܝܢ ܡܪܟܒܐ ܗܘ. ܐܝܬܝܗܝܢ ܡܕܝܢ (f. 105v) | ܐܦ ܡܢ̈ܘܬܐ ܕܡܢܗܝܢ ܡܪܟܒ. ܐܢ ܒܡܠܐ ܢܦܩ ܕܗܘܐ ܙܥܘܪܐ ܘܐܢ ܒܡܕܟܐ ܘܒܪܟܝܢܐ. ܘܐܢ ܗܕܐ. ܕܝܢܐ ܗܝ ܕܡܬܐܡܪܢ ܡܬܢ̈ܝܢ ܡܕܡܝܗܝ: ܒܡܬܕܡܝܢܘܬܐ ܕܒܢܝܐ ܐܘ ܕܡܕܟܐ ܡ̈ܢܘܬܐ ܕܡܢܗܝܢ ܐܬܪܟܒ. ܘܠܐ ܡܟܝܠ ܡܬܐܡܪ ܗܢܐ ܙܥܘܪܐ ܡܪܟܒܐܝܬ. ܐܠܐ ܡܢ̈ܘܬܐ ܗܠܝܢ ܕܡܢܗܝܢ ܐܬܪܟܒ. ܡܕܝܢ ܦܫܝܛܐ ܙܥܘܪ ܕܢܗܘܐ ܐܝܬܘܗܝ: ܘܗܘ ܕܐܝܬܘܗܝ ܙܥܘܪܐܝܬ ܙܥܘܪܐ.

7 ܘܡܦܣܩܢܝܬܐ scr.: ܘܡܦܣܩܣܢܝܬܐ cod. **8** ܕܗܘܢܐ scr.: ܕܗܘܠܐ cod. **9** ܒܡ̈ܬܒܪܝܢܘܬܗ scr.: ܒܡ̈ܬܒܪܝܢܘܬܗܝܢ cod.

§26 But pleasant order and beauty do not exist without harmony. And also harmony does not exist without proportion. And proportion does not exist without reason. And such reason does not exist without foresight and foreknowledge, while the latter two do not exist without intellect. Thus, when intellect sets in motion through its actions, it imprints, adjusts, arranges, and sets in order forms, qualities, and shapes.

§27 Thus, through the complex, the adding, and the attaching science, we found the active principle, which is Intellect. And because it is Intellect[10] that arranges, orders, and sets these things through its actions[11], its actions are thoughts. These thoughts we call Forms, Ideas, and prior definitions of the things, for through them, i.e. through their image and likeness, things are formed and set in order.

§28 Further, we have found also the third principle, in whose image things come to be. Thus, by means of the introductory science we have found Matter, and by means of the complex one the active cause, and through the activity of the latter we have found Idea and Form, according to whose image natures are formed. And because each one of these is a primary principle of existing things, we should first say what a principle is.

(3. Definition of a Principle)

§29 A principle is a primary limit of those things which are posterior to it and which from it initially come to be. And because all principles exist as something that is prior to everything, it is also characteristic of the principle that it is simple, unqualified, and also eternal.

§30 For if it is not simple, then it is compound. Consequently, there are also parts of which it is compound, whether we assume its composition to have occurred in time or in intellect and thinking. If this is so, then it is evident that the parts of which it is compound may be considered prior to it, either preceding it in time or in thinking. In this case, we cannot call it principle in the proper sense, but rather the parts of which it is compound. Therefore, something that is truly a principle must necessarily be simple.

10 A scribal mistake. Ms. has "Matter".

11 Ms. has "their actions", which is most likely a scribal mistake.

§31 ܗܟܢܐ ܕܝܢ ܐܦ ܕܠܐ ܚܫܐ. ܐܚܝܕ ܚܫܐ ܘܒܗ ܚܫܐ ܐܠܗܘܬܗ܆ ܐܦ ܗܟܢܐ ܗܘܐ ܠܗ ܡܬܚܒܒܢܐ܇ ܡܢ ܗܿܘ ܡܐ ܕܗܘܐ ܘܡܢ ܒܪܢܫܐ. ܕܐܝܟ ܗܢܐ ܒܪ ܡܕܡ ܐܠܗܘܬܗ܆ ܡܕܡ ܚܫܐ. ܡܕܝܢ ܕܠܐ ܚܫܐ ܐܠܗܘܬܗ܆ ܪܘܚܐ.

§32 ܐܡܪܢܐ ܕܝܢ ܐܦ ܡܬܘܡܝܢܐ. ܐܝ ܕܝܢ ܠܗ ܡܬܘܡܝܢܐ ܗܘ. ܡܢ ܙܒܢܐ ܘܒܙܒܢܐ ܡܕܡ ܗܘܐ. ܐܚܝܕ ܗܘܐ. ܐܠܐ ܐܝ ܕܐܦ ܐܝܬ ܠܗ ܥܠܬܐ ܕܗܘܝܗ ܗܘܐ. ܗܘ܆ ܡܬܡܕܪܢܐ ܡܬܪܒܝܢܐ ܡܕܝܢܗܘܢ܆ ܘܗܿܝ܆ ܐܠܗܘܬܗ ܪܘܚܐ ܚܫܝܫܐܝܬ. ܠܟܠ ܗܘܝܐ ܒܪ. ܡܕܡܝܢܐ ܠܗ ܥܠܬܐ ܒܒܪܝܬܐ. ܠܗܿܘ ܕܝܢ ܡܐ ܕܪܘܚܐ ܗܘ. ܠܐ ܙܒܢ ܕܢܗܘܐ ܐܝܬ ܡܕܡ ܕܡܕܝܢ ܠܗ. ܡܕܝܢ ܡܬܘܡܝܢܐ ܗܘ ܪܘܚܐ.

§33 ܬܘܒ ܕܝܢ ܠܪܘܚܐ ܕܗܘܝܐ. ܠܐ ܡܬܚܫܒܢܐ ܙܒܢ ܕܢܗܘܐ ܘܗܘܐ ܐܠܗܘܬܗ. ܐܝ ܒܪ ܢܐܡܪ ܐܚܕ ܕܡܬܚܫܒ ܪܘܚܐ. ܠܐ ܐܝܬ ܠܗ ܕܢܗܘܐ ܡܕܡ ܕܠܗ ܡܬܚܫܒ. ܠܐ ܒܪ ܠܝ ܬܘܬܐ ܦܫܝܛܬܐ ܥܠ ܟܠ ܒܗ ܢܬܚܫܒ. ܘܠܐ ܬܘܒ ܠܡܬܪܒܝܢܘܬܐ. ܐܝ ܕܝܢ ܢܐܡܪ ܕܠܦܫܝܛܘܬܐ ܡܬܚܫܒ. ܡܕܡܝܢܐ ܗܘ܆ ܕܐܦ ܠܗܠܝܢ ܐܦ ܠܐܚܪܢܝܬܐ ܡܬܚܫܒ. ܐܠܐ ܐܝ ܗܿܢ ܠܗܠܝܢ ܐܦ ܗܟܢܐ ܒܟܠ ܡܬܚܙܐ ܕܠܐ ܚܫܐ. ܘܐܝ ܬܘܒ ܠܡܕܡ ܐܚܪܢܐ ܦܫܝܛܐ. ܐܠܐ ܐܢ | ܕܐܦ ܟܠ ܗܢܐ. ܗܿܝ܆ ܒܗ <ܗܿܝ> ܒܥܠܬܐ ܬܘܗܐ. ܐܚܝܕ ܠܡܬܪܒܝܢܘܬܐ. ܡܕܡܝܢܐ ܗܘ܆ ܕܗܘܦܟ ܗܘ ܘܐܠܗܘܬܗ܆ ܒܗܝ. ܡܛܠ ܕܡܬܚܫܒ ܗܿܝ ܘܡܬܚܙܝܢ. ܒܟܠ ܡܬܪܒܝܢܐ ܒܪ. ܘܡܬܚܙܐ ܡܢ ܦܫܝܛܘܬܗ.

§34 ܐܠܐ ܘܐܦܠܐ ܠܠܐ ܡܕܡ ܡܢ ܕܢܬܚܫܒ. ܘܠܐ ܡܕܡ ܒܪ ܠܗܘ ܡܐ ܕܒܪܐܝܬ ܠܐܠܗܘܬܗ܆ ܡܬܚܫܒ. ܒܗ ܗܕܐ ܕܝܢ ܒܪܢܫܐ ܗܘܬ. ܕܢܬܪܡܐ ܠܗ ܟܠ ܡܐ ܕܐܠܗܘܬܗ܆ ܡܛܠ ܐܡܒܝܢ ܕܪܘܚܢܝܬܐ ܕܟܠ ܗܘܝܐ. ܘܠܐ ܗܿܝ܆ ܪܘܚܢܝܬܐ ܬܘܒ ܬܗܘܐ ܗܘܬ ܡܢ ܡܕܡ. ܡܛܠ ܕܠܐ ܐܝܬ ܗܘܬ ܪܘܚܢܝܬܐ ܕܡܕܝܢܗ ܬܗܘܐ ܗܘܬ. ܘܠܐ ܬܘܒ ܐܚܪܢܝܬܐ ܗܘܝܢ ܗܘ܆ ܡܕܝܢ ܕܗܘܐ: ܕܟܠ ܟܠܗ ܠܐܠܗܘܬܗ ܗܘܬ. ܡܕܝܢ ܐܬܚܙܝܬ ܕܠܐ ܐܠܗܘܬܗ܆ ܪܘܚܐ ܡܬܚܙܝܢܐ ܕܣܘܟܠܐ.

§35 ܡܛܠ ܗܟܢܐ ܕܐܬܐܡܪܬ ܕܢܒܗ ܪܘܚܐ܇ ܘܐܝܠܝܢ ܐܚܪܢ ܕܠܥܠܬܗ܆ ܘܕܐܝܬܘܗܝ ܟܠܗ ܗܠܝܢ ܡܟܢܫ ܐܚܕ܇ ܕܒܗ ܢܘܪܐ ܐܠܗܘܬܗ܆ ܪܘܚܐ ܡܕܡܝܢܐ ܕܡܕܝܢܗ ܗܘܐ ܗܘܝܐ܇ ܐܘ ܐܝܟܢܐ. ܐܘ ܫܡܝܐ. ܐܘ ܐܝܟܪ. ܐܚܝܕ ܐܚܕ ܢܐܡܪ ܕܚܕ ܡܢ ܗܠܝܢ ܐܦܘܩܠܣܝܣ ܐܠܗܘܬܗ܆ ܪܘܚܐ. ܒܪܢܫܐ ܠܗ ܕܠܗܘܝܐ ܦܐܪܡ ܕܐܠܗܘܬܗ܆ ܪܘܚܐ.

14 ܗܿܝ[2]] om. cod.   25 ܗܘܝܐ] add. in marg.: ܗܘܝܐ ܘܫܟܠܐ ܫܪܝܪܘܬܐ ܘܦܬܓܡܐ ܢܘܪܐ ܘܡܝܐ

§31 In the same way, it is also unqualified. For if it is qualified and has quality, it is likewise compound of a subject and an accident. For it is in this way that something becomes something qualified. Consequently, a principle is unqualified.

§32 I also call it eternal. For if it is not eternal, it will have started in time and existed for a particular time. If it is like that, it is necessary that it also had a cause from which it came to be. That (cause) would precede it and be considered prior to it, and would truly be a principle. For an active cause is prior to everything that comes to be. But it is proper that nothing should be prior to something that is a principle. Consequently, a principle is eternal.

§33 Further, it is proper that principles of existing things must be imperishable. For if someone were to say that a principle perishes, he would not be able to show anything into which it perishes, for after it has perished, it can neither be reduced to simple things nor to composite ones. Because if one were to say that it perished into simple things, it would be clear that it either perishes into itself or into something else. But if (it perishes) into itself, then in this way it is still preserved without perishing. And further, if (it perishes) into something else that is simple, also in this way it will necessarily be the ⟨same⟩ with the object of search. And if (it perishes) into composite things, then it is obvious that it is preserved and exists in those things, since they are compound of it. For the composition of everything compound is of simple things.

§34 But neither can it perish into nothing. For nothing perishes into what is completely nonexistent. What would follow from it is that we would negate everything that exists because of the destruction of the principle of every existing thing. Further, there would be no principle of anything, because there would be no principle from which it would come to be. Neither would anything else come to be from it, for it will be entirely nonexistent. Therefore, it is apparent that there is no principle which allows of perishing.

§35 Now, after it has been said what a principle is and what its properties are, it is necessary to inquire whether fire is the First Principle from which existing things come to be, or whether it is earth, water, or air[12]. If someone says that one of these elements (στοιχεῖα) is a principle, he errs by setting as a principle

12 A commentary in the right margin in the middle of the page: "Coming-to-be and perishing, singularity and plurality, fire and water."

ܐܢܐ ܕܝܢ ܐܡܪ ܐܢܐ. ܕܠܘܩܒܠܐ ܪܫܐ ܐܝܬ ܠܗ ܕܒܝܫܘܬܐ ܗܘܐ. ܪܫܐ ܕܝܢ ܠܐ ܐܝܬܘܗܝ ܗܘܝܐ.

§36 ܙܕܩ ܠܗܘܢ ܕܝܢ ܠܪ̈ܫܐ. ܕܟܕ ܟܝ ܚܕ ܬܪ̈ܝܢ ܢܗܘܘܢ ܐܝܬܝܗܘܢ ܪ̈ܫܐ ܩܕ̈ܡܝܐ. ܘܫܘܝܢ ܗܠܝܢ ܕܠܘܩܒܠܐ ܙܕܩ ܕܢܗܘܘܢ ܐܝܬܝܗܘܢ. ܗܟܢܐ ܓܝܪ ܣܓܝܐ ܘܐܢܫܝܢ ܡܢ ܗܠܝܢ ܕܡܕܡ ܦܠܓܘܢ. ܡܢܗܘܢ ܓܝܪ ܣ̈ܒܝܥܝܢ ܘܡ̈ܨܝܪܐ. ܐܚܪ̈ܢܐ ܕܝܢ ܙ̈ܘܓܝܐ ܘܡܬܢܝܐ ܐܡܝܪ ܕܐܝܬܝܗܘܢ ܪ̈ܫܐ ܕܗܘ̈ܝܐ. ܚܕ ܕܝܢ ܡܢܗܘܢ ܪܚܡܘܬܐ ܘܚܣܡܘܬܐ. ܐܚܪ̈ܢܐ ܬܘܒ ܚܕ ܘܣܓܝ ܓܒܐ. ܐܘ ܡܫܝܚܐ ܥܡܐ ܘܐܦܐ ܓܒܐ. ܗܕܐ ܕܝܢ ܐܝܬܝܗ ܠܡܕܒܪܢܘܬܐ ܘܬܪܝܨܘܬܐ. ܐܝܟ ܕܐܡܪܘ
f. 115r | ܗܠܝܢ ܕܟܣܠܬ ܦܠܛ ܓܒܘܪܘܣ. ܟܠܗܘܢ ܕܝܢ ܗܠܝܢ ܒܗܕܐ ܕܕܠܩܘܒܠܐ ܐܝܬܝܗܘܢ ܪ̈ܫܐ ܩܕ̈ܡܝܐ ܥܠܬܐ ܠܫܘ̈ܕܝܐ. ܦܠܛܝܢ ܕܝܢ ܒܗܕܐ. ܕܡܢܗܘܢ ܐܚܪ̈ܢܐ ܢܗܘܐ. ܘܡܢܗܘܢ ܡܩ̈ܕܡܝܐ. ܘܡܢܗܘܢ ܗ̇ܘܠܝܐ ܒܠܚܘܕ.

§37 ܐܠܐ ܕܝܢ ܘܐܦ ܠܝ ܥܦܪܐ: ܗ̇ܝ ܕܟܕ ܟܝ ܚܕ ܬܪ̈ܝܢ ܢܗܘܘܢ ܪ̈ܫܐ ܩܕ̈ܡܝܐ: ܘܕܠܘܩܒܠܐ ܬܘܒ ܢܗܘܘܢ. ܚܕ ܗ̇ܘ ܐܝܟ ܒܗܘܕܐ. ܐܚܪ̈ܢܐ ܕܝܢ ܐܝܟ ܗ̇ܘ ܡܐ ܕܢܐܡܪ ܡܢܗ. ܙܕܩ ܠܗܘܢ ܕܝܢ ܠܪ̈ܫܐ. ܕܠܐ ܡܢ ܐܚܪ̈ܢܐ ܢܗܘܘܢ ܐܝܬܝܗܘܢ. ܘܠܐ ܡܢ ܫܘ̈ܕܝܐ. ܗܠܝܢ ܕܝܢ ܬܬܐܝܬܝܗܝܢ ܠܕܠܘܩܒܠܝܬܐ ܩܕ̈ܡܝܬܐ ܢܩܦܢ. ܡܛܠ ܕܝܢ ܕܩܕ̈ܡܝܬܐ ܐܢܝܢ. ܠܝܬ ܐܢܝܢ ܡܢ ܐܚܪ̈ܢܝܬܐ. ܘܡܛܠ ܕܕܠܘܩܒܠܝܬܐ ܐܢܝܢ. ܠܝܬܝܗܝܢ ܡܢ ܫܘ̈ܕܝܐ. ܕܠܘܩܒܠܝܬܐ ܕܝܢ ܗ̇ܢܝܢ ܕܟܒܠ ܚܕ: ܠܚܕܐ ܐܢܝܢ. ܘܟܗ̇ܝ ܕܗ̇ܘܝܬܐ ܐܢܝܢ. ܡܢ ܒܠܦܘܪܣ ܐܦ ܡܢ ܫܘ̈ܕܝܐ ܗ̇ܘܝܢ. ܗܠܝܢ ܕܝܢ ܩܕ̈ܡܝܬܐ ܠܐ. ܡܛܠ ܕܐܦ ܗ̇ܘ̈ ܐܘ ܗܘ̈ܝܢ. ܠܐ ܡܟܝܠ ܐܝܬܝܗܝܢ ܩܕ̈ܡܝܬܐ ܡܪܢܐܝܬ.

§38 ܗܠܝܢ ܕܝܢ ܬܪ̈ܝܢ ܪ̈ܫܐ ܩܕ̈ܡܝܐ ܘܕܠܘܩܒܠܐ ܐܝܟ ܕܐܡܪܢ ܐܝܬ. ܚܕ ܒܗܘܕܐ ܘܚܕ ܚܘܣܪܢܐ. ܒܗܘܕܐ ܓܝܪ ܐܠܗܐ. ܚܘܣܪܢܐ ܕܝܢ ܗܘܠܐ. ܡܛܠ ܕܝܢ ܕܗ̇ܘ ܒܗܘܕܐ: ܐܠܝܟܐ ܗ̇ܝ ܠܗ ܕܒܕܡܘܬ ܪܘܫܡܐ ܘܨܘܪܬܐ ܘܣܘܟܠܐ ܕܒܗ ܢܒܕܘܢܗ̇ ܠܗ̇ܘ ܡܐ ܕܢܒܕ. ܐܬܝܕܥܬ ܠܗ̇ ܐܦ ܪܘܫܡܬܐ ܕܬܠܬ ܕܗܠܝܢ ܕܗ̇ܘܝܢ.

§39 ܗܠܝܢ ܡܕܝܢ ܬܠܬܐ ܐܝܬܝܗܘܢ ܪ̈ܫܐ ܩܕ̈ܡܝܐ ܕܗ̇ܘܝܐ. ܐܠܗܐ ܘܗܘܠܐ ܘܨܘܪܬܐ ܩܕ̈ܡܝܐ ܕܗ̇ܘܝܐ. ܘܐܠܗܐ ܡܢ ܐܝܬܘܗܝ ܪܫܐ ܕܟܝܢܗ ܩܕܡܝܐܝܬ

7 ܐܚܪ̈ܢܐ ܬܘܒ ܚܕ] add. in marg.: ܗܘܝܐ ܕܗܢܐ ܚܠܦ ܗܢܐ. ܐܟܘܬܐ ܕܚܠܦܐ ܕܣܠܬܐ ܗܘܝܐ ܕܚܠܦܐ. ܘܚܠܦܐ ܕܙܪܥܐ ܗܘܝܐ ܕܣܘܦܬܐ. 17 ܗ̇ܘܝܢ] add. supra lin.

that which comes to be. Instead, I say that coming-to-be has a principle from which it comes to be, but a principle is not a coming-to-be.

§36 In that case when the First Principles are reduced to two, it is necessary that they be opposite to each other. For this is also how some people before Plato taught. Some of them stated that principles of existing things are the hot and the cold, while others that they are the wet and the dry. One of them (stated that it is) Love and Victory[13]. Still, others (said) that it is One and Many[14], or Even and Odd (number). This is Monad and Dyad, as the Pythagoreans said. All of them agreed that the First Principles were opposite to each other, though they differed (from each other) in that some of them considered them as secondary, some as primary, and some only as material.

§37 However, it also seems good to us that, when the First Principles are reduced to two and are thus opposed to each other, one of them is like an active one and the other is like one that is affected by it. But it is necessary that these principles not originate from something else or from each other. And two of them that are characterised as being in primary opposition, because they are primary, cannot originate from something else, and because they are opposed, they cannot originate from each other. Those opposites in each of them exist in them by accident, in that they are generated things. And consequently, they originate from each other, while the primary ones do not. For if they had come to be or are coming to be, they would no longer be primary in the proper sense.

§38 So, of two First Principles which are opposed to each other, as we said, one is active and the other is passive. The active one is God, and the passive one is Matter. And because He is the active (cause), it is necessary that He performs His actions in accordance with the Idea, Form, and Thought that are in Him. This made apparent to us that there is a third principle of existing things.

§39 These are, namely, the three First Principles of existing things: God, Matter, and First Ideas of existing things. God is the principle by which origin-

13 I.e. love and *strife*. The same misinterpretation of the Greek form νεῖκος as νῖκος occurs in §13.

14 A commentary in the margin in the middle of the page: "The coming-to-be of something is the perishing of another, e.g. the death of wheat is the birth of an ear, and the death of a seed is the birth of a living being."

ܐܬܚܒܪ ܡܕܡ. ܘܪܘܫܡܐ ܡܕܡܝܐ ܐܝܬܘܗܝ، ܪܫܐ. ܕܒܕܡܘܬܗ ܐܬܚܒܪ ܗܘ ܕܐܬܚܒܪ. ܘܗܘܠܐ ܐܝܬܘܗܝ ܪܫܐ. ܕܡܢܗ ܡܕܡܝܐܝܬ: ܓܒܪ ܒܚܒܪܘܬܐ ܡܕܡ.

§40 ܡܛܠ ܕܝܢ ܕܗܠܝܢ ܗܘܝܐ ܐܬܬܣܝܡ. ܢܐܡܪ ܡܕܡܝܐܝܬ | ܥܠ ܗܘܠܐ. ܕܐܝܟܢܐ ܕܝܢ ܪܫܐ ܗܘܠܐ. ܫܦܝܪܐ ܘܠܗܠܝܢ ܕܒܝܫܬ ܦܝܫܬ ܠܒܪܘܣ. ܘܠܦܘܪܦܘܪܝܘܣ ܘܠܦܠܛܘܢ ܘܠܗܠܝܢ ܕܒܬܪ ܦܠܛܘܢ. ܘܠܐܦܝܩܘܪܘܣ. ܘܠܐܪܣܛܛܠܝܣ. ܦܪܐܘܗ ܕܝܢ ܗܠܝܢ ܕܒܬܪ ܦܠܛܘܢ. ܗܘܠܐ. (col. b)

§41 ܦܠܛܘܢ ܕܝܢ ܘܠܐ ܒܕܘܟ ܡܬܬܣܝܡܐ ܕܦܪܝܐ ܠܗ ܗܘܠܐ. ܐܠܐ ܒܒܘܢܝܐ ܐܣܝܪܐ ܡܚܒܐ ܠܗ. ܒܪ ܠܡܚܘܝܘ ܢܦܫ ܡܢܗ ܕܝܢ ܒܗܘܬܐ. ܘܠܡܚܘܝܘ ܡܢ ܫܟܐ ܕܝܢ. ܡܢܗ ܡܢ ܕܝܢ ܒܗܘܬܐ. ܐܒܘܢܐ ܕܦܪܝܐ ܠܗ ܫܬܐܣܬܐ ܡܕܡܝܬܐ: ܘܗܘ ܡܐ ܕܗܝܡܢ ܡܕܡܝܐܝܬ ܡܕܡ ܒܠܗܘܢ ܗ̈ܘܠܐ: ܐܘ ܡܩܒܠܢܬ ܟܠ. ܘܐܡܡܐ ܠܗ ܘܐܡܗܐ ܘܡܩܒܠܢܝܬܐ ܕܟܠ ܗ̈ܘܝܢ ܐܝܟ ܢܩܒܬܐ. ܡܢ ܫܟܐ ܕܝܢ ܕܡܢ ܡܚܒܐ ܠܗ: ܐܝܟ ܡܢܐ ܕܐܡܪ ܕܒܣܘܫܡܐ ܒܪܬܠܝܐ ܠܡܚܘܝܘ ܡܬܝܠܢܐ.

§42 ܗܠܝܢ ܕܝܢ ܕܡܢ ܐܦܠܛܘܢ. ܐܘܣܝܐ ܦܘܪܘܗ. ܘܡܬܬܣܝܡܢ ܠܗ ܗܘܝܐ. ܐܘܣܝܐ ܠܡ ܐܝܬܝܗ ܗܘܠܐ ܕܟܠ ܡܕܡ. ܘ ܒܐܝܢܐܝܬ ܡܢ ܡܬܬܕܪܐ ܠܟܠܗܘܢ. ܕܐܝܟܢܐ ܗܘܠܐ ܚܫܝܫܬܐ ܘܡܬܬܠܡܫܬܐ: ܘܒܠܗ ܒܟܠܗ ܡܬܠ ܚܫܝܫܬܐ. ܠܐ ܡܩܒܠ ܒܗ ܒܪ ܒܗ ܒܫܪ ܪܚܝܩܐ. ܗܠܝܢ ܕܝܢ ܕܡܢ ܐܦܠܛܘܢ. ܐܡܪܝܢ ܠܗ ܕܡܛܠ ܚܫܝܫܬܐ ܒܟܠܬܐ ܕܝܠܗ ܘܗܘܠܐ ܐܝܣܘܬܐ. ܒܪ ܠܐ ܢܦܩ ܠܗ ܡܕܡ. ܐܠܐ ܐܢ ܗܕܐ ܕܐܡܒܠܐ ܐܝܬܝܗ. ܐܝܟ ܕܬܗܘܐ ܡܕܡܐ. ܕܠܘ ܡܕܡ ܐܣܝܪ ܐܝܬܝܗ ܐܝܣܘܬܐ: ܠܒܪ ܡܢ ܗܘܠܐ. ܐܠܐ ܐܡܒܠܐ ܕܐܝܬܝܗ ܐܘܣܝܐ. ܐܝܬܝܗ ܐܝܣܘܬܐ: ܘܟܠ ܐܣܝܪܬܐ ܒܗ ܒܕܡܘܬܐ.

§43 ܠܐ ܕܝܢ ܠܘ ܗܘܝܐ ܡܬܬܣܝܡܐ. ܠܐ ܒܪ ܐܝܬܝܗ ܗܘܠܐ ܐܝܣܘܬܐ. ܐܠܐ (f. 115v) ܐܝܣܘܬܐ ܐܝܬܝܗ ܒܪܫܐ. ܗܘܠܐ ܕܝܢ ܗܘ ܡܐ ܕܗܝܡܢ ܕܒܗ | ܩܐܡ ܒܪܫܐ. ܡܬܐܡܪܐ ܕܝܢ ܫܘܫܒܘܬܐ ܒܗܕܐ. ܕܡܩܒܠܐ ܠܝܣܘܬܐ ܘܗܘܝܐ ܒܗ ܐܝܣܘܬܐ. ܫܘܫܠܦܐ ܕܗܘܝܢ ܒܗܘܠܐ. ܠܘ ܕܠܗ ܕܗܘܠܐ ܐܢܘܢ: ܐܠܐ ܕܙܢܝܐ ܕܒܗ. ܡܛܠ ܕܐܢܫܘ ܕܗ، ܒܠܬܗ ܡܬܬܠܡܫܐ ܗܘܬ. ܠܡܕܡ ܐܣܝܪ ܡܬܬܠܡܫܐ ܗܘܬ. ܕܕܡ ܗܘܝܐ ܒܪ ܕܢܦܫܐ ܐܝܬܘܗܝ، ܗܘܢܐ. ܘܐܢ ܡܬܠ ܚܫܝܫܬܐ ܗܘܬ ܗܝ، ܒܠܬܗ ܠܡܕܡ ܐܣܝܪ. ܦܫܝܛܐ ܗܘܬ ܠܗ ܡܢ ܗܕܐ ܕܗܘܠܐ ܐܝܬܝܗ. ܗܕܐ ܐܝܬܝܗ ܠܐ ܡܬܬܚܡܝܢ ܚܫܝܫܬܐ.

ally something was acted. The First Idea is the principle after the likeness of which something which was acted was acted. And Matter is the principle out of which originally some activity acted.

(4. Definition of Matter)

§40 As these things have been defined in this way, first we will speak about Matter. That Matter is a principle seems good also to the Pythagoreans, to Socrates and Plato, to those who were after Plato, to the Stoics, and to Aristotle. Those who were after Plato called it "matter" (ὕλη).

§41 But it seems that Plato nowhere calls it "matter", but uses other names for it, deriving some of them from the object itself, and others from affections in us. From the object itself, thus, he calls it the primary foundation, the first subject that is prior to all beings, or "all-receptive"[15], or "mould" (ἐκμαγεῖον)[16], or "mother" and "receptacle of all beings" which is like a female[17]. He names it from the affections in us when he says that it is difficult to consider it in pure thought[18].

§42 And the Stoics called it "substance" (οὐσία) and defined it as follows: substance is matter of everything. And in general, it is acknowledged by all of them that there is Matter which is passive and alterable and wholly and in all respects changeable. However, there is no unanimity on this question. For the Stoics consider (Matter) in the account of its essence to be changeable and becoming qualified, as nothing is associated with it, except in regard to how it exists. Thus, it should become apparent that quality is nothing else, except Matter. But in the way substance is, so is quality. And similarly about the rest.

§43 But it does not seem this way to us, for quality is not Matter. Rather, quality is an accident, while Matter is a subject in which an accident appears. It is called passive in the sense that it receives quality and through it becomes qualification. Those changes that occur in Matter are not its own, but are of the qualities in it. For if it were to be changeable in its essence, it might change into something else, (and) thus it would be necessary for the latter thing to exist. So, if it were to change in its essence into something else, it would cease to be Matter, which is impossible.

15 Plato, *Tim.* 51a7.
16 Plato, *Tim.* 50c2.
17 Plato, *Tim.* 51a4–5.
18 Plato, *Tim.* 52b2.

§44 ܬܘܒ ܐܚܪܢܐ ܕܡܪܘܬܐ ܕܝܢ ܡܫܬܠܛܐ ܒܐܘܣܝܐ ܕܡܠܬܐ: ܠܐ ܢܦܩܐ ܥܠ ܟܠܗ ܡܢ ܚܝܠܐ ܕܡܠܟܗ̇: ܐܠܐ ܡܟܬܪܐ ܗ̄ܝ ܡܪܘܬܐ: ܐܘܣܝܐ ܕܝܢ ܗܠܝܢ ܕܒܗ̇ ܗ̄ܘܘ ܕܡܫܬܠܛܝܢ ܠܫܪܪܐ. ܗܠܝܢ ܕܠܐ ܐܝܬܝܗܘܢ ܡܪܘܬܐ: ܘܒܗܘܢܐ ܐܝܟ ܡܬܐܡܪܢܐ ܗ̇ܝ ܡܪܘܬܐ ܚܫܚܬܐ. ܡܚܝܠܐ ܕܝܢ ܘܗܘܠܐ. ܒܪ ܒܠܥܕ ܠܐܘܣܝܐ ܐܚܪܢܐ ܘܐܢܫܘܬܐ ܡܫܬܠܩܬܐ ܡܡܠܠܐ ܒܗ̇. ܒܪ ܗ̄ܝ ܡܚܬܪܐ ܒܡܠܟܗ̇ ܕܠܐ ܚܘܠܦ: ܡܬܐܡܪܐ ܒܗܢܐ ܐܝܟ ܚܫܚܘܬܐ.

§45 ܬܘܒ ܕܝܢ ܒܐܢܫܘܬ ܐܡܪܝܢ. ܕܐܝܬܝܗ̇ ܒܡܠܟܗ̇. ܕܠܐ ܐܝܟ ܘܕܠܐ ܐܕܝܫܐ <ܘܕܠܐ> ܐܘܣܝܐ. ܠܘ ܐܝܟ ܕܐܝܬ ܐܢܫܐ ܕܠܝܬ ܒܗ̇ ܗܠܝܢ. ܐܠܐ ܐܦ ܕܒܡܠܬܐ ܕܐܝܬܗ̇ ܠܐ ܦܫܐ ܗܠܝܢ: ܘܠܐ ܚܕܐ ܐܢܫܘܬܐ ܕܠܝܬܗ̇. ܐܦ ܕܝܢ ܒܪܚܡܐ ܡܫܬܠܡܝܢ ܠܗ̇ ܡܢ ܐܢܫܘܬܐ ܒܡܠܟܗ̇. ܐܠܐ ܠܘ ܒܝ ܢܪܐܝܬ ܐܡܪܝܢ ܕܚܝܠܐ ܐܝܬܝܗܘܢ ܠܗ̇.

§46 ܗ̄ܝ ܕܝܢ ܗܕܐ ܕܚܝܠܐ. ܒܠܚܘܕ ܐܢܫܐ ܡܬܐܡܪܐ. ܚܕ ܓܝܪ ܐܝܟ ܡܐ ܕܐܡܪܝܢ ܕܐܝܬܝܗܘܢ ܒܪܘܚܐ ܓ̈ܒܠܐ ܟ̈ܠܗ ܕܗܠܝܢ ܕܩܘܝܢ ܡܢܗ ܒܚܝܠܐ. ܐܚܪܢܐ ܕܝܢ. ܗ̇ܘ ܕܒܡܠܟܗ ܠܐ ܦܝܫܐ ܒܗ ܟ̈ܠܗ ܗܠܝܢ: ܒܗ̇ ܕܝܢ ܕܡܢ ܠܡܡܠܠܘ ܐܚܝܢ ܘܠܡܬܬܠܒܒܘ ܒܗܘܢ: ܡܬܐܡܪ ܕܐܝܬܝܗܘܢ ܒܗ ܒܚܝܠܐ. ܐܝܟ ܡܪܘܬܐ
col. b ܘܫܘܚܐ | ܕܡܬܐܡܪܝܢ ܒܚܝܠܐ ܐܕ̈ܝܫܐ ܘܐܘܣܝܐ ܕܡܬܬܠܒܒܝܢ ܒܗܘܢ.

§47 ܐܝܟܢܐ ܗܟܝܠ ܕܒܗ̇ ܡܫܬܘܕܥܢܘܬܐ ܡܕܡܥܠܬܐ ܢܐܡܪ ܐܢܫ: ܕܡܫܝܚܐ ܗ̄ܝ ܒܗ̇ ܗܘܠܐ ܠܝܫܘܬܐ ܒܚܝܠܐ: ܘܒܗܢ ܗܠܝܢ ܬܘܒ: ܠܐܕ̈ܝܫܐ ܘܐܘܣܝܐ: ܐܝܟ ܓܝܪ ܕܡܢܗ̇ ܗܠܝܢ ܟܠܗܘܢ ܬܚܝܢ. ܘܠܘܬ ܫܘܚܠܦܐ ܐܬܝܢ. ܠܐ ܡܚܝܠ ܐܝܬ ܠܗ̇ ܦܘܢܝܐ ܥܠ ܒܥܘܕܪܐ ܠܘܬ ܦܘܪܩܢܗ ܕܚ̈ܒܪܐ. ܙܕܩ ܕܝܢ. ܕܒܗ ܗܘܠܐ ܢܗܘܐ ܐܦ ܒܥܘܕܪܐ: ܐܝܟ ܒܠܚܘܕ ܕܬܬܚܫܒ ܒܥܕܪܐ. ܐܟܚܕ ܒܗ̇ܘ ܘܠܐ ܕܐܬܝܢ: ܐܡܪܝܢ ܕܐܝܬܝܗܘܢ ܒܗ̇ ܗܠܝܢ ܒܚܝܠܐ. ܘܠܥܘܕܪܐ ܬܘܒ ܡܫܪܝܢ. ܘܡܫܪܪܬܐ ܘܠܐ ܚܕ ܢܦܩܐ ܠܡܠܬܐ.

§48 ܬܘܒ ܕܝܢ ܘܗܕܐ. ܕܒܗܐ ܗ̄ܝ ܠܗܘܢ: ܕܙܕܩ ܠܗ̇ ܠܗܘܠܐ ܒܟܠ ܦܘܪܫܢ ܕܡܬܬܘܡܝܬܐ ܬܗܘܐ ܐܝܬܘܬܗ̇. ܐܝܟ ܗ̇ܘ ܕܪܫܝܐ ܗ̄ܝ ܕܗ̈ܘܝܐ. ܗܕܐ ܕܝܢ ܕܡܫܬܡܠܝܬܐ ܗ̄ܝ. ܠܘ ܕܒܗܐ ܗ̄ܝ. ܐܟܚܕ ܗܕܐ. ܡܫܬܘܕܥܐ ܕܐܝܟ ܒܡܫܘܬܐ

8 ܘܕܠܐ] om. cod.   13 ܓ̈ܒܠܐ ܟ̈ܠܗ ܕܗܠܝܢ] fort. leg. ܟ̈ܠܗ ܕܓ̈ܒܠܐ ܗܠܝܢ   22 ܡܫܪܝܢ scr.: ܡܬܪܝܢ cod.

§44 Further, as in the case of the wax, while it changes in the shapes it receives, it does not depart totally from the faculty of its essence, but remains being wax, while the shapes in it change into one another, i.e. something that is not wax, and in this way is it said that wax is passible; so also in the case of Matter: while it constantly receives in itself various shapes and different qualities, it remains without change in its essence. It is in this way that we speak about passibility.

§45 Further, they say in general that it is unqualified, unspecified, ⟨and⟩ form⟨less⟩[19] in its essence. Not as though there is a time when these (categories) are absent from it, but rather in the account of its essence it does not possess them, nor even a single particular quality. But even if in (our) intellect we differentiate it in its essence from qualities, we nontheless say that it has them potentially.

§46 For there are two ways of saying that (something exists) potentially. One of them is when we say that in a seed there are principles of ears[20] that potentially come to be from it. Another is when something does not possess such principles in its essence, but may naturally receive them and be imprinted by them. It is stated that these exist potentially in it, just as forms and shapes are said to be potentially imprinted upon wax and brass.

§47 Now, if someone says according to the first meaning that Matter in itself potentially possesses qualities, and together with them also forms and shapes, so that all these appear from it and come to completion, then the active (cause) is not necessary for the constitution of the activity. But it is proper that there be an active (cause) together with Matter if an activity is to take place. And if in the second way we say that these exist potentially in it (i.e. Matter), then we also exclude the active (cause). But this is absurd and does not follow the reason.

§48 Further, both (meanings) have in common that it is necessary for Matter to be in every way eternal if it is a principle of existing things. For it is not a common (opinion) that it is finite. Because if it were, it would mean that

19 This seems to be the original meaning of the text, which in its present (probably corrupt) state may be translated as "of unspecified form".

20 Syriac text seems to be corrupt here. However, it is obvious that the author elaborates the Stoic idea of generative principles (λόγοι).

ܡܕܡ ܡܬܡܫܚܢܘܬܐ ܘܡܬܚܡܢܘܬܐ ܡܬܐܡܪܐ ܡܫܘܚܬܐ. ܒܡܫܘܚܬܐ ܕܝܢ ܡܬܡܫܚܢܘܬܐ. ܐܘ ܐܝܟ ܣܘܪܓܐ ܗ̣ܝ ܐܘ ܐܝܟ ܦܫܝܛܘܬܐ. ܐܘ ܐܝܟ ܒܡ̈ܢܝܢܐ. ܐܠܐ <ܠܐ> ܐܝܟ ܣܘܪܓܐ. ܘܠܐ ܐܝܟ ܦܫܝܛܘܬܐ ܡܬܐܡܪܐ ܡܫܘܚܬܐ. ܫܪܟܐ ܡܕܝܢ ܕܐܝܟ ܒܡܢܝܢܐ. ܐܚܪܝܢ ܐܝܟ ܒܡܢܝܢܐ. ܡܕܝܢ ܐܝܬ ܗܘ̣ ܠܗ̇ ܐܦ ܐܣܟܡܐ. ܗܟܢ ܕܝܢ ܕܒܡܢܝܢܐ. ܐܣܟܡܐ ܗܘ̣. ܘܐܣܟܡܐ ܐܕܫܐ ܗܘ ܡܕܡ ܕܙܘܥܬܐ.

§49 ܐܝܟܘ̇ ܡܕܡ ܕܒܗܢܐ ܙܢܐ ܐܝܬܝܗ̇ ܗܘܠܐ ܡܫܘܚܬܐ. ܙܢܝܬܐ ܐܝܬܝܗ̇ ܘܡܣܟܡܬܐ ܒܡܠܬܐ ܕܐܝܬܝܗ̇. ܐܠܐ ܡܛܠ ܕܕܠܐ ܙܢܐ ܘܕܠܐ ܐܣܟܡܐ ܣܟܡܗ̇ | ܒܡܠܬܐ ܕܐܝܬܝܗ̇. ܕܡܝܐ ܗ̣ܝ ܕܐܦ ܠܐ ܡܫܘܚܬܐ ܗ̣ܝ. ܐܠܐ ܠܐ ܡܫܘܚܬܐ. ܠܘ ܐܝܟ ܡܕܡ ܕܠܝܬ ܠܗ ܡܫܘܚܐ ܘܠܐ ܒܪܝܐ ܡܬܐܡܪܐ. ܐܠܐ ܐܝܟ ܗ̇ܘ ܡܢ ܕܡܬܚܙܐ ܕܢܩܒܠ ܗܟܢܐ: ܠܐ ܕܝܢ ܒܕܒܝܠ ܐܣܬܝܢ ܒܪܝܢܐ ܕܐܝܬܝܗ̇. ܘܐܡܝܢܐ ܕܠܐ ܙܢܐ ܘܕܠܐ ܐܣܟܡܐ ܡܬܐܡܪܐ. ܗܟܢܐ ܘܕܠܐ ܗܟܢܐ. ܐܝܟ ܡܢ ܕܠܐ ܒܕܒܝܠ ܡܠܬ ܗܟܢܐ.

§50 ܕܐܝܬ ܗܘ ܕܝܢ ܡܕܡ ܕܣܝܡ ܬܚܝܬ ܗܠܝܢ ܐܪ̈ܒܥܐ ܐܣܛܘ̈ܟܣܐ ܐܝܟ ܫܬܐܣܬܐ ܡܕܡܝܢܬܐ. ܕܠܗ ܩܕܡ ܗܘܠܐ ܕܡܝܐ ܗ̣ܝ. ܘܡܢ ܡܛܠ ܒܝܫܘܬܗܘܢ ܕܒܡ̈ܢܝܢܐ ܗܠܝܢ ܡܕ̈ܡܝܢܐ ܕܠܘܬ ܫ̈ܪܪܐ. ܘܡܢ ܡܫܬܚܠܦܘܬܗܘܢ ܕܙ̈ܢܝܐ.

§51 ܗܐ ܒܪ ܐܪ̈ܒܥܐ ܬܪ̈ܬܝܢ ܙܘܓܘܬܐ ܐܝܬ ܠܗ̇. ܝܒܝܫܘܬܐ ܘܩܪܝܪܘܬܐ. ܗܠܝܢ ܕܝܢ ܘܫ̈ܚܝܢܐ ܬܪ̈ܬܝܢ ܙܘܓܘܬܐ ܚܕ. ܪܛܝܒܘܬܐ ܘܩܪܝܪܘܬܐ. ܘܐܝܬܝܗ̇ ܕܠܝܬܐ ܡܢ ܕܐܪܥܐ ܝܒܝܫܘܬܐ. ܕܡ̈ܝܐ ܕܝܢ ܪܛܝܒܘܬܐ. ܩܪܝܪܘܬܐ ܕܝܢ ܕܟܘܠܐ ܠܬܪ̈ܬܝܗܘܢ ܗܠܝܢ ܒܡ̈ܢܝܢܐ. ܡܢ ܗܕܐ ܕܬܬܐܡܪ ܐܪܥܐ ܘܬܫܬܐ ܒܢܝܐ ܠܬ̈ܪܬܝܢ. ܗ̇ܝ ܕܝܢ ܝܒܝܫܘܬܗ̇ ܐܫܬܠܦܬ ܠܪܛܝܒܘܬܐ. ܩܪܝܪܘܬܐ ܕܝܢ ܕܐܝܬܝܗ̇ ܕ ܒܗ̇ ܐܝܟ ܡܬܚܪܐ.

§52 ܘܗ̇ܝ ܗܕܐ ܠܐ ܡܫܟܚ ܐܝܬܝܗ̇ ܒܐܪܥܐ. ܘܠܐ ܬܘܒ ܒܡ̈ܝܐ. ܘܒܐܪܥܐ ܡ̇ܢ. ܡܛܠ ܕܗ̇ܘ ܡܢ ܕܐܫܬ ܒܗ ܡܢ ܐܪܥܐ. ܠܐ ܡܫܟܚ ܐܝܬܘܗܝ ܐܪܥܐ. ܘܡ̈ܝܐ ܕܝܢ ܬܘܒ ܠܐ ܐܝܬܝܗ̇. ܡܛܠ ܕܠܐ ܒܕܒܝܠ ܗܘ̇ܐ. ܐܠܐ ܒܗܘܝܐ ܦܫܝܛ

3 ܠܐ] om. cod.

(Matter) were considered finite like some measurable and definable quantity. A measurable quantity is either like line, or like surface, or like bodies. But it is said to be finite ⟨neither⟩[21] like line nor like surface. What remains then is that it is like body. But if it is like body, then it also has shape. For the limit of a body is shape, and shape is one of the species of quality.

§49 If in this way Matter were finite, it would be qualified and formed in the account of its essence. But as they consider it to be without quality and without shape in the account of its essence, it is also obvious that it is not finite, but infinite. It is not said to be like something that has neither beginning nor end, but something that is able to receive a limit, yet which has not been limited in the account of its essence. Just as it is said to have no quality and no shape, in the same way it has no limit, like something that has not yet been limited.

§50 That there is something that underlies the four elements (στοιχεῖα) like the primary foundation which they call "matter" is obvious also from the transformation of the first bodies into one another, and from the changeability of the qualities.

§51 For, behold, earth has two qualities, dryness and coldness. Similarly, water has two qualities, wetness and coldness. Dryness is a peculiar characteristic of earth, and wetness is that of water, while coldness is a common characteristic of both bodies. Thus, when earth dissolves and transforms into water, its dryness is changed to wetness, while coldness, being the common characteristic, remains.

§52 And this (i.e. coldness) exists neither in earth anymore nor in water. It is not in earth because what has been transformed from earth is no longer earth. And neither is it water, because (water) has not yet come to be, but rather thus

21 The negative particle ܠܐ is not in the ms., but this seems to be the original meaning of the text.

ܒܕܒܥܠ. ܘܠܐ ܒܕܒܥܠ ܡܢܗ ܒܗܕܐ ܕܩܢܝܐ ܐܢܘܢ. ܢܦܩܐ ܗܟܝܠ ܕܒܡܕܡ ܬܗܘܐ ܐܠܗܘܬܗ ܡܪܘܬܐ. ܐܦܠܐ ܓܒܪ ܡܢ ܟܐ ܕܬܬܩܘܡ ܟܠܒܪ. ܗܘܿ ܡܢܐ ܕܒܗ ܐܠܗܘܬܗ. ܗܘܿ ܕܝܢ ܗܢܐ ܘܠܐ ܡܕܡ ܐܚܪܝܢ ܐܠܗܘܬܗ̇. ܐܠܐ ܐܢ ܗܘܠܐ ܕܗܘܝܢܐ ܠܒܢܗ̇ ܡܠܬܐ ܕܬܗܘܐ ܐܠܗܘܬܗ̇.

§53 ܬܘܒ ܐܡܪܝܢ. ܕܐܦ ܐܢܐ ܬܪ̈ܬܝܢ ܐܝܬܘܬܐ ܐܡܪܬ ܠܗ. ܡܫܝܚܘܬܐ. ܘܦܓܪܢܘܬܐ ܐܡܪ̈ܝܢ ܕܝܢ. ܕܐܦ ܩܢ̈ܘܡܐ | col. b ܡܚܝ ܦܓܪܢܘܬܐ ܘܡܪ̈ܘܬܐ. ܘܐܠܗܘܬܗ ܡܫܬܐܠܬ ܕܟܠܗܝܢ ܡܢ ܗܠܝܢ. ܕܩܢܝܐ ܗܿܢ ܡܪ̈ܘܬܐ. ܕܐܡܪ ܕܝܢ ܡܫܝܚܘܬܐ. ܒܐܝܠܬ ܕܝܢ ܕܬܪ̈ܝܗܘܢ ܦܓܪܢܘܬܐ. ܒܪ ܢܬܪ̈ܠܠܢ ܕܝܢ ܩܢܝܐ ܘܢܦܫ ܓܒܗܘܢ ܘܢܦܫܗܘܢ ܐܡܪ. ܡܪ̈ܘܬܗܘܢ ܗܿܢ ܐܬܚܠܦܬ ܠܡܫܝܚܘܬܐ. ܦܓܪܢܘܬܗܘܢ ܕܝܢ ܕܠܐ ܚܘܠܦ ܡܬܚܙܝܐ. ܒܪ ܠܐ ܐܠܗܘܬܗ ܘܠܐ ܒܡܕܡ ܐܚܪܝܢ. ܐܠܐ ܐܢ ܙܕܩ ܠܗ ܕܒܡܕܡ ܬܗܘܐ ܐܠܗܘܬܗ. ܒܗܘܠܐ ܡܕܡ ܐܠܗܘܬܗ.

§54 ܒܗ ܕܝܢ ܒܕܡܫܝܚܘܬܐ ܘܦܓܪܐ ܬܪ̈ܬܝܢ ܐܝܬܘܬܐ ܡܢܝܐ. ܡܫܝܚܘܬܐ ܘܡܫܝܚܘܬܐ. ܐܡܪ ܕܝܢ ܡܫܝܚܘܬܐ ܘܦܓܪܢܘܬܐ. ܕܒܗܢܐ ܕܝܢ ܕܬܪ̈ܝܗܘܢ ܐܠܗܘܬܗ. ܡܫܝܚܘܬܐ. ܡܫܬܐܠܬ ܕܝܢ ܕܐܡܪ ܦܓܪܢܘܬܐ. ܕܒܢܘܪܐ ܕܝܢ ܡܫܝܚܘܬܐ. ܡܢܐ ܕܢܣܒ ܕܝܢ ܐܡܪ ܘܢܦܫ ܓܒܢܐ ܠܒܢܘܪܐ. ܦܓܪܢܘܬܐ ܗܿܢ ܐܬܚܠܦܬ ܠܡܫܝܚܘܬܐ. ܡܫܝܚܘܬܐ ܕܝܢ ܐܠܗܘܬܗ ܕܒܗܢܐ ܠܐ ܐܠܗܘܬܗ ܘܡܫܝܚܐ ܘܠܐ ܒܗܢ ܡܫܝܚܘܗܝ. ܘܡܢܗ ܘܠܗ ܬܘܒ ܠܐ ܡܢ ܟܐ ܕܬܬܩܘܡ. ܢܟܝܐ ܗܿܝ ܡܕܡ ܕܒܗܘܠܐ ܐܠܗܘܬܗ.

§55 ܠܘ ܠܐ ܢܟܝܐ ܗܟܝܠ ܕܐܡܟܝܐ ܕܡܢ ܫܘ ܓܒܗܘܢ ܕܠܗܘܬ ܬܪ̈ܕܐ ܕܒܫܡܝܐ ܡܕ̈ܢܝܐ. ܡܬܚܒܢܝܐ ܗܘܠܐ ܕܐܠܗܘܬܗ ܐܝܟ ܡܕܡ ܡܫܝܚܐ: ܘܦܬܐܬܐ ܡܕܡܝܬܐ ܕܗܘܝܐ ܘܡܫܬܠܚܬ ܟܠ. ܘܡܫܬܠܚܬܐ ܘܡܬܚܒܢܬܐ ܕܟܠ ܗܘܩܡ ܐܝܟ ܢܫܡܬܐ.

§56 ܕܢܦܩܐ ܕܝܢ ܠܗܕܐ ܐܠܗܘܬܗ ܕܢܣܒ ܟܠܢܫ. ܕܒܪ ܓܒܝܬܐ ܗܿܝ ܗܘܠܐ ܐܘ ܠܐ ܓܒܝܬܐ. ܐܡܪ ܐܢܐ ܕܝܢ ܕܠܐ ܐܠܗܘܬܗ ܦܓܪܢܘܬ ܓܒܝܬܐ ܘܠܐ ܬܘܒ ܠܐ ܓܒܝܬܐ. ܐܠܐ ܒܢܫܠܐ ܓܒܝܬܐ ܗܿܝ ܘܡܕܡ ܓܒܝܬܐ.

§57 ܗܘܿ ܓܒܪ ܡܢܐ ܕܡܢܐܝܬ ܡܬܩܢܐ ܓܒܝܬܐ. ܡܢ ܗܘܠܐ ܡܢܒܒ ܘܡܢ ܢܫܘܬܐ. ܠܐ ܡܕܡ ܐܠܗܘܬܗ ܓܒܝܬܐ. ܬܘܒ ܕܝܢ ܠܢܬ ܓܒܝܬܐ ܕܠܘ ܢܫܐ ܗܘ. ܗܘܠܐ ܕܝܢ ܒܡܠܬܐ ܕܠܗ ܕܠܐ ܢܫܐ ܗܿܝ. ܠܐ ܡܕܡ ܐܠܗܘܬܗ ܓܒܝܬܐ.

far appears as coming-to-be and has not yet become what is water. It follows, thus, that coldness has to be in something, for it is not able to appear without that which it is in. And this is nothing other than Matter, which is a necessary reason for it to exist.

§53 Further, we say that air also has two qualities, hotness and wetness. And it is also said that water possesses wetness and coldness. There is something that each one of them has specifically: it is coldness for water, and hotness for air, while wetness is what both of them have in common. When water is rarefied, is transformed, and becomes air, its coldness changes then into hotness, while its wetness remains without change. Then it (i.e. wetness) is not present (in water anymore), neither is it in something else. But as it must be in something, thus it is in Matter.

§54 In the same way, fire also possesses two qualities, hotness and dryness, while air has hotness and wetness. What both of them have in common is hotness, while wetness belongs specifically to air and dryness to fire. When air becomes hot and transforms into fire, wetness changes into dryness, while hotness, which is common (to both), neither exists nor is (any longer) present in any of them. As it cannot be present by itself, it is obvious that it is in Matter.

§55 It is therefore not unclear how from the transformations of the primary bodies into each other it is found that Matter is something fixed, a primary foundation of beings, all-receptive, a receptacle and a nurse of all beings, like a female[22].

§56 It follows from this that we should consider whether Matter is embodied or not embodied. I state, namely, that it is not simply embodied, and neither is it unembodied, but rather it is potentially a body and something embodied.

§57 For that what is properly called body is composed of matter and quality. Therefore, it (i.e. Matter) is not a body. Further, there is no body which is not qualified. But Matter by its own definition has no quality. Therefore, it is not a

22 Cf. Plato, *Tim.* 51a4–5, 51a7, and 52d4–5.

f. 116v ܬܘܒ ܕܝܢ ܗܟܢܐ. ܟܠ ܓܘܫܡܐ ܩ̈ܠܝܠܐ | ܘܝܩ̈ܝܪܐ ܐܝܬ ܠܗ. ܗܘܠܐ ܕܝܢ ܠܝܬ ܠܗ̇ ܒܡܠܬܐ ܕܝܠܗ̇ ܩ̈ܠܝܠܐ ܘܝܩ̈ܝܪܐ. ܠܐ ܡܕܝܢ ܐܝܬܝܗ̇ ܓܘܫܡܐ.

§58 ܬܘܒ ܕܝܢ ܟܠ ܓܘܫ̈ܡܐ. ܡܬܐܡܪܝܢ ܘܡܬܝܕܥܝܢ ܐܢ ܓܢ̈ܣܐ ܩ̈ܕܡܝܐ ܕܡܠܟ ܓܢܘܣ. ܒܗܕܐ ܓܝܪ ܕܐܝܬܘܗܝ ܡܫܡܠܝܐ ܕܕܠܡܘܒܠܢܘܬܐ ܐܝܕܐ ܒܐܝܕܐ. ܐܘܣܝܐ ܗܘ. ܒܗܕܐ ܕܝܢ ܕܐܝܬ ܠܗ ܬܠܬܐ ܡ̈ܫܘܚܬܐ. ܡܢ ܒܡܫܘܚܬܐ ܗܘ ܘܒܦܬܝܐ. ܒܗܕܐ ܕܝܢ ܕܡܫܬܘܬܦ ܠܝܫܘܬܐ. ܐܝܢܐ ܗܘ. ܘܒܗܕܐ ܕܪܒ ܐܘ ܙܥܘܪ ܡܢ ܕܠܘܬ ܡܕܡ. ܘܡܛܠ ܬܘܒ ܡܠܟ ܓܢܘܣ ܐܣ̈ܛܘܟܣܐ ܡܫܟܚܬ. ܡܢ ܗܕܐ ܕܝܢ ܠܟܠܗܘܢ ܗܠܝܢ ܡܬܐܡܪܝܢ.

§59 ܬܘܒ ܗܘ ܗܢܐ ܕܐܢܫ. ܒܦܣܩܐܝܬ ܡܬܐܡܪ. ܘܗܘ̇ ܡ̇ܢ ܐܝܬܘܗܝ. ܗܘ ܕܗܘ ܝܬܗ ܡܫܚܬ ܓܢܣܐ ܘܡܫܬܚܠܦ. ܐܝܢܐ ܕܝܢ. ܗ̇ܘ ܕܗܘ ܡܢ ܝܬܗ ܠܐ ܡܫܚܬ ܓܢܣܐ ܘܠܐ ܡܫܬܚܠܦ ܐܠܐ ܡܛܠ ܕܡܫܡܠܝ ܒܗ ܗܠܝܢ ܕܡܫܚܬ ܓܢܣܝܢ ܘܡܫܬܚܠܦܝܢ ܡܬܐܡܪ ܕܐܢܫ. ܕܐܝܟ ܗܟܢ ܕܝܢ ܐܝܬܝܗ̇ ܗܘܠܐ.

§60 ܬܘܒ ܐܘܣܝܐ ܕܗܘ̇ ܡܫܡܠܝܐ ܕܟܢܫ ܠܐ ܐܝܬܘܗܝ ܓܘܫܡܐ: ܘܠܐ ܬܘܒ ܬܚܝܬ ܓܘܫܡܐ ܢܦܠ. ܗܟܢܐ ܘܗ̇ܘ ܡܫܡܠܝܐ ܕܐܢܫ. ܐܝܟ ܕܡܢ ܪ̈ܓܫܬܐ ܗܘ̇ ܘܠܐ ܬܘܒ ܬܚܝܬ ܓܘܫܡܐ ܢܦܠ. ܕܐܝܟ ܗܟܢ ܕܝܢ ܐܝܬܝܗ̇ ܗܘܠܐ ܘܒܕ ܓܘ ܐܝܟܘ ܕܪ̈ܓܫܬܐ. ܗ̇ܝ ܐܝܟ ܗܢܐ ܕܐܝܬܝܗ̇ ܪ̈ܓܫܬܐ. ܠܐ ܡܬܚܙܝܢܐ ܕܝܕܥܝܢ ܢܦܫܐ. ܓܘܫܡܐ ܡܕܡ ܘܡܫܚܬ. ܐܘܣܝܐ ܕܐܦ ܠܐ ܡܕܡ ܕܡܬܦܫܪ ܠܗ ܒܠܥܕܗ̇. ܐܢܫ ܗܕܐ. ܡܕܡ ܠܐ ܐܝܬܘܗܝ ܓܘܫܡܐ.

§61 ܬܘܒ ܟܠ ܓܘܫܡܐ ܡܬܪ ܓܒܝܐ ܗܘ. ܗܘܠܐ ܕܝܢ ܠܐ ܐܝܬܘܗܝ ܡܬܪ ܓܒܝܬܐ. ܡܕܝܢ ܠܐ ܐܝܬܘܗܝ ܓܘܫܡܐ.

§62 ܬܘܒ ܗܘܠܐ ܡܕܡ ܦܫܝܛܐ ܘܠܐ ܡܪ̈ܟܒܐ ܐܝܬܝܗ̇. ܓܘܫܡܐ ܕܝܢ ܠܐ
col. b ܐܝܬܘܗܝ ܦܫܝܛܐ ܐܠܐ ܡܪ̈ܟܒܐ. ܠܐ ܡܕܝܢ ܐܝܬܝܗ̇ | ܓܘܫܡܐ.

§63 ܬܘܒ ܐܢ ܗܘ̇ ܕܓܘܫܡܐ ܗܝ ܗܘܠܐ. ܐܝܬ ܠܗ̇ ܐܦ ܡܫܘܚܬܐ ܕܓܘܫܡܐ. ܗܢܘ ܕܝܢ ܕܐܝܬ ܠܗ ܬܠܬܐ ܡ̈ܫܘܚܬܐ. ܐܘ ܕܡܬܦܠܓ ܠܬܠܬܐ ܡ̈ܫܘܚܬܐ ܒܟܡ ܕܠܡܘܒܠܢܘܬ ܠܦܘܫܐ. ܠܐ ܕܝܢ ܐܝܬ ܠܗ̇ ܗܠܝܢ ܠܗܘܠܐ. ܘܐܢ

10 ܘܡܫܬܚܠܦ scr.: ܘܡܬܚܠܦ cod. 22 ܐܠܐ scr.: ܘܠܐ cod.

body. Further, similarly, every body has limits and boundaries. But Matter by its definition has no limits and boundaries. Therefore, it is not a body.

§58 Further, it is said about bodies that they are compounded by the first genera of categories. Thus, it is through substance (οὐσία) that they become receptive to all kinds of opposition. And quantity and amount are that through which they are three-dimensional. It is qualification that makes them partakers in quality. To be big or small is possible through relatives. And similarly with other categories. However, we deprive it (i.e. Matter) from all of them.

§59 Further, of something passive we may speak in two ways: one is (to say) that its essence transforms and changes, and another is that its essence does not transform or change, but it is called passive because it is receptive to something that transforms and changes – and Matter is like this.

§60 Further, just as the primary active thing is not a genus and does not fall under any genus, likewise the primary passive thing, which is a principle, also does not fall under any genus. Matter is also like this, and on that account, if it is a principle, like a principle it does not need to have an aim prior to itself, a certain genus before it, as likewise there is nothing that can be predicated of it. If it is like that, then it is not a body.

§61 Further, every body is perceptible. But Matter is not perceptible. Therefore, it is not a body.

§62 Further, Matter is something simple and not compound. A body is not simple, but compound. Therefore, it is not a body.

§63 Further, if Matter were a body, it would have the definition of a body, that is, it would have three dimensions, or it could be divided three-dimensionally and have resistance. But Matter does not have these, otherwise it too would be

ܠܐ ܗ̇ܘܝܐ ܐܦ ܗ̇ܘ ܒܡܫܘܚܬܐ ܘܐܢܫܘܬܐ. ܐܠܐ ܗܠܝܢ ܠܗܘܢ ܒܡܠܬܐ ܕܐܝܬܗ̇ ܠܐ ܐܝܬܘܗ̇. ܠܐ ܡܕܡ ܓܘܫܡܐ ܗܘ.

§64 ܐܠܐ ܕܝܢ ܘܐܦܠܐ ܠܐ ܓܫܡܢܝܬܐ ܗܘ. ܠܐ ܓܘܫܡܐ ܓܝܪ ܠܐ ܡܛܠ ܓܝܪ ܕܗܘܐ ܓܘܫܡܐ. ܗܘܠܐ ܕܝܢ ܒܪ ܬܘܟܠ ܐܪܥܐ. ܗܘܐ ܓܘܫܡܐ ܒܡܬܒܪܢܘܬܐ. ܡܕܡ ܠܐ ܐܝܬܘܗ̇ ܠܐ ܓܫܡܢܝܬܐ.

§65 ܬܘܒ ܐܢܫܘ ܕܓܘܫܡܐ ܗܘ. ܐܝܬܘܗ̇ ܡܬܬܕܝܢܢܘܬܐ ܠܬܘܕܝܢܬܐ ܥܡ ܪܓܫܬܐ ܕܠܐ ܡܠܬܐ. ܠܐ ܕܝܢ ܐܝܬܘܗ̇ ܗܘܠܐ. ܠܐ ܡܕܡ ܐܝܬܘܗ̇ ܓܘܫܡܐ.

§66 ܐܢܕܝܢ ܠܐ ܓܫܡܢܝܬܐ ܗܘ. ܐܝܬܘܗ̇ ܡܬܬܚܫܒܢܝܬܐ ܐܘ ܡܬܬܕܒܢܝܬܐ. ܠܗܘܢܐ ܐܘ ܠܬܪܒܝܬܐ ܥܡ ܡܠܬܐ ܐܘ ܗܘܢܐ ܡܬܬܪܒܝܢܝܬܐ ܘܡܬܕܒܢܝܬܐ ܒܡܕܒܪܐ ܐܘ ܒܬܪܒܝܬܐ ܥܡ ܡܠܬܐ. ܠܐ ܕܝܢ ܐܝܬܘܗ̇ ܗܘܢܐ. ܠܐ ܡܕܡ ܐܝܬܘܗ̇ ܠܐ ܓܫܡܢܝܬܐ.

§67 ܘܡܢܐ ܕܕܡܝܘܬ ܘܠܐ ܓܘܫܡܐ ܐܡܪܝܢ ܦܢܛܐܣܝܐ. ܘܠܐ ܬܘܒ ܠܐ ܓܫܡܢܝܬܐ. ܐܠܐ ܒܫܠܐ ܓܫܡܢܝܬܐ ܘܓܘܫܡܐ. ܒܫܠܐ ܕܝܢ ܡܬܐܡܪ. ܗ̇ܘ ܡܐ ܕܡܟܝܢ ܕܗܘܐ. ܗ̇ܘ ܕܝܢ ܕܡܟܝܢ ܕܗܘܐ ܠܐ ܒܪܒܠ ܐܝܬܘܗܝ. ܘܒܪ ܓܒܝ ܥܡ ܠܐ ܡܢ ܓܫܡܢܝܬܐ ܐܡܪܝܢ ܡܬܦܫܩܢܘܬܐ. ܘܒܫܘܦܢܐ ܠܡ ܒܐܠܦܐ ܠܚܫܒܐ ܡܬܗܡܢܢܐ. ܗܠܝܢ ܕܝܢ ܕܐܬܬܘܣܦ ܠܗ ܒܠ ܗܘܠܐ ܦܫܝܛܐ ܢܗܘܐ ܠܗ.

§68 ܟܕ ܗܠܝܢ ܕܝܢ ܕܡܫܪܝܬܐ ܘܥܒܘܪ ܡܬܓܠܝܢܘܬ | f. 98r ܐܬܐܡܪ. ܐܡܪܝܢ ܓܠܬܐ ܕܐܢܫܐ ܕܐܝܬܘܗ̇ ܗܘܠܐ. ܕܐܬܪܒܝܬܐ ܡܢ ܪܒܝܬܐ ܕܒܠ ܥܘ ܓܘܫܡܘܗܝ ܕܓܘܫܡܐ ܡܙܟܝܐ ܕܠܗܘܬ ܫܪܪܐ. ܐܬܐܦܪܬ ܕܝܢ ܐܦ ܕܐܡܪܝܢ ܦܠܛܘܢ ܪܘܚܢܝܐ ܠܐ ܗܘܬܐ ܢܦܩ ܠܗ̇ ܕܐܝܬܘܗ̇. ܘܦܫܝܛܘܬܐ ܬܘܒ ܘܕܠܐ ܗܢܐ ܒܡܠܬܐ ܕܐܝܬܘܗ̇.

§69 ܘܡܛܠ ܗܕܐ ܠܐ ܐܝܬܘܗ̇ ܓܘܫܡܐ ܐܠܐ ܒܫܠܐ ܓܘܫܡܐ. ܘܡܛܠ ܗܕܐ ܬܘܒ ܐܦܠܐ ܓܫܡܢܝܬܐ. ܘܠܐ ܬܘܒ ܗܘܦܬܐ. ܐܠܐ ܪܘܫܡܬܐ ܕܗܘܦܐ. ܘܠܐ ܬܘܒ ܫܘܫܒܬܐ. ܡܫܡܠܝܬܐ ܕܝܢ ܕܫܘܠܐ ܕܫܒܩ ܒܗ̇. ܘܠܐ ܡܛܠ ܓܫܡܢܝܬܐ ܬܘܒ ܘܠܐ ܡܫܡܠܝܬܐ. ܘܠܐ ܡܫܬܘܠܦܢܝܬܐ. ܒܪ ܐܝܬܘܗ̇ ܐܝܟ ܐܡܪܐ ܘܐܝܟ ܢܡܘܣܐ ܘܡܫܡܠܝܬܐ ܕܒܠܗܘܢ. ܐܝܟ ܕܐܡܪܝܢ ܗܠܝܢ.

quantified and qualified, but all this does not belong to the account of its essence. Therefore, it is not a body.

§64 However, neither is it incorporeal. For a non-body does not transform to become a body. But when Matter receives forms, it becomes a body in actuality. Therefore, it is not incorporeal.

§65 Further, if it were a body, it would be manifested to "belief supported by unreasoned sensation"[23]. But it is not like this. Therefore, it is not a body.

§66 And if it were incorporeal, it would be comprehensible and intelligible by intellect or by "thought with the support of a reasoned account"[24]. But it is not like this. Therefore, it is not incorporeal.

§67 Hence, we properly say that it is not simply corporeal, neither is it incorporeal, but rather it is potentially embodied and a body. And what is said to be in potentiality is capable of being. But what is capable of being is not yet there, and therefore it is said of it that it is associated with imperceptibility and that it may hardly be considered in pure thought[25]. These things which we have gathered concerning Matter may (here) come to an end for us.

(5. Plato's Concept of First Principles and Matter)

§68 Through these things which have been said clearly and very systematically, we stated the reason for Matter being necessary, which is derived from the concept of the transformation of the primary bodies into each other. It was also told how Plato counted it to be an ungenerated principle and, further, to be simple and unqualified in the account of its essence.

§69 And for this reason, it is not a body, but a body in potentiality. And for this reason, it is also incorporeal. Neither is it generated, but it is a principle of generated things. Further, it is impassible, but is receptive of faculties that are affected in it. Further, it is unchangeable, imperishable, and unalterable, being like a mother, like a female and a receptacle of all things like this[26].

---

23 Plato, *Tim.* 28a2–3.

24 Plato, *Tim.* 28a1–2.

25 Cf. Plato, *Tim.* 28a, 51a–b and 52b.

26 Cf. §§ 41 and 55, above.

§70 ܘܒܪ ܟܢ ܘܐܦ ܒܪ̈ ܗ̇ܘ ܒܥܠܬܗ̇ ܡܒܬܪܐ. ܡܡܠܠܐ ܠܗܠܝܢ ܒܠܗܘܢ. ܐܝܟ ܫܬܐܣܬܐ ܦܪܢܣܐ ܘܡܕܒܪܢܘܬܐ ܕܟܠ ܗܘ̈ܝܢ. ܘܣܘܟܠܐ ܒܪ̈ܝܬܐ ܠܡܣܒܪ ܡܬܝܠܦܐ. ܘܟܡ ܠܐ ܡܪ ܟܝܢܘܬܐ ܐܠܗܘܬܗ ܡܛܠ ܟܝܢܝܬܐ. ܘܚܝܠܐ ܟܠ ܡܕܡ ܐܠܗܘܬܗ. ܒܗ̇ ܕܡܚܝܠܐ ܠܡܡܠܠܘ ܒܠܗܘܢ ܐܝܩ̈ܪܬܐ ܘܐܣܟܡܐ ܘܡܫܘ̈ܚܬܐ.

§71 ܘܠܐ ܡܫܘܚܬܐ ܗܘܬ ܐܠܗܘܬܗ. ܠܘ ܐܝܟ ܡܕܡ ܕܠܝܬ ܠܗ ܡܫܘܚܬܐ ܘܚܕܪܐ. ܐܝܟ ܡܐ ܕܡܢ ܐ ܕܢܫܐ ܗܟܢܐ. ܠܐ ܕܝܢ ܒܕܚܠܐ ܒܪܚܡܘ ܡܚܠ ܗܟܢܐ: ܘܠܐ ܗܘܬ ܒܡܠܬܐ ܕܐܠܗܘܬܗ ܠܠܐ ܡܫܟܚܢܘܬܐ: ܐܘ ܠܐ ܡܫܟܚܢܐܝܬ ܡܬܦܫܩܐ. ܘܗܘܬ ܠܐ ܐܠܗܘܬܗ ܡܬܝܕܥܢܘܬܐ ܘܠܐ ܗܘܬ ܒܝ ܕܝܢܬܐ.

§72 ܐܬܐܡܪܬ ܕܝܢ ܘܟܠܬܐ ܕܡܬܠܠܬܗ̇ ܠܐ ܡܘܬܐ ܐܬܬܦܫܩܬ. ܘܠܐ ܟܪ ܡܢ ܐܪܝܢܐ ܡܢ ܐ ܕܬܗܘܐ ܒܪ ܐܠܗܘܬܗ ܪܫܝܬܐ. ܘܠܐ ܗܘܬ ܡܢ ܐܠܗܐ ܕܐܠܗܘܬܗ ܕܠܡܡܠܠܘ ܗ̇ܘ ܕܠܘܗ. ܘܬܪܝܗܘܢ ܕܠܡ̈ܠܠܐ ܩܕܡܝܐ. ܕܠܡ̈ܠܠܐ ܕܝܢ ܩܕܡܝܐ. ܡܢ ܫܪܪܐ ܠܐ ܡܢ ܐ ܕܢܗܘܘܢ. ܐܡܝܢܐ ܕܐܦܠܐ ܡܢ ܐܪܝܢܘܬܐ ܡܛܠ ܕܩܕܡܝܐ ܐܝܬܘܗܝ.

col. b §73 ܐܦܝܣܩܘ ܕܝܢ ܒܡܐܡܪܐ ܡܕܡܝܐ ܕܟܠ ܡܠܦܢܘܬܗ ܕܦܠܛܘܢ. | ܗܟܢܐ ܗܡ ܒܪ̈ܝܫܐ ܕܦܘܣܩܘܬܐ ܠܪܚܡܗ ܕܦܠܛܘܢ: ܕܟܠ ܪ̈ܫܐ ܩܕܡܝܐ. ܒܡܠܬܐ ܦܬ ܣܐܬܐ ܡܬܦܠܓܝܢ ܠܐܪ̈ܒܥܐ ܪ̈ܫܐ. ܠܚܕ ܕܐܠܗܘܬܗ، ܐܒܐ ܘܒܪܘܪܐ ܕܟܠ. ܘܠܐܣܝܢܐ ܕܐܠܗܘܬܗ، ܕܡܘܬܐ ܘܨܘܪܐ ܕܐܝܟܘܬܗ ܗܦ ܟܠ. ܘܠܗܘܠܐ ܕܐܠܗܘܬܗ ܡܡܠܠܢܘܬܐ ܕܟܠ ܗܘ̈ܝܢ ܘܡܬܬܕܒܪܢܘܬܐ ܐܘ ܠܢܘܟܪܝܐ ܗ̇ܘ ܕܐܟܚܕ ܟܡ ܗܘܠܐ ܐܝܬ ܗܘܐ: ܕܗ̇ܘ ܕܡܬܬܝܠܕ ܡܢ ܡܠܬܗ. ܠܗܘܠܐ ܕܝܢ ܡܬܬܝܠܕ ܡܢ ܡܠܬܗ ܡܬܚܡܝ ܢܦܫܐ.

§74 ܥܠܝܟ ܕܝܢ ܐܡܪ ܠܡܦܠܓܗ ܐܢܘܢ ܠܬܫܥܐ ܐܦ ܠܬܪ̈ܝܢ. ܠܚܠܬܐ ܚܒܘܪܬܐ ܘܠܗ̇، ܣܘܥܪܢܬܐ. ܗܘܬ ܟܠ ܚܕ ܡܢ ܗܠܝܢ ܠܬܪ̈ܝܢ ܡܬܦܠܓܢ. ܠܚܠܬܐ ܕܝܢ ܚܒܘܪܬܐ ܘܠܡܕܒܪܢܘܬܐ. ܠܗ̇، ܕܝܢ ܗܘܬ ܣܘܥܪܢܬܐ. ܡܦܠܓܝܢ ܠܗܘܠܐ ܘܠܨܘܪܐ ܕܡܬܬܝܠܕܐ ܡܢ ܡܠܬܗ. ܐܢܫܘ ܟܪ ܕܐܡܪ ܠܗܘ ܚܕ ܦܠܓܐ ܢܦܫܘܬܗ، ܕܠܐ ܦܠܓܐ: ܢܦܠܓ ܕܝܢ ܠܗܘ ܐܪܝܢܐ. ܐܦ ܗܟܢܐ ܗܠܬܐ ܠܬܐܡܪܘܢ ܬܫܥܐ.

§75 ܐܢܫܝܢ ܠܐ ܡܫܬܠܛܝܢ ܕܐܦ ܠܫܒܥܐ ܒܪ̈ܝܫܐ ܩܕܡܝܐ ܫܐܡ ܦܠܛܘܢ. ܘܗܟܢܐ ܗܠܬܐ ܬܫܥܐ ܫܡ. ܠܗܘܠܐ ܘܠܐܠܗܐ ܘܠܕܡܘܬܐ. ܠܘ ܟܪ ܗܟܢܐ

§70 And therefore, while it remains in its essence, it receives everything, like the primary foundation and a receptacle of all beings, and it may hardly be grasped in pure thought. And besides being imperceptible, it is changeable. It is everything in potentiality, for it may naturally receive all qualities, shapes, and measures.

§71 And further, it is infinite, not as something that has neither beginning nor end, i.e. as something which is able to have limits but has not yet received a limit in its notion. Neither is it divided to infinity or infinitely in the account of its essence. Also, it is neither great nor small.

§72 And the reason was explained as to why it is established as ungenerated. For, being a principle, it may come to be neither from something else, nor from God, who is its opposite, and it is his, so that both of them are primary opposites. And the primary opposites cannot come to be from one another, no from other things, because they are primary.

§73 Now, Atticus, in the first treatise on the teachings of Plato, sets out in the following concise and summary fashion the doctrine of Plato concerning First Principles:

> "By exact definition, they are divided into four principles: the one that is the Father and Creator of everything; the other that is the Form and Idea, according to which he formed everything; then Matter, which is receptive to all beings; and movability, or motion, which co-existed with Matter (and) which moves by itself. That which moves by itself he calls 'Soul'.
>
> §74 It is also permitted, he says, to divide the principles into two, the active cause and the passive one. Each of them may be further divided into two: (the first one) into the active cause and the Form; and the passive (cause) we may divide into Matter and Soul, which is moved by itself. If one would leave the first division undivided, but divide the other one, likewise in this way three principles would be stated.
>
> §75 Some people do not comprehend that Plato also puts Soul among the First Principles, and thus he set three principles: Matter, God, and Form.

ܡܬܚܙܝܐ ܕܣܐܡ. ܟܕ ܢܣܒ ܓܝܪ ܐܠܗܐ ܐܡܪ ܠܗܠܝܢ ܕܐܬܐܠܗܘ: ܟܕ ܟܠܠܐܝܬ ܘܠܐ ܡܬܚܡܐܝܬ ܐܬܐܠܗܘ ܗܘ̈ܘ. ܡܢ ܠܐ ܡܬܚܡܘܬܐ ܠܬܚܡܐ ܐܬܐ: ܐܝܟ ܕܬܗܘܐ ܡܕܝܢܐ ܡܢ ܡܠܬܗ ܕܦܠܛܘ. ܕܠܐ ܠܐ ܡܬܬܚܝܢܘܬܐ. ܘܠܐ ܬܗܘܐ ܕܠܐ ܙܢܐ ܢܗܘ̈ܐ ܠܗܘܠܐ.

§76 ܬܘܒ ܕܝܢ ܗܘ ܦܠܛܘ ܒܟܠܕܘܢ ܡܚܘܐ ܕܡܝܢܐ ܘܪܫܝܬܐ ܕܟܠ ܡܬܬܪܚܝܫܢܘܬܐ ܕܒܟܠ ܝ ܒܗ ܢܦܫܐ ܗ̇. ܕܡܢ ܗܠܝܢ ܟܕܝܫܐ ܗܕܐ ܕܐܦ ܟܠܠܐܝܬܐ ܘܠܐ ܡܬܚܡܘܬܐ ܗ̇. ܕܡܢ ܩܕܡ ܕܒܗܘܠܐ. ܡܢ ܢܦܫܐ ܗ̇.
f. 98v ܕܗܕܝܢ ܕܠܐ ܡܕܒܪܐ ܐܬܐܡܪܗ̇ ܗܘܬ ܒܗܘܠܐ | ܐܝܟ ܪܫܐ ܡܕܒܪܐ. ܐܚܝܕ ܠܟܠ ܡܡܟܠܐ ܕܗܘܠܐ ܢܣܒܗ̇ ܠܬܪܬܝܗܝܢ. ܡܛܠ ܕܐܦܠܐ ܡܬܦܪܫܢܝܬܐ ܐܢܫ ܡܢ ܫܪܪܐ ܢܦܫܐ ܘܗ̇. ܕܡܬܪܐܝܐ ܡܬܡܪܐ ܗܘܠܐ. ܡܕܒܪܐ ܗܝ ܕܬܪܝܢ ܐܝܬ ܐܬܐܡܪܗ̇ ܕܡܒܝܐ ܬܠܬܐ ܒܬܐܡܪܘܢ ܪ̈ܫܐ.

§77 ܒܠܗܘܢ ܕܝܢ ܐܝܠܝܢ ܕܐܠܗܐ ܗܢ ܘܠܕܡܘܬܐ ܡܬܒܢܝܢ ܠܗܕ: ܡܩܠܝܢ ܕܝܢ ܠܗܘܠܐ ܘܠܢܦܫܐ. ܡܬܪܐܝܬ ܗܠܝܢ ܢܬܬܒܪܘܢ ܕܐܬܐܡܪܘܢ ܡܢ ܪ̈ܚܝܩܘ ܕܦܠܛܘܢ. ܓܠܒ ܓܝܪ ܒܦܠܣܘܦܘ ܡܒܝܢܐ. ܕܗܠܝܢ ܬܠܬܐ ܐܬܐܡܪܘܢ. ܐܬܐܡܪܗ̇ ܘܕܡܘܬܐ ܘܗܘܠܐ. ܘܡܕܡ ܕܢܣܒܘܢ ܫܡܝܐ. ܐܬܐܡܪܗ̇ ܦܪܐ. ܠܒܠ ܡܢ ܕܐܬܐܡܪܗ̇ ܠܐ ܗܘܝܐ ܘܠܐ ܡܬܚܒܠܢܐ: ܘܐܡܬܝܢܐܝܬ ܒܗܝܢ ܒܪ ܒܗܝܢ ܘܗ̇ܘ ܗܒܘܬ ܐܬܐܡܪܗ̇ ܕܒܗ ܡܬܬܚܡ ܘܐܬܐܡܪܗ̇ ܐܠܗܐ ܡܕܒܪܐ ܘܕܡܘ̇ܬܐ ܒܢܫܬܐ.

§78 ܕܗܒܬܐ ܕܝܢ ܦܪܐ ܠܗܘܠܐ. ܗܒܝܐ ܕܝܢ ܡܫܒܚܗ ܗܘܐ ܠܗ̇. ܒܡ ܒܪ̈ܢܝܐ ܐܣܪܢܐ. ܠܐ ܓܝܪ ܒܕܒܠ ܫܒܝܐ ܕܗܘܠܐ ܐܬܦܫܛ ܗܘܐ ܒܠ ܐܘܣܝܐ: ܕܐܝܟ ܫܬܐܘܬܐ ܡܕܒܪܬܐ ܫܒܝܐ ܬܫܝܬ ܒܠܗܘܢ ܗ̈ܘܝܐ. ܗܘܝܐ ܕܝܢ ܦܪܐ ܠܪܫܝܬܐ ܕܒܠ ܗܘܝܐ ܘܙܘܝܐ ܘܙܒܝܐ ܡܕܒܪܐ. ܕܠܗ ܠܗܘܝܐ ܙܘܝܐ ܐܡܪ ܕܐܬܐܡܪܗ̇ ܒ<ܢ>ܦܫܐ.

§79 ܡܬܬܘܠܝܢ ܕܝܢ ܗܠܝܢ ܐܡܪ. ܡܢ ܬܘܕܝܬܐ ܘܫܠܡܘܬܐ ܕܬܪܝܢܘܬܐ ܡܕܒܪܬܐ. ܘܡܬܠܒܒܐ ܗܒܝܐ ܕܢܫܠܡ. ܕܒܠ ܡܐ ܕܫܦܝܪܐܝܬ ܐܬܐܡܪܗ̇. ܒܟܕܐ ܐܝܬ ܗܘ ܠܗ. ܡܬܠܒܒܐ ܠܗ ܓܝܪ ܠܗܘ ܐܝܢܐ ܕܒܠܒܕܡ ܫܦܝܪܐܝܬ

11 ܪ̈ܫܐ] corr. in cod. 23 ܒܢܦܫܐ] parum cl. in cod.

But it does not seem that he postulates this. For he says: 'Taking over all existing things, which were in a discordant and disorderly state, God brought them to order from disorder'[27]. It is clear, then, from the words of Plato that Matter, which (God) took over, was neither unmovable nor unqualified.

§76 For Plato also demonstrates everywhere that Soul is a source and principle of every sort of movability in all things. From this follows that the discordance and disorder which were in Matter from the beginning were from irrational Soul, which at that time was in Matter as a First Principle. And if one agrees to call both of them 'matter', because Soul and what is properly called Matter were unseparated from each other, then it is clear that it is right to speak in this way about three Principles.

§77 Now, all those, who unite God and Form and make a distinction between Matter and Soul, should be considered those who especially follow Plato's opinion. For he wrote thus in the *Timaeus*: 'There were three things, being, place, and coming-to-be, three in threefold way, before the heavens came to be'[28]. He calls 'being' everything that exists without coming-to-be and corruption and that firmly remains the same. That is how the primary God and the universal Form are defined and exist.

§78 He calls Matter 'place'. He referred to it by this term, alongside others, for until then the name 'matter' had not been fixed upon the substance (οὐσία) which as the primary foundation underlies all beings. He calls 'coming-to-be' the principle of every generation and the primary movement, and this movement, he says, is ⟨due to⟩[29] Soul.

§79 He also says that these things are formed in agreement with and in adherence to the primary design. It is thus necessary that we conclude that everything that exists beautifully has a creator. And it is necessary that the one who creates everything beautifully should also have some

27 Plato, *Tim.* 30a3–6. The Syriac text omits the word ὁρατὸν. Cf. another rendering of the same passage in §85.

28 Plato, *Tim.* 52d2–4.

29 Ms. is barely readable at this place, however it is evident that the word ܢܦܫܐ has some prefix and it is most likely ܒ.

ܒܪܐ. ܕܢܫܘܐ ܐܝܬ ܠܗ ܘܪܚܡܬܐ ܡܢܗ ܕܐܠܗܘܬܗ، ܕܠܘܬܗ ܘܒܗ ܡܢܝ ܕ ܘܐܒܗܘܬܗ ܒܠܚܘܕ ܒܪܐ. ܐܢܫ ܠܐ ܢܣܘܕܥ ܠܬܪܥܐ: ܘܠܐ ܢܣܘܕܥ ܚܝܐ. col. b ܕܐܝܟ ܐܡܝܢܐ ܙܕܩ ܕܢܫܘܐ | ܗܘ ܕܒܠܬܘ ܠܡܫܘܐ ܥܒܪܐܝܬ. ܠܐ ܡܢܝ ܐ ܕܒܪܐ ܒܒܕܝܗ ܠܚܡܐܝܬ.

§80 ܘܡܢܐ ܕܗܘ ܕܒܪܐ ܐܠܗܘܬܗ، ܙܕܩ ܗܘ ܡܢ ܒܠܦܪܘܦ ܕܢܫܘܐ ܐܠܗܘܬܗ،. ܘܗܘ ܕܗܘܐ ܘܡܬܒܪܐ ܘܡܬܬܗܝܢ. ܐܠܐ ܘܐܦ ܙܒܢܐ ܡܢܗ ܙܕܩ ܕܢܫܘܐ ܠܐܠܗܐ: ܕܒܡܢ ܕܢܫܘܬܗ ܡܒܪܐ. ܘܬܘܪܐܝܬ ܡܢܐ ܕܡܠܠܬܐ ܡܩܪܒܬܐ ܒܒܘܕܝܬܐ ܠܐ ܡܬܬܘܡܝܬܐ ܘܩܕܡ ܒܪ ܩܘܡ ܗܘ ܡܒܘܬ ܡܒܠܬܝ. ܠܐ ܒܪ ܡܢ ܐܢܐ ܕܡܢ ܠܐ ܡܬܬܘܡܝܐ ܩܕܡܝܐ ܢܫܘܐ ܘܡܝܬܐ ܕܡܬܬܘܡܝܐ.

§81 ܐܝܟ ܬܪܥܝܬܐ ܕܦܠܛܘܢ. ܕܠܐ ܒܡܬܚܬܐ ܐܠܗܘܬܗ ܗܘܠܐ ܘܕܠܐ ܙܢܐ: ܡܢ ܕܬܬܪܡܝ ܡܢܗ ܒܠܗܘܢ ܗܠܝܢ ܕܐܠܗܘܬܗܘܢ ܒܗ. ܒܡܬܦܬܬܐ ܒܪ ܕܡܢܬ ܠܗܬ ܙܝܘܬܐ ܘܣܝܠܐ ܕܠܗܬ ܗܕܐ. ܡܥܝܠܦܐܝܬ ܡܒܠܢܐ ܠܗ ܦܠܛܘܢ. ܡܡܠܠܬܐ ܒܪ ܘܐܣܛܬܐ ܫܬܬܬܐ. ܘܐܡܡܐ ܘܢܡܒܬܐ ܘܡܡܠܠܬ ܒܗܠ. ܘܡܣܘܣܝܬܐ ܘܕܒܘܬܐ ܘܐܬܪܐ.

§82 ܐܡܪܝܢ ܬܘܒ ܕܒܕ ܗܒܢܐ ܐܡܪ ܠܗ ܕܠܐ ܙܢܐ. ܐܠܐ ܠܐ ܡܬܘܡ ܐܡܪ ܠܗ ܕܐܠܗܘܬܗ ܒܠܒܕ ܙܝܘܬܐ. ܡܛܠ ܕܝܢ ܕܐܡܟܢܐܝܬ ܐܠܗܘܬܗ ܒܗ ܢܦܫܐ ܕܐܠܗܘܬܗ ܡܬܬܘܡܝܬ ܡܢ ܗܠܗ. ܐܠܝܢ ܐ ܕܐܦ ܗܝ ܬܬܘܡܝ. ܗܕܐ ܕܝܢ ܕܬܬܘܡܝ ܠܗܘܠܐ ܐܠܗܘܬܗ ܕܬܡܒܠ ܙܢܐ. ܐܦܠܐ ܒܪ ܙܒܢܐ ܕܒܐܬܪܐ ܡܢܝ ܡܐ ܕܢܫܘܐ: ܐܝ ܠܐ ܢܫܘܘܢ ܡܢܝ ܗܟܢܐ ܡܕܡ ܒܬܘܒܬ ܗܠܝܢ ܕܡܬܬܘܡܝܢ ܘܐܬܩܒܡܐ. ܒܪ ܗܠܝܢ ܕܝܢ ܢܫܘܘܢ ܢܩܦܢ ܘܐܠܗܘܬܗܝܢ ܠܗܘܠܐ. ܠܐ ܡܒܠ ܡܬܒܘܡܐ ܠܡܒܬܪ ܒܡܣܝܡܗ ܒܬܘܡܐ.

§83 ܡܬܚܙܝܐ ܕܝܢ ܕܐܝܬ ܗܘ ܠܡܣܒ ܦܘܣܐ ܒܠܝܢܐ ܒܠ ܗܘܠܐ. f. 99r | ܘܡܢ ܡܥܬ ܒܝܢܬܗܘܢ ܕܒܡܫܡܝܐ ܩܕܡܝܐ ܠܫܕܕܐ. ܡܢ ܒܪ ܕܡܥܬ ܒܝܢܐ ܙܝܘܬܐ. ܠܐ ܡܒܢܐ ܙܝܘܬܐ ܗܝ ܡܕܡܝܬܐ ܠܡܡܠܠܘ ܒܗ ܠܙܝܘܬܐ ܗܝ ܕܬܪܬܝܢ. ܙܕܩ ܡܢܝܢ ܕܢܫܘܐ ܐܝܬ ܡܢܗ ܡܡܠܠܢܐ ܕܬܬܘܡܝܢ. ܘܗܘ ܗܢܐ.

7 ܕܒܡܢ ܕܢܫܘܬܗ scr.: ܕܒܡܢ ܕܠܗ cod. 19 ܕܡܬܬܘܡܝܢ scr.: ܕܡܬܬܘܡܝܢ cod.

idea upon which and through which he would gaze, and according to which he would create everything. For if he does not foreknow and foresee in what way something should come to be which will beautifully come to be, he will not be able to start his work properly.

§80 And if there is the one who creates, it is by all means necessary that there is also that which comes to be, is created, and formed. But it is also necessary that God have a certain movement through the gazing at which he creates, especially when the primary generative causes are motionless and thus remain the same. For it is impossible that a structure which is in motion should appear from the primary things which are motionless.

§81 According to Plato's view, Matter is incorporeal and unqualified when everything that exists in it is removed from it. But because of its association with quality, which it acquires, and of its potential ability to (acquire) it, Plato calls it in various ways, i.e. 'receptacle', 'exact foundation', 'mother', 'female', 'all-receptive', 'manifestator', 'space', and 'place'.

§82 Some also say that, though he in this way states that it is unqualified, yet he never says that it is without quality. For because Soul, which is moved by itself, is constantly in it, it is necessary that it be also moved. Thus, the ability of Matter to be moved allows it to receive quality. For even in space no movement may occur unless those things that are moved should properly possess some limit and shapes. Since these things are associated with and belong to Matter, it may no longer remain in its proper condition.

§83 Now, it seems necessary to take a comprehensive explanation concerning Matter also from the ability of the primary bodies to transform into one another. For when a quality changes, the first quality is not naturally able to receive in itself the second quality. Therefore, it is necessary that there should be something receptive to both of them, and this

ܗܟܢܐ ܡܢ ܗܘܝܐ ܡܕܡ. ܗܟܢܐ ܕܝܢ ܐܚܪܢܐ ܡܕܡ ܢܗܘܐ ܠܦܘܬ ܐܢ̈ܫܘܬܐ ܡܫ̈ܠܡܘܬܐ ܕܡܟܠ.

§84 ܐܦܝܩܘܪܘܣ ܕܝܢ ܟܕ ܢܣܒ ܠܦܠܘܛܪܟܘܣ. ܐܦ ܠܚܢܢܐ ܕܢܦܫܐ ܕܐܝܬܘܗܝ ܠܐ ܗܘܝܐ ܡܢ ܫܐܡ. ܠܐ ܡܬܦܣܩܐ ܕܝܢ ܘܠܐ ܡܬܡܢܝܐ. ܘܕܡܢ ܟܠܡ ܡܢ ܐܝܬܘܗܝ ܗܘ ܘܟܠ ܟܡ ܗܘܠܐ. ܘܟܕ ܗܕܐ ܕܐܝܬܘܗܝ ܒܥܠܝܬ ܟܡ ܗܘܠܐ: ܘܡܢ ܦܠܓܘܬܐ ܘܡܬܕܡܟܐ ܒܐܕ̈ܫܐ ܘܒܣܘܪܐ ܡܕ̈ܝܢܐ ܕܒܐܠܗܐ. ܡܢ ܐܠܗܐ ܡܢ ܦܠܓܘܬܐ ܐܦ ܗܘܠܐ.

§85 ܘܒܠܬܐ ܗ̇, ܒܣܘܡܐ ܘܠܐ ܡܬܦܪܢܣܬܐ: ܕܐܡܟܢܐ ܗ̇ܘ̈ܠܐ ܐܬܛܒܥܬ ܠܣܘܪܐ ܩܪ̈ܝܬܐ. ܒܗܘܢܐ ܪܒܢܐ ܦܥܡܬ, ܠܥܪܒܐ ܗܘܬ. ܘܠܗ̇, ܠܡ ܒܥܪ ܕܐܬܐܡܪܬ ܡܢ ܦܠܛܘܢ. ܕܟܕ ܐܡܪ, ܐܠܗܐ ܠܟܠ ܡܟܐ ܕܡܬܝܚܐ: ܠܐ ܟܕ ܒܠܐ ܢܣܒܗ. ܐܠܐ ܟܕ ܡܬܬܪܝܒ ܒܠܠܐܝܬ ܘܠܐ ܡܬܦܣܩܐܝܬ: ܘܡܢ ܠܐ ܡܬܦܣܩܘܬܗ ܠܘܬ ܦܣܩܐ ܐܝܬܘܗ.

§86 ܟܕ ܠܗ̇, ܕܡܢܝܐ ܗܘܠܐ ܘܪܒܐ. ܒܠ ܡܬܬܪܝܒܘܬܐ ܒܠܠܐܝܬܐ ܕܢܦܫܐ ܕܐܝܬ ܒܗ̇ ܢܦܫܡ ܠܗ̇. ܘܗܟܢ ܠܐ ܦܪܫܝܢ: ܕܐܚܪܢܐ ܗܘ ܡܢ ܩܘܡܐ ܕܚܠܡܐ: ܐܚܪܢܐ ܗܘ ܕܝܢ ܕܒܣܘ̈ܟܠܐ. ܠܩܘܡܐ ܕܝܢ ܕܚܠܡܐ ܐܝܟ ܒܠܡܐ ܐܬܝܗܘܢ ܕܪܒܐ. ܒܣܘ̈ܟܠܐ ܩܪ̈ܝܬܐ. ܠܗ̇ܘ ܕܝܢ ܕܒܣܘ̈ܟܠܐ ܐܝܟ ܒܣܘ̈ܟܠܐ ܗܘܠܐ. col. b | ܘܐܕܪܝܐ ܘܐܣܛܘ̈ܟܐ. ܗܠܝܢ ܕܝܢ ܠܟ̈ܠܗܝܢ ܕܐܬܐܡܪ ܡܢ ܦܠܛܘܢ ܒܠ ܩܘܡܐ ܕܚܠܡܐ. ܒܠ ܩܘܡܐ ܕܒܣܘ̈ܟܠܐ ܡܣܒܪܝܢ ܕܐܬܐܡܪ. ܘܐܬܬܚܝܕ ܒܦܣܘܬܐ ܗܦܟܐܬܐ ܫܢܘܢ ܘܗܠܝܢ ܕܢܣܒܘ ܠܗܘܢ. ܟܕ ܠܪ̈ܒܢܐ ܕܢܘܟܪ̈ܝܢ ܠܢܟܫ ܕܦܠܛܘܢ ܢܣܒܘ.

§87 ܐܠܐ ܒܠ ܗܠܝܢ ܡܢ ܡܟܐ ܕܢܨܪܐ ܕܒܟܕ ܒܣܘܡܐ ܕܬܩ̈ܘܪܬܐ ܕܬܪܝܢ ܫܬܐܡܬ ܡܬܬܒܝܢ: ܕܐܡܟܢܐ ܦܥܡܗ ܣܒܪܘܗܝ ܠܗܕܐ ܡܠܬܐ ܕܦܠܛܘܢ. ܣܒܪܘܗܝ ܗܟܠ ܒܡܐܡܪܐ ܩܕܡܝܐ ܕܗܠܝܢ ܕܟܒܪ ܦܠܛܘܢ ܠܘܬ ܦܝܬܓܘܪܘܣ: ܟܕ ܡܦܫܩ ܕܟܝܢܐ ܗܘ ܡܟܐ ܕܐܡܪ ܦܠܛܘܢ: ܕܡܬܬܪܝܒ ܗܘܐ ܡܕܡ ܗܘܝܐ ܕܚܠܡܐ ܠܐ ܡܬܦܣܩܐܝܬ: ܘܡܢ ܐܡܪܐ ܠܐ ܡܬܦܣܩܘܬܐ ܠܐܡܪܐ ܡܬܦܣܩܘܬܐ ܡܢ ܐܠܗܐ ܐܬܐ, ܐܡܪ.

3 ܐܦܝܩܘܪܘܣ scr.: ܐܦܝܩܘܘܪܘܣ cod. 23 ܦܝܬܓܘܪܘܣ scr.: ܦܝܬܐܬܓܘܪܘܣ cod.

will be at one moment one thing and at another moment something else, according to the changing qualities it receives."[30]

§84 Now, Atticus, who follows Plutarch, also states that the nature of Soul is ungenerated, unordered, and unformed, and that it appeared by itself from eternity and came together with Matter. And because it exists naturally with Matter, is set in order, and imitates the First Forms and Ideas which are in God, also Matter is set in order by God.

§85 There is a difficult and irresolvable problem regarding how Matter partook of the First Ideas. It may be easily solved by the following argument. For it was said by Plato that when God brought forth "all that is visible, he gave it not in a state of rest but moving in a discordant and disorderly manner, and he brought it to order from disorder"[31].

§86 While they (i.e. Atticus and Plutarch) assume that Matter possesses movement due to the discordant motion of Soul that is in it, they completely fail to differentiate (two things): one thing is the constitution of the world, and another is that of the bodies. For the constitution of the world as world has primary bodies as principles, while that of bodies as bodies has matter, form, and shapes. So, they assume that the words which Plato uttered about the constitution of the world refer to the constitution of bodies. And they and those who followed them were sized by great error, following opinions that are foreign to Plato's aim.

§87 Instead, when in regard to these matters we start to do inquiry among (different) opinions, we discern more exactly how Severus interpreted this utterance of Plato. Now, in the first treatise which he wrote on the questions concerning Plato's *Timaeus*[32], when Severus was explaining what it was about which Plato said that it was moving in an unordered way before the generation of the world, and from what kind of disorder to what kind of order it was brought by God, he said:

---

30 It is not clear where the quotation from Atticus ends. It is possible that §83 does not belong to it, but should be rather considered a commentary of the author of the treatise (i.e. Porphyry) on Atticus' words.

31 Plato, *Tim.* 30a3–6.

32 The text of the manuscript is corrupt. Literally: "in the first treatise concerning those things which Plato has accomplished to Timotheus". The last form is an evident corruption of Timaeus.

§88 ܕܐܠܝ ܐ ܗܟܢܐ ܐܝܬܘܗܝ ܠܡܕܒܪ. ܕܗܢܐ ܚܕ ܦܝܠܣܘܦܐ ܒܕܘܟܬܐ ܗܕܐ ܡܢ ܥܘܪܐ ܕܡܠܬܐ ܕܟܠ ܚܢܢܐ: ܒܕܡܘܬܐ ܠܗ̇ ܕܡܬܬܘܪܐ ܠܒܪܘܬ ܢܦܫܐ. ܐܘܪܐ ܠܘ ܠܚܠܡܐ ܒܥܡܐ ܡܬܠܡ ܒܪܚܡܘ. ܘܗܘܐ ܠܘ ܐܣܪܐܝܬ ܡܬܚܫܐ ܕܢܚܕܐ ܠܗܢܐ. ܐܘܪܐ ܠܘ ܡܢ ܐܘܪܚܐ ܒܥܘ̈ܡܩܐ ܡܙܒܢ. ܐܠܐ ܗܕܐ ܡܫܝܚܐ. ܕܢܦܩܐ ܗܟܢܐ ܐܝܬܘܗܝ ܕܢܗܪܐ. ܕܐܝܬܘܗܝ ܗܘܐ ܩܕܡ ܗܢܐ ܗܠܝܢ ܐܘܪܚܐ ܒܥܘ̈ܡܩܐ.

§89 ܡܬܝܕܥܢܐ ܕܝܢ ܐܘ ܠܐ ܡܬ̈ܝܕܥܢܐ ܐܝܬܝܗܘܢ ܗܘܘ. ܐܠܐ ܕܐܢܫܝ̈ ܐܝܠܝܢ ܡܬ̈ܝܕܥܢܐ ܠܐ ܫܪܝܪܐ. ܐܝܟ ܒܪ ܡܬ̈ܝܕܥܢܐ ܗܘܘ. ܒܠܚܘܕ ܡܕܡ ܐܝܬܘܗܝ ܗܘܐ ܗ̇ܘ ܕܡܢ ܗܠܝܢ ܡܬ̈ܝܕܥܢܐ ܐܬܝܕܥ. ܠܗܢܐ ܕܝܢ ܒܠܚܘܕ ܩܕܡ ܗܘܐ ܕܒܠܚܘܕ ܕܡܢܗ ܗܘܐ ܗܢܐ ܕܒܗܘܪܬܐ ܗ̇ܝ. ܫܪܝܪܐ ܗܟܢܐ ܕܢܗܪܐ. ܕܗܠܝܢ ܐܘܪܚܐ ܒܥܘ̈ܡܩܐ ܡܢ ܩܕܡ ܡܬܬܐܡܪܝܢ ܗܘܘ | [f. 99v] ܠܐ ܡܬܝܕܥܢܘܬ. ܗܕܐ ܕܝܢ ܐܝܬܘܗܝ ܕܠܘ ܒܝܕܥܬܐ ܒܒܕܝܢ ܗܘܘ ܠܡܬܬܐܡܪܢܘܬܗܘܢ. ܘܠܐ ܡܢ ܒܬܪ ܗܘܘ. ܘܠܐ ܬܘܒ ܒܠܚܘܕ ܡܫܬܡܠܝܢ ܗܘܘ ܡܢ ܡܬܬܐܡܪܢܘܬܗܘܢ.

§90 ܠܠܐ ܡܬܝܕܥܢܘܬܐ ܕܒܗܘܢ ܐܝܟ ܠܒܠܝܘܬܐ ܕܝܕܥܬܐ ܕܗܘ ܠܡܫܒܚܘ. ܐܝܟ ܡܢ ܕܠܐ ܒܪܒܝܐ ܡܫܬܘܕܥ ܠܝܕܥܬܐ ܕܗܘ ܗܘܐ ܠܗܘܢ ܘܠܚܠܡܐ. ܘܠܘ ܠܡܫܬܘܕܥܘܬܐ ܘܠܚܠܝܠܘܬܐ ܕܐܝܬܘܗܝ ܫܘܚܠܦܐ ܠܝܕܥܬܐ ܒܣܠܩܐ ܘܒܢܝܐ: ܗ̇ܝ ܕܐܝܬܘܗܝ ܪܫܐ ܕܒܫܘܬܐ. ܡܛܠ ܕܝܢ ܕܗܘ ܒܟܠܗ ܕܡܬܪ ܗܠܝܢ ܟܠ ܗܘܠܐ ܘܐܦ ܟܠ ܩܘܡܐ ܕܗܠܝܢ ܒܥܘ̈ܡܩܐ ܡܬܚܒܢܐ. ܐܡܪ ܕܠܐ ܡܬܝܕܥܢܘܬ ܡܢ ܡܬܬܐܡܪܝܢ ܗܘܘ.

§91 ܕܗܘ ܗܟܢܐ ܠܡܕܒܪ. ܕܒܠܚܘܕ ܐܝܠܝܢ ܕܒܠܝܘܬܐ ܘܡܫܬܡܫܢܘܬܐ ܡܬܐܡܪܝܢ: ܐܝܟ ܗ̇ܝ. ܕܠܐ ܥܩܪ ܘܠܐ ܫܪܐ ܘܠܐ ܡܬܝܕܥ. ܘܟܠ ܕܐܝܟ ܗܠܝܢ. ܘܠܐ ܡܕܡ ܡܬܐܡܪ ܗ̇ܘ ܫܘܫܒܠܐ ܡܫ̈ܬܕܠܝܢ ܐܘ ܗ̇ܘ ܡܢܐ ܕܐܝܬܘܗܝ. ܡܢ ܒܥܐ ܕܐܡܪܐ. ܡܢܐ ܗܟܢܐ ܕܢܐܡܪ ܠܐ ܥܩܪܐ. ܒܗܝ ܓܝܪ ܠܫܘܝܐ ܡܫܬܕܠܝܢ. ܒܗܝ ܕܝܢ ܠܗ̇ܘ ܕܐܝܬܘܗܝ. ܡܢ ܒܥܐ ܕܫܘܝܐ ܘܕܥܩܪܐ.

§92 ܗܟܢܐ ܘܒܥܘܢܝܐ ܘܠܐ ܫܪܐ ܘܠܐ ܡܬܝܕܥ ܠܘ ܡܢ ܒܠܥܕܘܗ̇ ܠܗ̇ܘ ܫܘܫܒܠܐ ܡܫܬܕܠܝܢ ܐܘ ܕܠܫܘܒܠܐ. ܐܠܐ ܒܗܟܐ ܕܟܠܗܝܢ ܘܠܗܝܢ ܒܥܐ ܕܗܠܝܢ. ܡܛܠ ܕܐܦ ܠܡܫܘܕܥܘܬܐ ܕܐܝܟ ܗܠܝܢ ܕܟܠܗܝܢ ܕܡܬܝܕܥܢܐ ܢܬܒ̈ܝܢ ܒܗ: ܠܐ

§88 “Now, it is necessary to understand what the philosopher did in this place, i.e. from the beginning of the passage on nature until that one which is called ‘generation of Soul’. Had not he (i.e. God) established the corporeal world in his mind? But behold, does it not seem that he creates this (world) in a different manner? Does he not compose it from the four bodies? But it is evident that the way of understanding this, which we should follow, is that these four bodies existed prior to this (world).

§89 Were they there ordered or disordered? But to say that they were ordered would not be correct. For if they were ordered, then the world would have been that which is composed of these ordered things. But it is a fallacy to think that there was a world before the generation of this world, which came to be from it. Then it remains that we think that the four bodies were from the beginning moving disorderly. That means that they accomplished their motion without order and that they were not settled. And they also have not brought about the world from their movability.

§90 The disorder in them should be understood as privation of order, as if they have yet partaken neither in the order which was due to them and to the world nor in the disturbance and confusion which are contrary to order in potentiality and in kind and which are the beginning of evil. But because in the words after that he (i.e. Plato) speaks about Matter and also about the constitution of bodies, he says that they were moving disorderly.

§91 Now, we must understand that all those things that are said by the way of privation and negation – e.g., ‘unattractive’, ‘unseen’, ‘unordered’, and all the like – either signify to a greater extent something contrary or that which is intermediate to the extremes. Thus, when we say ‘unattractive’, sometimes we denote the ugly, and sometimes the intermediate to the ugly and the beautiful.

§92 Similarly with the terms ‘unseen’ and ‘unordered’, we do not always designate the contrary or the opposite, but sometimes the intermediate to them. For when a bunch of plants is intended to be planted in some order,

ܡܫܡܫܢܘܬܐ ܐܚܪܢܐ. ܠܘ ܒܗ̇ ܕܡܢܝ ܠܡܣܟܢܘܬܐ ܘܠܒܨܝܪܘܬܐ. ܐܠܐ ܒܗ̇ ܕܠܐ ܒܕܒܠ ܢܩܒܠ ܠܗܘ ܫܡܫܐ ܕܒܪ ܡܠܟܝܢ ܒܢ ܩܕܝܡ.

§93 ܠܐ ܡܫܡܫܐܝܬ ܗܒܝܠ ܡܬܬܪܒܝܢ ܗܘܘ ܗܠܝܢ ܐܪ̈ܒܥܐ ܒܢ̈ܝܢܫܐ
col. b ܒܗܢܐ ܙܒܢܐ. ܕܠܐ ܒܕܒܠ ܢܫܒܩܘܢ ܗܘܘ | ܠܫܡܫܐ ܘܙܗܐ ܘܚܒܪ ܒܠܗܐ.

§94 ܒܬܪ ܗܠܝܢ ܕܝܢ ܗܕܪܗ ܚܬܬܐܝܬ ܦܩܕܗ̇ ܠܕܘܒܪܬܐ. ܒܪ ܚܘܝ ܕܠܘ ܒܠ ܗܘܠܐ ܐܡܪ ܦܠܛܘܢ ܠܟܠܗ ܗܠܝܢ. ܐܦܠܐ ܗܝܢ ܒܠ ܡܘܡܐ ܕ ܒܢ̈ܝܢܫܐ. ܐܠܐ ܒܠ ܬܘܡܢܐ ܘܡܢ ܒܬܪ ܕܟܠܗܐ ܕܡܢ ܒܢ̈ܝܢܫܐ. ܐܝܟ ܕܬܘܗܐ ܗ̇, ܕܐܡܪܝܢ. ܕܐܚܪܢܐ ܗܘ ܙܒܢܐ ܕܒܠ ܡܘܡܐ ܕܟܠܗܐ ܐܝܟ ܟܠܗܐ. ܘܐܚܪܢܐ ܗܘ ܕܒܠ ܡܘܡܐ ܕ ܒܢ̈ܝܢܫܐ ܐܝܟ ܒܢ̈ܝܢܫܐ: ܗܠܝܢ ܕܒܪܘܗܝ ܡܢ ܟܠܗܐ.

§95 ܠܗܢܐ ܕܝܢ ܙܒܢܐ ܢܦܩ ܐܦ ܦܠܛܘܢ ܡܠܦܝܢ ܒܪ ܡܦܩܩ ܠܛܒܬܗܘܢ. ܒܬܘܗܘ ܕܝܢ ܕܠܗ ܢܦܩ ܠܘܬܗܘܢ ܗ̇ܘ ܡܠܦܝܢ ܒܠ ܗܘܠܐ ܦܩܕ ܕܐܒܪܐ ܐܚܪܝܢ ܠܗܠܝܢ ܦܠܛܘܢ: ܒܪ ܡܦܩܩ ܕܡܛܠ ܡܢܗܐ ܡܬܬܪܒܝܢܘܬܐ ܘܠܘ ܠܐ ܡܬܬܪܒܝܢܘܬܐ ܐܟܠܗ ܠܗܘܠܐ ܦܠܛܘܢ: ܘܦܩܕܗ̇ ܠܒܕܘܒܪܬܐ ܐܠܗܝܬܐ.

§96 ܒܪ ܡܫܒܚ ܕܝܢ ܠܟܠܬܐ ܐܡܪ. ܕܠܐ ܡܢ ܐ ܡܕܡ ܕܢܚܙ ܡܢ ܐܚܪܢܐ: ܐܢ ܠܐ ܢܗܘܐ ܦܢܐ ܐܦ ܗܘ ܘܗܒܐ ܡܕܡ ܒܬܚܬܐ. ܐܦܠܐ ܓܒܪ ܠܐܒܫܡܘܫܐ ܡܢ ܚܕ ܠܡܫܘܝܘ. ܘܠܐ ܡܕܡ ܡܢ ܕܐܝܟ ܗܠܝܢ. ܡܛܠ ܗ̇, ܕܠܐ ܩܢܝܢ ܗܠܝܢ ܒܬܚܬܝܢ ܘܗܒܐ. ܡܢ ܐ ܕܝܢ ܠܡܫܘܕܐ ܒܐܦܐ ܠܟܠ. ܗ̇ܘ ܕܐܝܬ ܗܘ ܠܗ ܢܝܠܐ ܠܘܬ ܡܢ ܒܬܐ.

§97 ܠܐ ܗܒܝܠ ܐܡܪ ܡܢ ܕܐ ܗܘܬ ܡܬܬܘܡ ܗܘܠܐ ܕܬܬܪܒܐ ܡܢ ܐܠܗܐ: ܐܢ ܠܐ ܐܝܬ ܗܘܐ ܡܬܬܪܒܝܢܘܬܐ ܡܕܡ ܒܬܚܬܗ̇. ܕܠܗ̇ ܠܗܕܐ ܬܦܢܝܗ̇ ܘܫܡܫܗ̇ ܐܠܗܐ. ܡܬܚܙܝܐ ܗܒܝܠ ܐܦ ܗܢܐ. ܕܐܝܟ ܬܪܒܝܬܗ ܕܦܠܛܘܢ. ܡܬܬܪܒܝܢܘܬܐ ܒܚܝܠܐ ܡܫܒ ܠܗ̇ ܠܗܘܠܐ. ܐܝܟ ܗܝ ܕܒܠܒܪ ܗܕܐ. ܠܐ ܡܢ ܐ ܗܘܬ ܕܬܬܢܝܚ ܠܘܬ ܒܟܘܪܘܬܐ. ❖

we also call them unordered, not because they possess disturbance and confusion, but because they do not yet possess the order which they acquire when being planted.

§93 Therefore, these four bodies were moving disorderly in such a sense that they had not yet acquired the necessary order which makes up the world."

§94 With these (arguments) Severus precisely explained this passage, having shown that with these words Plato did not refer to Matter, and certainly not to the state of bodies, but rather to the formation and setting in order of the world from bodies. This is how it comes that we say that the opinion concerning the constitution of the world as world is one thing, and that concerning the constitution of the bodies as bodies from which the world appeared is another.

§95 Our teacher Plotinus also shared this view, when he interpreted the *Timaeus*. Boethus, instead, who was followed by our teacher Longinus, thought that these words of Plato refer to Matter while he was explaining why Plato provided Matter with movability rather than with immovability and attributed creation to God.

§96 Giving a reason (for this) he (i.e. Boethus) says:

"Something cannot be affected by something else unless it also possesses some motion of its own. We are even unable to deliver a statement (ἀξίωμα) about similar things, if they do not possess a movement of their own. For it is possible to throw a stone up, but by itself it will fall down towards the centre."

§97 That's why, he says[33], Matter would have never been able to be moved by God unless there was some movability in itself, so that God could have formed it and set in order. Therefore, it seems also that, according to the opinion of Plato, he gave natural motion to Matter, for without it, it would have not been possible to utilise it for creation.

33 It is possible that the last paragraph also belongs to the quotation from Boethus. In this case, "he" would refer to Plato.

Syriac and Greek Glossary

Given the fact that no Greek original for the Syriac translation has been found thus far, we have no direct basis for comparison between the Syriac and Greek terminology. Thus, the Greek terms in the following glossary should not be taken as actual equivalents to the Syriac ones, but rather as hypothetic variants that derive from the extant Syriac translations of Greek philosophical and scientific works.

Following published glossaries of the Syriac translation of Greek philosophical texts have been consulted:

DeM	*De Mundo*: Adam McCollum, *A Greek and Syriac Index to Sergius of Reshaina's Version of the De Mundo* (Gorgias Handbooks, 12; Piscataway: Gorgias, 2009).
DeV	*De Virtutibus et vitiis*: Sebastian P. Brock, "An Abbreviated Syriac Version of Ps.-Aristotle, *De Virtutibus et vitiis* and *Divisiones*", in: E. Coda & C. Martini Bonadeo (eds.), *De l'Antiquité tardive au Moyen Age: Mélanges offertes à Henri Hugonnard-Roche* (Études Musulmanes, 44; Paris: Vrin, 2014), 91–112.
HippAph	*Aphorismi Hippocratis*: Henri Pognon, *Une version syriaque des aphorismes d'Hippocrate* (Leipzig: Hinrichs, 1903).
Hof	Johann G.E. Hoffmann, *De Hermeneuticis apud Syros Aristoteleis* (Leipzig, 1869).
Pol	Isidor Pollak, *Die Hermeneutik des Aristoteles in der arabischen Übersetzung des Ishak ibn Honain* (Abhandlungen für die Kunde des Morgenlandes, XIII.1; Leipzig, 1913).
SRInt	*Sergius of Reshaina, Introduction to Aristotle and his Categories*: Sami Aydin (ed.), *Sergius of Reshaina, Introduction to Aristotle and his Categories, Addressed to Philotheos: Syriac Text, with Introduction, Translation, and Commentary* (Aristoteles Semitico-Latinus, 24; Leiden/Boston: Brill, 2016).

Additionally, the following Syriac translations from the Greek were analysed on the basis of the online editions in the HUNAYNNET database[1]:

AnPrG	Aristotle, *Analytica Priora*, translation of George of the Arabs (ed. HUNAYNNET, based on the collation of cod. and the edition of Furlani);

1 <https://hunaynnet.oeaw.ac.at/>

https://doi.org/10.1515/9783110747027-003

AnPrP	Aristotle, *Analytica Priora*, translation of Proba (critical edition of HUNAYNNET);
CatAn	Aristotle, *Catogories*, anonymous translation (critical edition of HUNAYNNET);
CatG	Aristotle, *Categories*, translation of George of the Arabs (ed. HUNAYNNET, based on the collation of cod. and the edition of Furlani);
CatJ	Aristotle, *Categories*, translation of Jacob of Edessa (critical edition of HUNAYNNET);
DeInAn	Aristotle, *De Interpretatione*, anonymous translation (ed. HUNAYNNET, based on the edition of Hoffmann);
DeInG	Aristotle, *De Interpretatione*, translation of George of the Arabs (ed. HUNAYNNET, based on the collation of cod. and the edition of Furlani);
DeSim	*De Simplicium medicamentorum temperamentis et facultatibus*, liber VI (ed. HUNAYNNET, based on the edition prepared within the project "The Syriac Galen Palimpsest: Galen's On Simple Drugs and the Recovery of Lost Texts through Sophisticated Imaging Techniques" at the University of Manchester);
IsagAn	Porphyry, *Isagoge*, anonymous translation (ed. HUNAYNNET, based on the edition of Brock);
IsagAth	Porphyry, *Isagoge*, translation of Athanasius of Balad (critical edition of HUNAYNNET).

Two Greek texts may be considered as containing close parallels to the Syriac:

Pl.*Tim.*	Plato, *Timaeus*;
SextEmp	Sextus Empiricus, *Adv. Math.*, Book X.

In two cases, no references to the extant Syriac translations from the Greek appear near the Greek aquivalents: (1) by loanwords from the Greek (then the sign " < " is applied), (2) when a term is not attested in the Syriac translations listed above, but is reconstructed with a high degree of probability (the presumed Greek aquivalents were suggested by the editor by means of the sign " ≈ "):

<	Greek source of the Syriac loanword;
≈	presumed Greek equivalent, not attested in the extant sources.

The following glossary contains lexemes, which belong to philosophical and scientific terminology[2]. It includes nouns, adjectives, verbs, and adverbs, but also some prepositions and pronouns, which assume terminological meaning. Prefixes, suffixes, and most of the pronouns, prepositions, and conjunctions are excluded.

---

2 For the definition of philosophical and scientific terminology, cf. Leicht & Veltri, "The Study of Pre-Modern Philosophical and Scientific Hebrew Terminology".

The Syriac glossary is organized according to Syriac roots, established on the basis of Sokoloff's lexicon[3].

References are to the paragraph numbers of the Syriac edition published in the present volume.

3 Sololoff, *A Syriac Lexicon*. Cf. Kindt et al., "La concordance bilingue grecque-syriaque".

Syriac Glossary

ܐ

ʾʾr		
ܐܐܪ	§7, 13, 21–23, 35, 52, 54	< ἀήρ
ʾbʾ		
ܐܒܐ	§6, 73	πατήρ (IsagAn)
ʾbd		
ܐܒܕܢܐ	§34	≈ ἀπώλεια
ʾdšʾ		
ܐܕܫܐ	§5, 11, 14, 17, 23–26, 47, 48, 64, 84, 86	< εἶδος; ἰδέα (DeM)
ܕܠܐ ܐܕܫܐ	§45	≈ ἀνείδεος
ʾwsyʾ		
ܐܘܣܝܐ	§15, 42, 58, 78	< οὐσία
ʾḥd		
ܐܬܬܚܕ *Ethpe.*	§86	ἐπιλαμβάνομαι (DeSim)
ʾḥr		
ܐܚܪܝ	§17, 20	ὕστερος, ὕστατος (IsagAn, IsagAth), τελευταῖος (AnPrG)
ܐܚܪܢܐ	§10, 17, 33, 34, 36, 37, 41–44, 46, 58, 59, 72 74, 78, 83, 86, 94, 96	ἄλλος (IsagAn, IsagAth, DeInG), ἀλλοιόω (CatG)
ܐܚܪܝܬ	§3	τελευταῖον (IsagAn), ὕστερον (IsagAn)
ܐܚܪܢܐܝܬ	§88	ἄλλως (IsagAn, IsagAth), ἑτέρως (DeM)
ʾydʾ		
ܒܝܕ	§17, 24, 68, 84, 94	διά *c. gen.* (IsagAn, IsagAth, CatAn, etc.), κατά *c. acc.* (IsagAn, CatAn)
ʾyk		
ܕܐܝܟ ܐܡܪ	§21, 79	οἷον (CatAn, CatJ, CatG, etc.)
ܕܐܝܟ ܗܢܐ	§4, 26, 31	τοιοῦτος (IsagAth, DeInG, AnPrP)
ܐܟܘܬܐ	§27, 73, 79	
ʾyn		
ܐܝܢܐ (*f.* ܐܝܕܐ)	§79, 87	ποιός (CatAn, IsagAn, IsagAth), οἷον (Hof, DeInG)
ܐܝܕܐ ܒܐܝܕܐ	§58	κατὰ μέρος (IsagAn)

ʾyt		
ܐܝܬ	§1, 3–5, 7–15, 17–40, 42–73, 75–84, 86, 88–91, 96, 97	εἰμί (DeInAn, DeInG); ἔχω (DeInG); ὑπάρχω (Hof, DeInG)
ܐܝܬܘܗܝ	§77	τὸ ὄν (Pl.*Tim.*)
ܐܝܬܘܬܐ	§4	ἕξις (CatAn)
ܠܝܬ	§11, 22, 24, 34, 37, 45, 57, 71	οὐκ εἰμί (IsagAn, DeInAn, DeInG), μὴ ὑπάρχω (AnPrP)
ʾkḥd		
ܐܟܚܕ	§19, 73	συν- and προσ- in composite words (Hof); ἅμα (DeM, IsagAn, DeInG, etc.); πᾶν (DeInG)
ʾksywmʾ		
ܐܟܣܝܘܡܐ	§96	< ἀξίωμα
ʾlh		
ܐܠܗܐ	§6, 15, 38, 39, 72, 75–77, 80, 84, 85, 87, 95, 97	θεός (Pl.*Tim.*)
ʾlṣ		
ܐܠܝܨܐ	§18, 19, 32, 33, 38, 82, 88	ἀνάγκη (DeM, IsagAn, AnPrP), ἀναγκαῖος (CatAn, IsagAn)
ʾmʾ		
ܐܡܐ	§41, 69, 81	μήτηρ (Pl.*Tim.*)
ʾmn		
ܐܡܝܢܐ	§11	συνεχής (DeM)
ܐܡܝܢܐܝܬ	§19, 77, 82	συνεχής (CatAn, AnPrG, DeM), συνεχῶς (DeM), ἀεί (IsagAth)
ʾmr		
ܐܡܪ	§1–6, 8–16, 18, 23, 25, 28, 32, 33, 35, 36, 38, 40–42, 45, 47, 52, 53, 56, 67, 68, 74, 75, 78, 79, 82, 87, 89–92, 94–97	λέγω (Hof, DeInG, AnPrP, etc.)
ܐܬܐܡܪ *Ethpe.*	§30, 35, 43, 44, 46, 48, 49, 58, 59, 67, 68, 71, 74, 76, 85, 86, 91	λέγομαι (IsagAn, IsagAth, AnPrP, etc.)
ܡܐܡܪܐ	§73, 87	λόγος (DeInAn, AnPrP), ῥῆμα (DeInG)

ʾn		
ܐܢ	§18, 19, 30–33, 35, 37, 42, 43, 45, 47–49, 52, 53, 60, 62, 63, 65, 66, 74, 76, 79, 82, 89, 96, 97	εἰ (IsagAn, IsagAth, CatAn, etc.), ἐπεί (IsagAn, CatAn)
ʾnnqʾ		
ܐܢܢܩܐ	§2, 23, 68	< ἀνάγκη
ʾnšʾ		
ܐܢܫܐ	§6, 18, 33, 35, 36, 47, 74–76	τίς (DeM, DeInG), ἄνθρωπος (CatAn)
ʾsṭwksʾ		
ܐܣܛܘܟܣܐ	§4, 35, 50	< στοιχεῖον
ʾskmʾ		
ܐܣܟܡܐ	§11, 12, 14, 23, 25, 26, 44–49, 70, 82, 86	< σχῆμα
ܡܣܟܡܐ	§49	≈ ἐσχηματισμένος
ʾsr		
ܡܐܣܘܪܬܐ	§92	≈ δεσμός
ʾpzgʾ		
ܐܦܙܓܐ	§36	≈ ἄνισος
ʾqmʾgwn		
ܐܩܡܐܓܘܢ	§41	< ἐκμαγεῖον
ʾrʾ		
ܐܪܐ	§88	< ἄρα
ʾrbʿ		
ܐܪܒܥ	§1, 13, 50, 73, 88, 89, 93	τέσσαρες (IsagAn, IsagAth, DeInAn, etc.), τέταρτος (CatJ, DeSim)
ʾrʿʾ		
ܐܪܥܐ	§13, 21–23, 35, 51, 52	γῆ (DeM)
ܐܪܥܢܐ	§22	χθόνιος (DeM)
ʾšd		
ܐܬܐܫܕ *Ethpe.*	§51	ἀναχεῖται (DeM)
ʾštʾ		
ܐܫܬܐ	§81	
ܫܬܐܣܬܐ	§41, 50, 55, 70, 78	στοιχείωσις (DeSim)
ʾty		
ܐܬܝ	§47	εἰμί (DeInAn), ἥκω (DeSim)
ܐܝܬܝ *Af.*	§75, 85	ἄγω (Pl.*Tim.*)
ܐܬܬܝܬܝ *Ettaf.*	§87	προσέρχομαι (IsagAth)

ʾtrʾ		
ܐܬܪܐ	§81, 82	χώρα (DeM, DeSim), τόπος (CatJ, CatG, DeM)

ܒ

bṭl		
ܒܛܠ *Pa.*	§8	ἀναιρέω (CatAn), συναναιρέω (IsagAn, CatAn)
bwr		
ܒܘܪܘܬܐ	§89	≈ μωρία
byš		
ܒܝܫܬܐ	§90	τὸ κακόν (CatAn)
bytʾ		
ܒܝܬܐ	§16, 36, 40, 96, 97	≈ οἶκος, οἰκεῖος
ܒܝܬܝܐ	§82, 96	οἰκεῖος (CatJ, CatG, IntG, IsagAth)
ܒܝܬܝܬ	§82	οἰκείως (CatJ, CatG)
bll		
ܒܠܝܠܐ	§86	≈ πλημμελής
ܒܠܝܠܐܝܬ	§25, 75, 85	πλημμελῶς (Pl.*Tim.*)
ܒܠܝܠܘܬܐ	§76, 90, 92	
blʿd		
ܒܠܥܕ	§22, 26, 52, 82, 97	χωρίς (DeM), ἄνευ (IsagAn, CatAn, DeInG)
bʿy		
ܐܬܒܥܝܐ *Ethpe.*	§60, 79	ζητοῦμαι (AnPrG)
ܒܥܬܐ	§33, 85	ἀπορία (SRInt)
bṣr		
ܒܨܝܪܐ	§36, 37, 71	ἧττον (IsagAn, IsagAth, CatAn)
ܒܨܝܪܐܝܬ	§45	ἧττον (IsagAn, IsagAth, CatJ)
brʾ		
ܠܒܪ ܡܢ	§42	παρά *c. acc.* (CatJ), ἐκτός *c. gen.* (DeInAn, DeInG)
btr		
ܒܬܪ	§24, 29, 35, 40, 90	μετά *c. acc.* (CatAn, CatJ, CatG, etc.), ἑξῆς *c. gen.* (DeM)
ܒܬܪܟܢ	§12	εἶτα (CatAn, DeInAn, DeInG, etc.), ἔπειτα (DeInAn, DeInG, DeSim)

ܓ

gdš		
ܓܕܫܐ	§3, 4, 31, 34, 43, 76	συμβαίνω (CatAn, CatJ, CatG, etc.); τὸ συμβεβηκός (CatAn, CatJ, CatG)
ܓܕܫܐܝܬ	§37	κατα συμβεβηκός (DeInAn, DeSim)
gwʾ		
ܓܘܐ	§48, 51, 54	κοινός (IsagAn, CatAn, CatJ, CatG), καθόλου (DeInAn, DeSim, SRInt)
ܓܘܝܐ	§77	κοινός (CatJ), καθόλου (DeInAn)
ܓܘܝܐܝܬ	§42, 45, 53	ἁπλῶς (Hof, AnPrP), κοινός (IsagAn, IsagAth, CatAn, CatJ), κοινῶς (IsagAn), καθόλου (IsagAn, DeSim)
gwn		
ܒܓܘܢ	§9, 60, 67, 70	διό (IsagAn, IsagAth), ὥστε (IsagAn)
glz		
ܐܬܓܠܙ *Ethpe.*	§4	στεροῦμαι (Hof, CatAn, CatJ, etc.)
ܓܠܝܙܘܬܐ	§14, 90, 91	στέρησις (CatAn, CatJ, CatG)
gmr		
ܓܡܝܪܐܝܬ	§34	τελέως (DeSim)
gnsʾ		
ܓܢܣܐ	§11, 58, 60	< γένος
gšm		
ܓܘܫܡܐ	§14, 23, 48, 50, 51, 55–58, 60–65, 67–69, 83, 86, 88–90, 93, 94	σῶμα (IsagAn, IsagAth, CatAn, etc.)
ܓܫܝܡܐ	§56, 64, 67, 88	≈ σωματωθεῖσα (sc. ἡ ὕλη)
ܠܐ ܓܫܝܡܐ	§56, 64, 66, 67, 69, 81	≈ ἀσώματος

ܕ

dbq		
ܕܒܩ	§12	κολλάω (DeSim)
dwk		
ܒܟܠܕܘܟ	§76	πανταχοῦ (DeInG)
ܠܐ ܒܕܘܟ	§41	≈ μηδαμοῦ
ܕܘܟܬܐ	§77, 78, 81, 88, 94	τόπος (IsagAth, CatAn), χώρα (Pl.*Tim.*)

dyl		
ܕܝܠ	§23, 43, 57, 72	αὐτός (DeInAn, DeInG), τὸ ἴδιον (IsagAn)
ܕܝܠܝܘܬܐ	§17, 35	τὸ ἴδιον (IsagAn, IsagAth, CatAn, etc.), ἰδιότης (IsagAn, IsagAth)
ܕܝܠܝܐ	§45, 45	ἴδιος (CatAn, CatJ, CatG, etc.), ἰδικός (Hof)
dll		
ܐܬܕܠܠ *Ethpa.*	§53	ἀραιοῦμαι (DeM)
dmy		
ܕܡܝ	§12	ἔοικα (IsagAn, IsagAth, CatAn, etc.), ὅμοιος (CatJ)
ܐܬܕܡܝ *Ethpa.*	§84	
ܕܡܝܢ ܡܢܘ̈ܬܐ	§10	≈ ὁμοιομερής
ܡܬܕܡܝܢܐ ܒܐܕ̈ܫܐ	§84	≈ ὁμοιοειδής
ܕܡܘܬܐ	§27, 73, 74–77	μορφή (CatJ, CatAn)
ܒܕܡܘܬܐ	§23, 27, 28, 38, 39, 42, 54	ὁμοίως (DeInAn, DeInG, AnPrP, etc.), ὡσαύτως (CatAn)
drk		
ܡܬܕܪ̇ܟܢܐ	§66	

ܗ

h'		
ܗܐ	§51, 88	ἤδη (Hof)
hwy		
ܗܘܝ	§3–6, 13, 17–19, 21, 28–37, 39, 42, 46–48, 52, 53, 64, 67–69, 72, 73, 75–80, 82–85, 87–90, 93, 94, 96, 97	εἰμί (IsagAn, IsagAth, CatAn, etc.), γίγνομαι (Pl.*Tim.*, CatAn, DeSim), ὑπάρχω (AnPrP)
ܗܘܝܐ	§8, 10, 11, 19, 35, 43, 52, 77, 78, 87, 89	γένεσις (Pl.*Tim.*; CatAn, CatJ)
ܕܠܐ ܗܘܝܐ	§84	≈ ἀγέννητος
ܗܘ̈ܝܐ	§6, 28, 33, 35–37, 39, 41, 48, 55, 69, 70, 73, 78	τὰ ὄντα (DeM), τὰ γενόμενα (Pol)
hwl'		
ܗܘܠܐ	§9, 14, 15, 24, 25, 28, 38–44, 47–50, 52–57,	< ὕλη

	60–64, 67, 68, 73–76, 78, 81–88, 90, 94, 95, 97	
ܗܘܠܝܐ	§24, 36	< ὑλικός
ܗܘܠܢܝܐ	§3, 4, 6, 7, 10	ἔνυλος (SRInt)
hwn’		
ܗܘܢܐ	§10, 26, 27, 66	νοῦς (Hof, DeM)
hymn		
ܐܬܗܝܡܢ *QuadRef.*	§67	≈ πιστεύω (cf. ܗܝܡܢ in DeM)
hkyl		
ܗܟܝܠ	§6, 18, 29, 35, 42, 47, 51, 52, 55, 79, 87–89, 91, 93, 97	οὖν (CatAn, CatJ, CatG, etc.)
ܥܕܟܝܠ	§33, 49, 52, 67, 71, 78, 90	ἔτι (DeSim)
ܠܐ ܥܕܟܝܠ	§52, 92, 93	οὔπω (CatAn, CatJ, DeInAn, etc.), οὐδέπω (CatJ, CatG)
hrysys		
ܗܪܣܝܣ	§2	< αἵρεσις
hš’		
ܗܫܐ	§17, 83	νῦν (IsagAn, IsagAth, CatJ, etc.)

ܘ

wrd		
ܘܪܝܕܐ	§22	φλέψ (DeSim, HippAph), φλέβιον (HippAph)

ܙ

zbn		
ܙܒܢܐ	§30, 32, 45, 92	χρόνος (CatAn, DeInAn, DeInG, etc.), καιρός (DeM)
ܙܒܢ ܡܢ ... ܙܒܢ ܕܝܢ	§91	ὁτὲ μὲν ... ὁτὲ δέ (DeInAn, DeInG)
zdq		
ܙܕܩ	§17, 25, 30, 32, 33, 36, 37, 43, 47, 48, 53, 79, 80, 83, 90, 91	δεῖ (IsagAn, IsagAth, CatAn, etc.)
ܙܕܩܐܝܬ	§35, 67	εἰκότως (DeSim, CatJ, CatG)

zwʿ		
ܐܬܬܙܝܥ *Ettaph.*	§12, 26, 73, 74, 82, 85, 87, 89, 90, 93, 97	κινοῦμαι (IsagAn, IsagAth, DeM, etc.)
ܡܬܬܙܝܥܢܐ	§1, 80	κινητός (DeInAn, DeInG)
ܠܐ ܡܬܬܙܝܥܢܐ	§1, 2, 8, 9, 75, 80, 95	ἀκίνητος (DeM)
ܙܘܥܐ	§78, 80, 82, 86, 96	κίνησις (CatJ, DeM)
ܡܬܬܙܝܥܢܘܬܐ	§8, 73, 76, 86, 89, 97	κίνησις (CatJ, AnPrG, DeM), τὸ κινεῖσθαι (IsagAn, IsagAth, DeM)
zky		
ܙܟܘܬܐ	§13, 36	≈ νῖκος (a corruption for νεῖκος)
znʾ		
ܙܢܐ	§24, 31, 44, 46, 47, 49, 82, 90	ποιός (IsagAn, CatAn), τρόπος (CatJ)
ܕܠܐ ܙܢܐ	§29, 31, 45, 49, 57, 68, 75, 81, 82	≈ ἄποιος
ܙܢܝܐ	§43, 50	τρόπος (CatAn, CatJ), ποιός (CatAn)
ܙܢܝܘܬܐ	§23–26, 42–45, 47, 48, 51, 53, 54, 57, 58, 70, 81–83	≈ ποιότης
ܙܢܢܝܐ	§31, 42, 49, 57, 58	
ܙܢܢܝܘܬܐ	§23, 43, 63	
zʿr		
ܙܥܘܪܐ	§58	ὀλίγος (CatAn, CatJ), μικρός (CatAn, CatJ, DeM)
zrʿ		
ܙܪܥܐ	§46	σπέρμα (DeSim), γόνος (HippAph)

ܚ

ḥbl		
ܚܒܠ	§33	≈ φθείρομαι
ܐܬܚܒܠ *Ethpa.*	§3, 4, 33, 34	φθείρομαι (DeM)
ܚܘܒܠܐ	§8, 10, 13, 34	φθορά (CatAn, Hof, SRInt, etc.)
ܠܐ ܡܬܚܒܠܢܐ	§33, 69, 77	≈ ἄφθαρτος
ḥbš		
ܚܒܫ	§2, 22	περιέχω (IsagAn, IsagAth, DeM, etc.), περιλαμβάνω (CatAn, CatJ), διαλαμβάνω (DeM)

ḥd		
ܚܕ	§1, 2, 5, 7–9, 11, 17, 24, 28, 35–38, 42, 45–47, 54, 73, 74, 76	εἷς (IsagAn, IsagAth, CatAn, etc.)
ܟܠܚܕ	§53, 74	ἕκαστος (CatAn, CatJ, CatG, etc.), ἑκάτερος (IsagAn, IsagAth, AnPrP, etc.)
ܚܕܕܐ	§10, 12, 18, 36, 37, 44, 50, 55, 68, 72, 76, 83	ἀλλήλων (CatAn, IsagAn, IsagAth, etc.)
ܝܚܝܕܐ	§23	ἴδιος (IsagAn)
ܝܚܝܕܐܝܬ	§53, 54	ἰδίως (IsagAn), ἴδιον (IsagAn), μοναχῶς (AnPrG)
ḥwy		
ܚܘܝ *Pa.*	§17, 33, 76, 94	ἀποδείκνυμι (AnPrP), ἀναφαίνω (DeM)
ܐܬܚܘܝ *Ethpa.*	§34	δείκνυμαι (DeInAn, DeInG, AnPrG)
ܡܚܘܝܢܐ	§17, 81	ἀποδεικτικός (Hof)
ḥwr		
ܚܘܪܐ	§27, 28, 38, 73, 84, 85	≈ εἶδος
ḥzy		
ܚܙܐ	§5, 79	βλέπω (CatAn, CatJ), ὁράω (DeSim)
ܩܕܡ ܚܙܐ	§79	≈ προοράω
ܠܐ ܚܙܝܐ	§91, 92	ἀόρατος (DeM)
ܡܬܚܙܝܐ *Ethpe. part.*	§24, 41, 43, 75, 83, 85, 88, 97	φαίνομαι (CatAn, DeInAn, CatJ, etc.), θεωροῦμαι (DeM, CatAn, CatJ, etc.), ἔοικα (IsagAth), σαφής (IsagAn), φανερός (DeM), ὁρατός (Pl.*Tim.*)
ܡܬܚܙܝܢܐ	§21, 22	≈ ὁρατός
ḥyl’		
ܚܝܠܐ	§15, 18, 44–47, 56, 67, 69, 81, 90	δύναμις (CatAn, IsagAn, IsagAth, etc.)
ḥkm		
ܚܟܡ	§36	οἶδα (DeSim)
ḥlṭ		
ܚܠܛ *Pa.*	§10	≈ μίγνυμι
ܐܬܚܠܛ *Ethpa.*	§10	≈ μίγνυμαι
ܚܘܠܛܐ	§13	μῖξις (Hof)
ḥmm		
ܚܡܡ	§54	θερμαίνω (CatAn)
ܚܡܝܡܐ	§21, 22, 36	θερμός (CatJ)

ܚܡܝܡܘܬܐ	§5, 23, 53, 54	θερμότης (CatAn, DeSim), θέρμα (DeM), θερμασία (DeSim)
ḥsn		
ܠܚܘܣܢ *adv.*	§41, 70	μόλις (HippAph)
ḥšb		
ܚܫܒ	§9, 68	ἀγέομαι (DeSim), ἀξιόω in ἀπαξιόω (DeM)
ܚܘܫܒܐ	§38, 41, 67, 70	≈ ἰδέα (Platonic); νόημα (DeInAn, DeInG)
ܦܪܢܣܘܬ ܚܫܒܬܐ	§26	≈ πρόνοια
ḥšḥ		
ܐܬܚܫܚ *Ethpa.*	§17	χρῶμαι (IsagAn, IsagAth, DeInAn, etc.)
ḥšš		
ܚܫܫ	§15, 37, 58–60, 69, 96	πάσχω (CatAn, CatJ, SRInt, etc.)
ܚܫܐ	§41	πάθημα (DeInAn, DeInG), πάθος (Hof)
ܚܫܘܫܐ	§38, 41, 44, 69, 74	παθητικός (Hof), παθητός (DeM)
ܚܫܘܫܘܬܐ	§43, 44	≈ πάθημα
ḥtt		
ܚܬܝܬܐ	§73, 81	≈ ἀκριβής
ܚܬܝܬܐܝܬ	§86, 94	ἀκριβῶς (CatAn, CatJ), δι' ἀκριβείας (DeM)

ܛ

ṭbʿ		
ܛܒܥ	§24	ἐντυπόω (DeM)
ܐܬܛܒܥ *Ethpa.*	§46, 84	
ṭwps'		
ܛܘܦܣܐ	§63	< τύπος
ܕܠܘܩܒܠܘܬ ܛܘܦܣܐ	§63	≈ τὸ ἀντίτυπον, ἡ ἀντιτυπία
ṭks'		
ܛܟܣܐ	§25, 26, 75, 85, 89, 90, 92, 93	< τάξις
ܛܟܣ *Pa.*	§26, 27, 97	τάσσω (DeM)
ܡܛܟܣܐ	§89	τάσσομαι (AnPrP, AnPrG), τεταγμένος (AnPrG), ἐν τάξει (DeM)
ܠܐ ܡܛܟܣܐ	§84, 89, 91, 92	ἄτακτος (DeM, AnPrG)

ܡܛܟܣܘܬܐ	§87	
ܠܐ ܡܛܟܣܘܬܐ	§75, 85, 90	ἀταξία (Pl.*Tim.*)
ܡܛܟܣܐܝܬ	§68	οὐκ ἀτάκτως (DeM)
ܠܐ ܡܛܟܣܐܝܬ	§25, 75, 76, 85, 87, 89, 90, 93	ἀτάκτως (Pl.*Tim.*)
ṭʿy		
ܛܥܐ	§10, 35	ἐξαπατάω (DeSim)
ܛܥܝܘܬܐ	§86	ἀπάτη (DeInG)

ܝ

ybš		
ܝܒܝܫܐ	§36	ξηρός (DeM)
ܝܒܝܫܘܬܐ	§23, 51, 54	ξηρότης (SRInt), τὸ ξηρόν (Hof)
ydy		
ܐܬܬܘܕܝ *Ettaf.*	§18, 19, 42	ὁμολογοῦμαι (Hof)
ܡܬܬܘܕܝܢܐ	§65	δοξαστός (Pl.*Tim.*; DeInAn), ὁμολογούμενος (CatJ, AnPrG)
ܬܘܕܝܬܐ	§6, 19, 65, 79, 87	δόξα (Pl.*Tim.*; DeInAn)
ydʿ		
ܝܕܥ	§17, 25, 88, 91	οἶδα (CatAn, CatJ, DeSim)
ܝܕܝܥܐ	§22, 30, 33, 42, 49, 50, 54, 55, 75, 76, 88	δῆλον (CatAn, CatJ, DeM, etc.), φανερὸν (CatJ)
ܐܬܝܕܥ *Ethpe.*	§19, 39	περιληπτός (Pl.*Tim.*), θεωροῦμαι (DeM), δηλοῦμαι (DeSim)
ܡܕܥܐ	§18, 30, 66, 76	διάνοια (Hof), γνώμη (Hof)
ܝܕܘܥܬܐ	§18	≈ γνῶσις, νόησις
ܡܬܝܕܥܢܐ	§66	ἐπιστητός (CatJ)
ܡܬܝܕ̈ܥܢܝܬܐ	§19, 20	≈ τὰ νοητά
ܩܕܝܡܘܬ ܝܕܥܬܐ	§26	≈ πρόγνωσις
yhb		
ܝܗܒ	§85, 96, 97	δίδωμι (Hof), ἀποδίδωμι (CatAn, IsagAth)
yld		
ܝܠܝܕܘܬ ܢܦܫܐ	§88	≈ ψυχογονία
ylp		
ܐܬܝܠܦ *Ethpe.*	§70	ἀποτελοῦμαι (DeSim)
ܝܘܠܦܢܐ	§73	μάθησις (DeM), ἐπιστήμη (Hof)
ܡܠܦܢܐ	§95	≈ διδάσκαλος
ܡܠܦܢܘܬܐ	§17, 24, 25, 27, 28	διδασκαλία (IsagAn, IsagAth)

ym’		
ܝܡܐ	§6	θάλασσα (DeM)
y‘y		
ܝܥܐ	§47	≈ φύομαι
yqr		
ܝܩܪ *Pa.*	§6	τιμάω (DeM)
ܝܘܩܪܐ	§12	βρῖθος (DeM)
ysp		
ܐܬܬܘܣܦ *Ettaf.*	§67	προστίθεμαι (IsagAn, IsagAth, AnPrP)
ܡܘܣܦܢܐ	§25, 27	
yt’		
ܝܬܐ	§4, 33, 42–45, 49, 59, 63, 70	ἑαυτοῦ (CatAn, DeM)
ܡܢ ܝܬܗ	§73, 74, 82, 84	καθ’ ἑαυτήν (DeM)
ytr		
ܝܬܝܪ	§21, 87	μᾶλλον (IsagAn, CatAn, DeM), μάλιστα (IsagAth, CatAn), comparative (CatAn, CatJ, CatG, etc.), superlative (IsagAth)
ܝܬܝܪܐܝܬ	§11, 77, 80, 91	μᾶλλον (IsagAn, IsagAth, CatJ, etc.), μάλιστα (DeM, IsagAn, IsagAth, etc.)

ܟ

k’p’		
ܟܐܦܐ	§96	λίθος (AnPrP, AnPrG), πέτρος (DeM)
kd		
ܗܘ ܟܕ ܗܘ	§5	αὐτός (AnPrG)
ܒܗ ܟܕ ܒܗ	§77, 80	αὐτός (CatAn, CatJ, DeInAn, etc.), οὕτως (IsagAth)
kwn		
ܡܟܝܢ *Af. part. pass.*	§46, 67, 70	πέφυκα (IsagAn, IsagAth, DeM, etc.)
ܟܝܢܐ	§3, 5, 20, 22, 28, 84, 88	φύσις (IsagAn, IsagAth, DeM, etc.)
ܟܝܢܝܐ	§1, 14, 97	φυσικός (CatAn, CatJ, DeM)
ܟܝܢܐܝܬ	§84	φύσει (IsagAn, DeInAn), κατὰ φύσιν (DeM)

kl		
ܟܠ	§5–8, 18, 21, 23, 24, 28, 29, 32–34, 36, 37, 41, 42, 47, 56, 57, 59, 61, 63, 69, 70, 73, 74, 76–79, 81, 85, 91	πᾶς (IsagAn, IsagAth, CatAn, etc.), ὅσος (CatAn, CatJ)
ܟܠ ܟܠܗ	§34, 44	ὅλως (CatAn, CatJ)
ܟܠܐ	§23, 81	τὸ ὅλον (IsagAn, CatAn)
ܟܠܢܝܐ	§83	καθόλου (DeInAn, DeInG)
ܟܠܕܘܟ → dwk		
ܟܠܚܕ → ḥd		
ܟܠܡܕܡ → mdm		
ܟܠܦܪܣ → prs		
km'		
ܟܡܝܘܬܐ	§48, 58, 63	ποσόν (CatAn, CatJ), ποσότης (SRInt)
ܟܡܝܐ	§58	ποσόν (CatG)
kny		
ܟܢܝ *Pa.*	§41, 81	≈ ὀνομάζω; κατηγορέω (CatAn)
ܟܘܢܝܐ	§41, 78, 92	ὄνομα (IsagAn, DeSim), κατηγορία (CatAn)
knš		
ܐܬܟܢܫ *Ethpa.*	§76	συνᾴδω (DeM)
ܟܘܢܫܐ	§17	συμπέρασμα (AnPrG)
ktb		
ܟܬܒ	§77	≈ γράφω
ktr		
ܟܬܪ *Pa.*	§3, 10, 33, 44, 51, 53, 70, 80, 82	μένω (DeM), ὑπομένω (CatJ), παραμένω (CatJ), διαμένω (CatJ, DeM), ἐπιμένω (DeM), στηρίζομαι (DeM)

ܠ

lbk		
ܡܬܠܒܟܢܐ	§21, 22	≈ περιλαμβανόμενος

lwt		
ܠܘܬ	§10, 12, 19–21, 47, 50, 55, 58, 68, 79, 81, 85, 87, 96, 97	πρός *c. acc.* (IsagAn, IsagAth, CatAn, etc.)
ܕܠܘܬ ܡܕܡ	§19	πρός τι (CatAn, CatJ, Hof)
lḥd		
ܒܠܚܘܕ	§36	μόνος (IsagAn, CatAn, CatJ, etc.)
ܠܚܘܕܝܘܬܐ	§36	≈ μονάς
lḥm		
ܠܚܡ *Pa.*	§26	ἁρμόζω (DeM), ἐφαρμόζω (CatJ)
ܠܚܡܘܬܐ	§26	συστοιχία (AnPrG)
ܠܚܡܐܝܬ	§79	
lpwt		
ܠܦܘܬ	§83	πρός *c. acc.* (CatAn, DeM), παρά *c. acc.* (DeM), κατά *c. acc.* (DeM)

ܡ

mʾ		
ܡܕܝܢ	§22–24, 26–28, 30–32, 34, 39, 48, 49, 53, 54, 57, 60–66, 83, 89	ὥστε (IsagAn, IsagAth, CatAn, etc.), ἄρα (IsagAn, CatAn, AnPrP), οὖν (IsagAn, CatAn), δέ (IsagAn, DeInAn), γάρ (DeInAn), οὐκοῦν (CatAn, CatJ, AnPrP), οἷον (DeInAn)
mdm		
ܡܕܡ	§11, 19, 21, 22, 24, 25, 31–34, 39, 42, 43, 48–50, 52, 53, 55, 56, 58, 60, 62, 70, 71, 79, 80, 82, 83, 91, 96, 97	τίς (IsagAn, IsagAth, CatAn, etc.)
ܟܠܡܕܡ	§3, 5, 8, 42, 70, 79	τὰ πάντα (CatAn, DeM, CatJ, etc.), ὅσα (IsagAn), ἕκαστος (IsagAn)
ܠܐ ܡܕܡ	§17, 34, 42, 60, 96	οὐδείς (IsagAn, CatAn, CatJ, etc.)
mzg		
ܡܘܙܓܐ	§21	κρᾶσις (DeSim)
mṭl		
ܡܛܠ	§4, 17, 23, 25, 27–29, 33–35, 37, 38, 40, 43, 49, 52, 59, 69, 72, 76, 82, 90, 92, 95, 96	ὅτι (IsagAn, IsagAth, DeInAn, etc.), ἐπεί (IsagAn, IsagAth, CatAn, etc.), διό (CatAn, CatJ, CatG, etc.), περί *c. gen.* (IsagAn, IsagAth, CatJ, etc.), διά *c. acc.* (IsagAth, CatAn, CatJ, etc.)

my’		
ܡ̈ܝܐ	§5, 6, 13, 21–23, 35, 51–53	ὕδωρ (CatAn, DeM), ἔνυδρος (CatAn, CatG)
mkyl		
ܡܟܝܠ	§30, 52	λοιπόν (IsagAth)
ܠܐ ܡܟܝܠ	§37, 47, 82, 83	οὐκέτι (IsagAn, DeSim)
mll		
ܡܠܠ	§6	≈ λέγω
ܡܠܬܐ	§9, 16, 17, 19, 20, 26, 42, 45–47, 49, 52, 57, 63, 66, 68, 71, 73, 75, 86–88, 90, 94	λόγος (Pl.*Tim.*; CatAn, IsagAn, etc.), ῥῆμα (DeInAn)
ܕܠܐ ܡܠܬܐ	§19, 65	ἄλογος (Pl.*Tim.*; IsagAn, DeInAn)
mn		
ܡܢܐ	§28	τίς (IsagAn, IsagAth, CatAn, etc.)
mny		
ܡܢܝܢܐ	§5, 9, 36	ἀριθμός (IsagAn, IsagAth, CatAn)
ܡܢܬܐ	§10, 22, 23, 30	μέρος (DeM, IsagAth, CatAn, etc.), μόριον (CatG)
ܕܠܐ ܡܢܘ̈ܢ	§12	≈ ἀμερής
ܡ̈ܢܘܢ ܡ̈ܢܘܢ	§13	κατὰ μέρος (DeM)
mṣy		
ܡܨܝ	§34, 49, 52, 54, 71, 72, 79, 82, 96, 97	δύναμαι (IsagAn), optative (IsagAn, DeM)
ܡܬܡܨܝܢܝܬܐ	§43	τὸ ἐνδεχόμενον (DeInAn, AnPrP, AnPrG)
mṣ‘		
ܡܨܥܬܐ	§23, 96	μέσον (DeM, IsagAn, IsagAth, etc.), μεταξύ (IsagAn)
ܡܨܥܝܐ	§91, 92	μέσος (CatAn)
mr’		
ܡܪܐ	§13	δεσπότης (CatAn, CatJ, CatG)
ܡܪܐܝܬ	§20, 30, 37, 57, 67	κυρίως (IsagAth, CatAn, CatJ), ἁπλῶς (Hof), οἰκείως (CatAn)
mšḥ		
ܡܬܡܫܚܢܐ	§48	
ܡܫܘܚܬܐ	§70	μέτρον (DeM)
mtwm		
ܠܐ ܡܬܘܡ	§82, 97	ποτέ (IsagAn, IsagAth, CatJ, etc.), οὐδέποτε (CatAn, CatJ, CatG, etc.)
ܡܬܘܡܝܐ	§32, 48	ἀίδιος (DeInAn, DeInAth)

ܡܬܘܡܐܝܬ	§29	≈ ἀεί
mtḥ		
ܡܬܚܐ	§58, 63	διάστημα (AnPrG), μέτρον (Hof)
ܬܠܬܐ ܡܬܚ̈ܐ	§58, 63	≈ τὰ τρία διαστήματα

ܢ

nhr		
ܢܗܝܪܘܬܐ	§23	≈ τὸ σαφές
ܢܗܝܪܐܝܬ	§68	σαφής (IsagAn), ἀκριβής (DeSim)
nwr’		
ܢܘܪܐ	§7, 13, 22, 23, 35, 54	πῦρ (CatAn, CatJ, DeM, etc.)
ܢܘܪܢܐ	§22	πυρώδης (DeM)
nzl		
ܢܠ	§96	≈ πίπτω
nḥš’		
ܢܚܫܐ	§46	χαλκός (IsagAn, IsagAth, DeM)
nṭr		
ܢܛܪ	§4, 33	φυλάσσω (DeM)
nyš’		
ܢܝܫܐ	§60, 86	≈ τέλος, σκοπός
nkr		
ܢܘܟܪܝܐ	§86	ἀλλότριος (CatAn, CatJ, CatG), ἑτεροῖος (DeM)
nsb		
ܢܣܒ	§30, 36, 41, 75, 83, 86, 92, 93	λαμβάνω (IsagAn, CatAn, CatJ, etc.), παραλαμβάνω (Pl.*Tim.*), προσλαμβάνω (AnPrP), περιαιρέω (CatAn)
ܐܬܢܣܒ *Ethpe.*	§97	λαμβάνομαι (IsagAn, IsagAth, AnPrP, etc.)
ܡܬܢܣܒܢܐ	§66	
npl		
ܢܦܠ	§60	ἐκπίπτω (DeSim)
npq		
ܢܦܩ	§44	προσέρχομαι (IsagAn)
ܡܦܩܢܐ	§49, 70	ἔξοδος (DeM)
npš		
ܢܦܫܐ	§73–76, 78, 82, 84, 86, 88	ψυχή (CatAn, CatJ, DeInAn, etc.)

nṣb		
ܐܬܢܨܝܒ ܒ *Ethpe.*	§92	
ܢܨܝܒܬܐ	§92	φυτόν (CatAn, CatJ, DeM)
nqb		
ܢܩܒܬܐ	§41, 55, 69, 81	τὸ θῆλυ (DeM, DeSim)
nqp		
ܢܩܦ	§11, 25, 29, 37, 42, 47, 56, 82, 84, 86, 88, 95	ἀκολουθέω (CatJ, DeInAn, DeInG, etc.), πάρειμι (IsagAn, IsagAth), συνάπτω (CatAn, CatJ, DeM), ἕπομαι (IsagAth, DeInAn, DeInG)
ܐܩܦ *Af.*	§25	συνάγω (DeM)
ܐܬܢܩܦ *Ethpa.*	§10	σύνειμι (IsagAn), ἀκολουθέω (CatAn, DeM)
ܡܩܦܢܐ	§27	
ܡܬܢܩܦܢܐ	§67	

ܣ

sbr		
ܐܣܒܪ *Af.*	§3, 6, 86	οἴομαι (IsagAn, IsagAth, DeM), δοκέω (CatAn, CatJ, DeM), φρονέω (DeM), διαλαμβάνω (IsagAth), ὑπολαμβάνω (IsagAn)
ܐܬܣܒܪ *Ethpe.*	§6, 77	δοκέω (CatJ, CatG)
sgy		
ܣܓܝ	§1, 2, 3, 71, 86	πολύς (IsagAn, CatAn, CatJ, etc.), πλείων (IsagAn, AnPrP, CatAn, etc.), πλεῖστος (CatAn, CatJ, IsagAth), πάνυ (CatAn, CatJ), μέγας (CatAn), πλῆθος (CatAn, CatJ)
ܣܘܓܐܐ	§36	τὸ πολύ (CatAn, CatJ, AnPrP, AnPrAth), πολύς (DeInAn), πλείων (DeInAn), πλῆθος (DeM, CatG)
swk		
ܣܘܟ	§8, 48	≈ περαίνω
ܐܣܬܝܟ *Ethpe.*	§49	περαίνομαι (DeM)
ܡܣܝܟܐ	§1, 2, 9, 13, 48, 49	πεπερατωμένος (DeM), τὸ πεπερατῶσθαι (DeM)
ܠܐ ܡܣܝܟܐ	§1, 2, 9–12, 49, 71	ἄπειρος (DeInG)

ܣܟܐ	§29, 49, 57, 71, 82	πέρας (CatJ, DeM), ἄκρα (IsagAn, AnPrP), ἄκρον (AnPrP)
ܠܐ ܡܣܬܝܟܢܘܬܐ	§71	
ܠܐ ܡܣܬܝܟܢܐܝܬ	§71	
ܣܟ *adv.*	§86, 94	ὅλως (DeInAn, DeSim, CatJ), οὐδαμῶς (CatJ, CatG, DeInG)
swlwgysmw		
ܣܘܠܘܓܝܣܡܘ	§17	< συλλογισμός
sybr		
ܣܝܒܪܬܐ	§5	τροφή (DeSim)
sym		
ܣܝܡ	§1, 2, 7–10, 35, 49, 73–75, 84, 95	προτίθημι (IsagAn), ὑπόκειμαι (AnPrP, AnPrG)
ܗܘ ܕܣܝܡ	§24, 31, 41, 43, 50	τὸ ὑποκείμενον (IsagAn, IsagAth, CatAn, etc.)
ܐܬܬܣܝܡ *Ethpe.*	§72, 78	τίθεμαι (AnPrG), κεῖμαι (IsagAn, IsagAth), σύγκειμαι (DeInAn, DeInAth), ὑποτάσσομαι (IsagAn), τὸ ὑποκείμενον (CatAn), θέσις (CatAn), διάθεσις (CatAn)
ܣܝܡܐ	§78, 82	θέσις (CatAn, CatJ, AnPrP, etc.), διάθεσις (CatAn), ὑπόθεσις (AnPrP, AnPrG)
skl		
ܐܣܬܟܠ *Ethpe.*	§75	νοέω (DeInAn, DeInG)
slq		
ܣܠܩ	§20	ἀνάγω (AnPrP, AnPrG), ἀναφέρω (DeM)
sny		
ܣܢܝܐ	§91	χείρων (CatG)
snq		
ܣܢܝܩܐ	§52	δέομαι (IsagAn), τὸ προσδεόμενον (AnPrP), χρεῖος (IsagAn, AnPrP)
ܣܘܢܩܢܐ	§47	δέομαι (DeM)
spq		
ܣܦܝܩܘܬܐ	§12	τὸ κενόν (SRInt, Hof)
sqbl		
ܣܩܘܒܠܐ	§90–92	τὸ ἀντικείμενον (IsagAn, IsagAth)
srṭ		
ܣܪܛܐ	§48	γραμμή (CatAn, CatJ, CatG, etc.)

ܥ

ʿbd		
ܥܒܕ	§1, 10, 15, 38, 39, 60, 79, 80, 87, 88, 89, 93	ποιέω (IsagAn, IsagAth, DeM, etc.)
ܐܥܒܕ *Af.*	§80	ἐνεργέω (DeM, DeInAn, DeInG)
ܐܬܥܒܕ *Ethpe.*	§39, 80	ποιοῦμαι (CatAn)
ܥܒܘܕܐ	§10, 27, 28, 32, 37–39, 47, 73, 74, 79, 80	ποιητικός (CatAn, CatJ)
ܥܒܕܐ	§47, 79	ἔργον (DeV)
ܥܒܘܕܘܬܐ	§95, 97	
ܡܥܒܕܢܘܬܐ	§18, 26–28, 64	ἐνέργεια (DeM, IsagAn, IsagAth, etc.)
ʿbr		
ܥܒܪܐ	§49, 57, 71	συμπέρασμα (AnPrG)
ʿzl		
ܐܬܥܪܙܠ *QuadRef.*	§12	πεπλεγμένος (DeInG)
ʿṭp		
ܥܛܦ	§10	ἀντιστρέφω (CatAn, DeInG)
ʿyn		
ܡܥܝܢܐ	§76	≈ πηγή
ʿly		
ܡܥܠܝܐ	§25	ἀνώτερος (DeM), ἐπαναβεβηκός (IsagAn, IsagAth)
ʿll		
ܥܠ	§84	≈ εἰσέρχομαι
ܐܥܠ *Af.*	§10, 95	≈ εἰσάγω
ܥܠܬܐ	§10, 28, 32, 68, 72, 74, 80, 96	αἰτία (AnPrP, AnPrG, DeV), αἴτιον (CatAn, CatJ, DeM, etc.)
ʿlmʾ		
ܥܠܡܐ	§12, 86–90, 93, 94	κόσμος (CatAn, CatJ, DeM), αἰών (DeM)
ܡܢ ܥܠܡ	§84	εἰς αἰῶνα (DeM)
ʿsq		
ܥܣܩܐ	§85	χαλεπός (CatAn, CatJ, CatG), δυσ- (CatAn, CatJ)
ʿpp		
ܥܦܝܦܐܝܬ	§59	≈ διπλῷ
ʿqb		
ܥܩܒ *Pa.*	§3, 5, 24, 35, 56	σκέπτομαι (SextEmp)
ܥܘܩܒܐ	§1, 87	ἐξέτασις (IsagAn)

ʿqr		
ܥܩܪܐ	§13	ῥίζα (DeSim)
ʿrṭl		
ܥܪܛܠܝܐ	§41, 67, 70	≈ γυμνός
ʿtd		
ܥܬܝܕ	§47, 79, 92	μέλλον (CatAn, CatJ, DeM, etc.)

ܦ

pʾʾ		
ܦܐܐ	§25, 26	κρείσσων (DeM), πρέπω (DeM)
pʾwṭʾ		
ܦܐܘܛܐ	§6	< ποιητής
pgr		
ܦܓܪܐ	§21	σῶμα (DeSim, CatJ)
pwš		
ܦܘܫ	§43	≈ μένω
pḥm		
ܦܘܚܡܐ	§23, 26	≈ ἀναλογία, σύγκρισις
pylswpʾ		
ܦܝܠܣܘܦܐ	§3, 18, 88	< φιλόσοφος
ܦܝܠܣܘܦܘܬܐ	§5	< φιλοσοφία
pys		
ܦܝܣܐ	§83	< πεῖσις
plg		
ܦܠܓ *Pa.*	§23, 36, 74	διαιρέω (Pol), ἀντιδιαιρέω (CatAn)
ܡܬܦܠܓ *Ethpa.*	§63, 73, 74, 76	διαιροῦμαι (IsagAn, IsagAth, CatAn, etc.), διαλύομαι (AnPrP, AnPrG)
ܦܘܠܓܐ	§2, 74	διαίρεσις (IsagAn, IsagAth, CatAn, etc.), διαιρετικός (IsagAn), διάστασις (CatG), διανέμησις (DeM)
ܕܠܐ ܦܘܠܓ	§74	≈ ἀδιάφορος
plṭ		
ܦܠܛ ܡܢ	§2	συγχέω (DeSim)
psq		
ܐܬܦܣܩ *Ethpa.*	§71	τέμνομαι (CatAn, IsagAth)
ܠܐ ܡܬܦܣܩܢܐ	§12	ἄτομος (CatAn, CatJ, IsagAth, etc.)
ܒܦܣܝܩܘܬܐ	§73	κεφαλαιωδῶς (DeM), σύντομον (IsagAth)

prs (< πόρος)		
ܡܢ ܟܠܦܘܪܘܣ	§37, 80, 92	πάντως (IsagAn, IsagAth, CatJ, etc.)
ܒܟܠ ܦܘܪܣܝܢ	§48	≈ πάντως
prš		
ܦܪܫ *Pa.*	§10, 23, 86	ὁρίζω (IsagAn, IsagAth), διορίζω (CatAn, CatJ), προσδιορίζω (DeInAn), διαφέρω (IsagAn, CatAn), διαλαμβάνω (CatAn)
ܐܬܦܪܫ *Ethpa.*	§10	ὁρίζομαι (CatAn, DeInAn, DeInG), ἀφορίζομαι (IsagAth), κατηγοροῦμαι (IsagAn)
ܦܘܪܫܢܐ	§13	διαφορά (IsagAn, CatAn), ἀφορισμός (CatG)
ܦܪܝܫܐ	§11, 14, 15, 18, 23	ἀφορίζω (CatAn), διορίζω (CatAn), διαφέρω (IsagAn, CatAn)
ܡܬܦܪܫܢܐ	§76	χωριστός (IsagAn)
pšṭ		
ܦܫܝܛܐ	§29, 30, 33, 62, 68	ἁπλός (CatJ, DeSim)
ܦܫܝܛܐܝܬ	§4, 56, 67	ἁπλῶς (IsagAn, CatAn, CatJ, etc.)
pšq		
ܦܫܩ *Pa.*	§85, 87, 94, 95	≈ ἑρμηνεύω

ܨ

ṣbw		
ܨܒܘܬܐ	§1, 27, 28, 33, 41, 76	πρᾶγμα (IsagAn, DeSim)
ṣbt		
ܨܒܬ *Pa.*	§26, 27, 89	διακοσμέω (DeM)
ܐܨܛܒܬ *Ethpa.*	§27	
ܨܒܬܐ	§94	κόσμος (DeM)
ṣdd		
ܐܨܕ *Af.*	§79	≈ θεωρέω
ܡܨܕܝܢܘܬܐ	§80	≈ θεώρησις
ṣly		
ܐܨܛܠܝ *Ethpe.*	§12	≈ κλίνω, κλίνομαι

ܩ

qbl		
ܩܒܠ *Pa.*	§24, 41, 43, 44, 46, 49, 55, 59, 64, 70, 71, 76, 81–83	δέχομαι (CatAn, CatJ, CatG), ἐπιδέχομαι (IsagAn, IsagAth, CatAn, etc.), παραδέχομαι (CatAn, CatG), ἐνδέχομαι (DeInG), ὑποδέχομαι (DeM), δεκτικός (IsagAn, CatAn)
ܡܩܒܠܬ ܟܠ	§41	πανδεχής (Pl.*Tim.*)
ܡܩܒܠܢܐ	§34, 41, 55, 58, 69, 70, 73, 81, 83	δεκτικός (IsagAn, IsagAth, CatJ, etc.), ὑποδοχή (Pl.*Tim.*)
ܕܠܘܩܒܠܐ	§72, 92	ἐναντίος (IsagAn, CatAn, DeM), ἀντίκειμαι (IsagAn, CatAn, CatG, etc.)
ܕܠܘܩܒܠܝܐ	§36–38, 58, 72	ἐναντίος (CatAn), ἀντίκειμαι (CatAn, DeInAn, DeInG, etc.)
ܕܠܘܩܒܠܝܘܬܐ	§11	τὸ ἐναντίον (CatAn), ἐναντιότης (CatAn), ἀντίθεσις (CatAn, CatJ)
ܕܠܘܩܒܠܝܘܬ ܛܘܦܣܐ	§63	≈ τὸ ἀντίτυπον, ἡ ἀντιτυπία
qbʿ		
ܩܒܝܥܐ	§55	κεῖμαι (DeM)
ܩܒܝܥܘܬܐ	§23	
qdm		
ܩܕܡ	§7, 60, 79	≈ πρό-
ܩܕܡ ܚܙܐ	§79	≈ προοράω
ܩܕܡ ܐܬܪܥܝ	§79	≈ προνοέω
ܐܬܩܕܡ *Ethpe.*	§30, 32	≈ πρό-
ܩܕܝܡܐ	§32	πρότερος (IsagAn, CatAn, CatJ, etc.)
ܩܕܝܡܘܬ ܡܚܫܒܬܐ	§26	≈ πρόνοια
ܩܕܝܡܘܬ ܝܕܥܬܐ	§26	≈ πρόγνωσις
ܡܩܕܡܘܬܐ	§30	≈ πρόθεσις
ܩܕܡܝܐ	§1, 3, 5–7, 17, 20, 21, 27–29, 35–39, 41, 47, 50, 55, 58, 60, 68, 70, 72, 73, 75–80, 83–87	πρότερος (IsagAn, IsagAth, CatAn, etc.)
(ܦܠܩܘܣܐ) ܩܕܡ̈ܝܐ	§3	οἱ πρεσβύτεροι (IsagAn), οἱ παλαιοί (IsagAn)
ܩܕܡ *prep.*	§17, 29, 30, 32, 36, 41, 77, 87–89	πρίν (Pl.*Tim.*); πρό *c. gen.* (IsagAn, IsagAth, CatAn, etc.), πρότερος (IsagAn, IsagAth), πρῶτος (DeM)

ܡܢ ܩܕܝܡ	§76, 89	πρότερον (DeM)
ܩܕܡܝܬ	§3, 5, 28, 29, 39–41	πρότερον (IsagAn, CatAn, CatJ, etc.), πρῶτον (DeInAn, AnPrP, AnPrG, etc.), προηγουμένως (IsagAn, IsagAth)
qwm		
ܩܘܡ	§4, 24, 52, 54, 84, 94	πάρειμι (DeInAn), κεῖμαι (CatAn), καθέζομαι (IsagAn)
ܐܩܝܡ *Af.*	§27	συνίστημι (IsagAn), ὑφίστημι (IsagAth)
ܐܬܩܝܡ *Ethpa.*	§47	συνίσταμαι (IsagAn, DeM), ὑφίσταμαι (IsagAn, IsagAth)
ܩܘܡܐ	§23, 94	στάσις (CatAn, CatJ, CatG)
ܩܝܡܐ	§24	
ܩܘܝܡܐ	§47, 80, 86, 90, 94	ὑπόστασις (IsagAth), σύστασις (IsagAn, IsagAth, CatJ, etc.), διάθεσις (CatAn, CatJ, CatG), τὸ ὑφιστάμενον (IsagAn), σύστημα (DeM)
qṭ'gryws		
ܩܛܐ ܓܪܝܘܣ	§58	< κατηγορία
qṭrg		
ܐܬܩܛܪܓ ܠ *QuadRef.*	§60	< κατηγοροῦμαι
qll		
ܩܠܝܠܘܬܐ	§23	ταχύς (DeM)
qny		
ܩܢܐ	§11, 19, 45, 46, 47, 51, 53, 54, 71, 81, 82, 86, 92, 96	ἔχω (IsagAn, DeM)
qrb		
ܩܪܒ	§21	προσεχής (IsagAn, IsagAth), ἐγγίων (CatAn), πάρειμι (DeInG)
qry 1		
ܩܪܐ	§6, 13, 19, 24, 27, 40–42, 50, 77, 78	καλέω (IsagAn, IsagAth, AnPrP)
ܐܬܩܪܝ *Ethpe.*	§19, 20, 24, 57, 67, 88	λέγεται (IsagAn, IsagAth, DeM)
qry 2		
ܩܪܘܬܐ	§44, 46	< κηρός

qrr		
ܩܪܝܪܐ	§36	ψυχρός (CatAn, CatJ, CatG), παγετώδης (DeM)
ܩܪܝܪܘܬܐ	§23, 51–53	ψυχρότης (CatAn, CatJ, CatG, DeM)
qšy		
ܩܫܝܐ	§21, 22	σκληρός (CatAn, CatJ, CatG)

ܪ

rby		
ܪܒܐ	§58	μέγας (IsagAn, AnPrP, AnPrG), αὐξόμενος (CatAn, CatJ)
ܪܒܘܬܐ	§12	μέγεθος (CatAn, CatJ, CatG, DeM)
ܡܪܒܝܢܝܬܐ	§55	τιθήνη (Pl.*Tim*)
rdy		
ܪܕܝ	§20	πορεύομαι (DeM), ῥέω (DeM)
rgš		
ܪܓܫܐ	§18–20, 65	αἴσθησις (DeM)
ܡܬܪܓܫܢܐ	§61	αἰσθητός (IsagAth, CatAn, CatJ, etc.)
ܡ̈ܬܪܓܫܢܝܬܐ	§19–21	τὰ αἰσθητά (IsagAth, CatAn, CatJ, etc.)
ܪܓܫܬܐ	§19	αἴσθησις (Pl.*Tim.*)
ܪܓܘܫܘܬܐ	§18	≈ αἴσθησις
ܡܪܓܫܢܘܬܐ	§67, 70	τὸ αἰσθητικόν (IsagAth)
rwḥ		
ܪܘܚܐ	§22	πνεῦμα (DeM, HippAph), ἄνεμος (DeM)
rwm		
ܐܪܝܡ *Af.*	§25, 58	ἀναιρέω (IsagAth), ἀφαιρέω (DeSim), ἀπόφημι (DeInG)
ܐܬܬܪܝܡ *Ettaf.*	§34, 81	ἀναιροῦμαι (IsagAn, IsagAth, CatJ, etc.), συναιροῦμαι (IsagAth, CatG), περιαιροῦμαι (CatAn, CatJ, CatG)
ܡܪܝܡܢܐ	§25	ἀποφατικός (CatJ)
ܡܪܝܡܢܘܬܐ	§91	ἀπόφασις (CatJ)
rḥm		
ܪܚܡܘܬܐ	§13, 36	≈ φιλία
rṭb		
ܪܛܝܒܐ	§22, 36	ὑγρός (DeM)
ܪܛܝܒܘܬܐ	§5, 6, 51, 53, 54	τὸ ὑγρόν (DeM), ὑγρότης (SRInt)

ryšʾ		
ܪܝܫܐ	§1–4, 9–17, 20, 28–40, 48, 73–76, 86, 90, 91	ἀρχή (IsagAn, IsagAth, DeM, etc.), ἄκρον (IsagAth, AnPrG), κεφαλή (CatJ, CatG)
ܪܫܝܬܐ	§4–7, 24, 27, 28, 34, 39, 60, 68, 69, 72, 76, 78	ἀρχή (AnPrP)
rkb		
ܪܟܒ *Pa.*	§25, 57, 88	συντίθημι (SRInt)
ܐܬܪܟܒ *Ethpa.*	§30, 58, 68, 89	συντίθεμαι (IsagAn, IsagAth, DeInAn, etc.), περιτίθεμαι (CatAn), ἀντίκειμαι (DeInAn)
ܪܘܟܒܐ	§17, 30, 33	σύνθεσις (Hof, Pol)
ܡܪܟܒܐ	§30, 31, 33, 62	σύνθετος (DeSim), πεπλεγμένος (DeInG), προαιρούμενος (DeInAn, DeInAth)
ܡܪܟܒܢܐ	§25, 27, 28	≈ σύνθετος
rny		
ܪܢܐ	§88, 89	φρονέω (DeM)
ܐܬܪܢܝ *Ethpe.*	§17, 30, 32, 41, 48	ἐπινοοῦμαι (IsagAn, IsagAth)
rʿy		
ܐܬܪܥܝ *Ethpa.*	§79	δοξάζω (CatAn), φρονέω (DeM)
ܩܕܡ ܐܬܪܥܝ	§79	≈ προνοέω
ܪܥܝܢܐ	§13, 16, 19, 23, 25, 27, 30, 42, 45, 49, 68, 71, 73, 77, 85, 86, 88, 93–95	νόησις (Pl.*Tim.*), δόξα (CatAn), ἐπίνοια (IsagAn)
ܬܪܥܝܬܐ	§66, 79, 81, 97	διάνοια (DeInAn, DeInAth, DeM)
ršm		
ܪܘܫܡܐ	§27, 28, 38, 39	≈ ἰδέα

ܫ

šbl		
ܫܒܠܐ	§46	
šbq		
ܫܒܩ	§74	ἀφίημι (HippAph)
ܐܫܬܒܩ *Ethpe.*	§82	καταλείπομαι (CatAn, CatJ, CatG), ἀφίημι (DeInAn, DeInG)

šgny		
ܫܓܢܝ *Quad.*	§3	ἀλλοιόω (CatG)
ܐܫܬܓܢܝ *QuadRef.*	§3, 4, 42, 43, 51–54, 59, 83	ἀλλοιοῦμαι (CatAn, CatJ)
ܫܘܓܢܝܐ	§4, 8, 11, 55, 68	ἀλλοίωσις (CatAn, CatJ)
ܡܫܬܓܢܝܢܐ	§42, 69, 70	
ܡܫܬܓܢܝܢܘܬܐ	§50, 83	
šgš		
ܫܓܝܫܘܬܐ	§90, 92	
šdy		
ܫܕܝ	§96	ἀποβάλλω (IsagAth), ῥίπτω (DeM)
šwdʿ		
ܫܘܕܥ *Quad.*	§48, 91, 93	σημαίνω (CatAn, CatJ, DeInAn, etc.), προσημαίνω (DeInAn, DeInAth), δηλόω (DeSim)
ܡܫܘܕܥܘܬܐ	§47	≈ τὸ σημαινόμενον
šwy		
ܫܘܝܐ	§36	ἴσος (CatAn, CatJ, CatG, etc.)
šwzb		
ܫܘܙܒ *Quad.*	§96	
šwtpʾ		
ܫܘܬܦ *Quad.*	§58, 90	κοινωνέω (SRInt)
ܐܫܬܘܬܦ *QuadRef.*	§85	κοινωνέω (CatAn, CatG), μετέχω (IsagAn, IsagAth), μέτειμι (DeM)
ܫܘܬܦܘܬܐ	§81	κοινωνία (IsagAn, IsagAth, DeM), μέθεξις (IsagAn, IsagAth), μετουσία (IsagAn, IsagAth), ἄθροισις (IsagAn)
šḥlp		
ܫܚܠܦ *Quad.*	§44	διαφέρω (IsaAn, IsagAth, CatJ, etc.)
ܐܫܬܚܠܦ *QuadRef.*	§43, 44, 51, 53, 54, 59, 83	μεταβάλλω (CatAn, CatJ)
ܫܘܚܠܦܐ	§4, 43, 44, 53	μεταβολή (CatAn, IsagAn), διαφορά (CatJ, IsagAn, IsagAth), ἀλλοίωσις (Pol, SRInt)
ܡܫܬܚܠܦܢܐ	§42, 69	
ܡܫܬܚܠܦܢܘܬܐ	§50	
ܡܫܚܠܦܐܝܬ	§81	μετα- (DeInAn), ἄλλως (DeSim)
šṭḥ		
ܫܛܝܚܘܬܐ	§48	ἐπιφάνεια (CatAn, CatJ)

škḥ		
ܐܫܟܚ *Af.*	§24	εὑρίσκω (DeM, DeSim), ἐξευρίσκω (DeSim), ζητέω (DeM), ἐνδέχομαι (DeInAn), δυνατός (CatJ, CatG, DeInAn, etc.)
ܐܫܬܟܚ *Ethpe.*	§27, 28, 55	εἰμί (DeM), εὑρίσκομαι (DeSim)
ܡܫܟܚܢܐ	§5	δυνατός (DeInAn, AnPrP)
škr		
ܫܟܝܪܘܬܐ	§47	ἄτοπος (DeInAn, DeInAth)
šlṭ		
ܫܠܛ	§74	ἄρχω (DeM)
šly		
ܫܠܐ	§85	παύομαι (IsagAn, IsagAth), ἠρεμέω (Hof)
šlm		
ܫܠܡ	§12, 36, 79	ὁμολογέω (DeM)
ܫܘܠܡܐ	§67	τέλος (Hof), ἀποτέλεσμα (DeM), τελευτή (DeM)
ܫܠܡܘܬܐ	§79	συνθήκη (DeInAn, DeInAth), τὸ σύμφωνον (DeM), ὁμολογία (DeM)
šmʾ		
ܫܡܐ	§78	ὄνομα (IsagAn, CatAn, CatJ, etc.)
šmhʾ		
ܫܡܗ	§73, 76, 78	καλέω (DeM), ὀνομάζω (DeM)
šmyʾ		
ܫܡܝܐ	§77	οὐρανός (Pl.*Tim.*, DeM)
šmly		
ܫܡܠܝ *Quad.*	§10, 12, 89	συμπληρόω (IsagAth), ἀποτελέω (IsagAth, DeM), ἐπιτελέω (DeM)
ܫܘܡܠܝܐ	§47	συμπληρωτικός (IsagAn)
šmʿ		
ܫܡܥ	§90	ἀκούω (DeM, DeInAn, DeInG)
šʿy		
ܐܫܬܥܝ *Ethpa.*	§87, 90	προφητεύω (DeM)
špr		
ܫܦܪܐ	§37, 40	≈ καλός
ܫܘܦܪܐ	§25, 26	κάλλος (DeM)
ܫܦܝܪܐ	§68, 91	καλός (CatAn, CatJ, CatG, etc.)
ܫܦܝܪܐܝܬ	§79	καλῶς (DeInAn, DeV), μετρίως (CatAn)

šry		
ܫܪܝ *Pa.*	§16, 20, 79, 87	ἄρχομαι (IsagAn, IsagAth), λύω (CatAn, CatJ, CatG), ἱδρύω (DeM)
ܫܪܘܝܐ	§17, 20, 24, 25, 28	≈ πρῶτος
ܫܪܝܐ	§85	
ܡܫܪܝܢܐ	§6	
ܡܫܬܪܝܢܐ	§85	
ܫܘܪܝܐ	§87	ἀρχή (IsagAn, CatAn, CatJ, etc.)
šryn᾽		
ܫܪܝܢܐ	§22	≈ ἀρτηρία
šrk		
ܫܪܟ	§33, 48, 89	καταλείπω (CatAn)
šrr		
ܫܪܝܪܐ	§18, 89	ἀληθής (IsagAn, IsagAth, CatAn, etc.)
ܫܪܝܪܐܝܬ	§20, 30, 32	ἀληθῶς (CatAn, CatG), ἀληθές (DeInG)
ܡܫܪܪܘܬܐ	§23	

ܬ

tḥwm᾽		
ܬܚܘܡܐ	§27	ὅρος (IsagAth, CatAn, DeM, etc.), ὁρισμός (IsagAn, IsagAth, CatJ), ὑπογραφή (IsagAn), πέρας (DeM), λόγος (IsagAn, DeInAn)
ܬܚܡ *Pa.*	§42	ὁρίζω (CatAn, CatJ, CatG), ἀφορίζω (IsagAn, IsagAth), διορίζω (AnPrP), ἀποδίδωμι (IsagAn, CatAn, CatJ, etc.)
ܐܬܬܚܡ *Ethpa.*	§15, 40, 48, 77	ὁρίζομαι (CatAn, CatJ, CatG), ἀφορίζομαι (IsagAn, IsagAth), διορίζομαι (DeM, DeInAn, DeInG, etc.)
tlt		
ܬܠܬܐ	§1, 28, 39, 58, 63, 74–77	τρεῖς (Pl.*Tim.*)
ܬܠܬܐܝܬ	§77	τριχῆ (Pl.*Tim.*), τριχῶς (AnPrG)
tnn		
ܬܢܢ	§23	ὁμοῦ (DeM)

tqn		
ܬܩܢ *Pa.*	§73, 88, 97	≈ κοσμέω
ܐܬܬܩܢ *Ethpa.*	§27, 28, 79, 80	κεκοσμῆσθαι (DeM), διατάσσομαι (DeM)
ܠܐ ܡܬܩܢܐ	§85	≈ ἀκόσμητος
ܬܘܩܢܐ	§94	κόσμος (DeM), διακόσμησις (DeM), κατασκευή (DeM)
tryn		
ܬܪ̈ܝܢ	§1, 17, 23, 35, 37, 46, 47, 51, 53, 54, 72, 74, 76, 83	δύο (IsagAn, IsagAth, DeInAn, etc.), ἀμφότερος (AnPrG)
ܬܪܝܢܐ	§20	δεύτερος (CatAn, CatJ)
ܬܪܝܢܘܬܐ	§36	≈ δυάς
ܬܪܬܐ	§37	
trṣ		
ܬܪܝܨ ܐܝܬ	§67, 76	εὐθύς (CatJ, DeM)

Greek Glossary

ἀγέννητος : hwy
ἀγέομαι : ḥšb
ἄγω : ʾty,
ἀδιάφορος : plg
ἀεί : ʾmn, mtwm
ἀήρ : ʾʾr
ἄθροισις : šwtpʾ
ἀίδιος : mtwm
αἵρεσις : hrysys
αἴσθησις : rgš
αἰσθητικός : rgš
αἰσθητός : rgš
αἰτία : ʿll
αἴτιον : ʿll
αἰών : ʿlmʾ
ἀκίνητος : zwʿ
ἀκολουθέω : nqp
ἀκόσμητος : tqn
ἀκούω : šmʿ
ἄκρα : swk
ἀκρίβεια : ḥtt
ἀκριβής : ḥtt, nhr
ἄκρον : swk, ryšʾ
ἀληθής : šrr
ἀλλήλων : ḥd
ἀλλοιόω : ʾḥr, šgny
ἀλλοίωσις : šgny, šḥlp
ἄλλος : ʾḥr
ἀλλότριος : nkr
ἄλλως : ʾḥr, šḥlp
ἄλογος : mll
ἅμα : ʾkḥd
ἀμερής : mny
ἀμφότερος : tryn
ἀναγκαῖος : ʾlṣ
ἀνάγκη : ʾlṣ, ʾnnqʾ
ἀνάγω : slq
ἀναιρέω : bṭl, rwm
ἀναλογία : pḥm
ἀναφαίνω : ḥwy
ἀναφέρω : slq
ἀνείδεος : ʾdšʾ
ἄνεμος : rwḥ
ἄνευ : blʿd
ἄνθρωπος : ʾnšʾ
ἄνισος : ʾpzgʾ
ἀντιδιαιρέω : plg
ἀντίθεσις : qbl
ἀντίκειμαι : sqbl, rkb
ἀντιστρέφω : ʿṭp
ἀντίτυπον : ṭwpsʾ, qbl
ἀνώτερος : ʿly
ἀξιόω : ḥšb
ἀξίωμα : ʾksywmʾ
ἀόρατος : ḥzy
ἀπάτη : ṭʿy
ἄπειρος : swk
ἁπλός : pšṭ
ἁπλῶς : gwʾ, mrʾ
ἀποβάλλω : šdy
ἀποδείκνυμι : ḥwy
ἀποδεικτικός : ḥwy
ἀποδίδωμι : yhb, tḥwmʾ
ἄποιος : znʾ
ἀπορία : bʿy
ἀποτέλεσμα : šlm
ἀποτελέω : ylp, šmly
ἀπόφασις : rwm
ἀποφατικός : rwm
ἀπόφημι : rwm
ἀπώλεια : ʾbd
ἄρα : ʾrʾ, mʾ
ἀραιόω : dll
ἀριθμός : mny
ἁρμόζω : lḥm
ἀρτηρία : šrynʾ
ἀρχή : ryšʾ, šry
ἄρχω : šlṭ, šry
ἀσώματος : gšm
ἄτακτος : ṭksʾ

ἀταξία : ṭks'
ἄτομος : psq
ἄτοπος : škr
αὐξάνω : rby
αὐτός : dyl, kd
ἀφαιρέω : rwm
ἄφθαρτος : ḥbl
ἀφίημι : šbq
ἀφορίζω : prš, tḥwm'
ἀφορισμός : prš
βλέπω : ḥzy
βρῖθος : yqr
γάρ : m'
γένεσις : hwy
γένος : gns'
γῆ : 'r''
γίγνομαι : hwy
γνώμη : yd'
γνῶσις : yd'
γόνος : zr'
γραμμή : srṭ
γράφω : ktb
γυμνός : 'rṭl
δέ : m'
δείκνυμι : ḥwy
δεκτικός : qbl
δεσμός : 'sr
δεσπότης : mr'
δεύτερος : tryn
δέχομαι : qbl
δέω : zdq, snq
δῆλος : yd'
δηλόω : yd'
διά : 'yd', mṭl
διάθεσις : sym, qwm
διαίρεσις : plg
διαιρετικός : plg
διαιρέω : plg
διακοσμέω : ṣbt
διακόσμησις : tqn
διαλαμβάνω : ḥbš, sbr, prš
διαλύω : plg
διαμένω : ktr
διανέμησις : plg
διάνοια : yd', r'y
διάστασις : plg
διάστημα : mtḥ
διατάσσω : tqn
διαφέρω : prš, šḥlp
διαφορά : prš, šḥlp
διδασκαλία : ylp
διδάσκαλος : ylp
δίδωμι : yhb
διό : gwn, mṭl
διορίζω : prš, tḥwm'
διπλῷ : 'pp
δοκέω : sbr
δόξα : ydy, r'y
δοξάζω : r'y
δοξαστός : ydy
δυάς : tryn
δύναμαι : mṣy
δύναμις : ḥyl'
δυνατός : škḥ
δύο : tryn
δυσ- : 'sq
ἑαυτοῦ : yt'
ἐγγίων : qrb
εἰ : 'n
εἶδος : 'dš', ḥwr
εἰκότως : zdq
εἰμί : 'yt, 'ty, hwy, škḥ
ἔοικα : ḥzy
εἷς : ḥd
εἰσάγω : 'll
εἰσέρχομαι : 'll
εἶτα : btr
ἕκαστος : ḥd, mdm
ἑκάτερος : ḥd
ἐκμαγεῖον: 'qm'gwn
ἐκπίπτω : npl
ἐκτός : br'
ἐναντίος : qbl
ἐναντιότης : qbl

ἐνδέχομαι : mṣy, qbl, škḥ
ἐνέργεια : ʿbd
ἐνεργέω : ʿbd
ἐντυπόω : ṭbʿ
ἔνυδρος : myʾ
ἔνυλος : hwlʾ
ἐξαπατάω : ṭʿy
ἐξέτασις : ʿqb
ἐξευρίσκω : škḥ
ἑξῆς : btr
ἕξις : ʾyt
ἔξοδος : npq
ἔοικα : dmy
ἐπαναβαίνω : ʿly
ἐπεί : mṭl
ἔπειτα : btr
ἐπιδέχομαι : qbl
ἐπιλαμβάνω : ʾḥd
ἐπιμένω : ktr
ἐπινοέω : rny
ἐπίνοια : rʿy
ἐπιστήμη : ylp
ἐπιστητός : ydʿ
ἐπιτελέω : šmly
ἐπιφάνεια : šṭḥ
ἕπομαι : nqp
ἔργον : ʿbd
ἑρμηνεύω : pšq
ἑτεροῖος : nkr
ἑτέρως : ʾḥr
ἔτι : hkyl
εὐθύς : trṣ
εὑρίσκω : škḥ
ἐφαρμόζω : lḥm
ἔχω : ʾyt, qny
ζητέω : bʿy, škḥ
ἤδη : hʾ
ἥκω : ʾty
ἠρεμέω : šly
ἧττον : bṣr
θάλασσα : ymʾ
θεός : ʾlh
θέρμα : ḥmm
θερμαίνω : ḥmm
θερμασία : ḥmm
θερμός : ḥmm
θερμότης : ḥmm
θέσις : sym
θεωρέω : ḥzy, ydʿ, ṣdd
θεώρησις : ṣdd
θῆλυ : nqb
ἰδέα : ʾdšʾ, ḥšb, ršm
ἰδικός : dyl
ἴδιος : dyl, ḥd
ἰδιότης : dyl
ἰδίως : ḥd
ἱδρύω : šry
ἴσος : šwy
καθέζομαι : qwm
καθόλου : gwʾ, kl
καιρός : zbn
καλέω : qry, šmhʾ
κάλλος : špr
καλός : špr
κατά : ʾydʾ, ʾyn, lpwt
καταλείπω : šbq, šrk
κατασκευή : tqn
κατηγορέω : kny, prš, qṭrg
κατηγορία : kny, qṭʾgryws
κεῖμαι : qbʿ, sym, qwm
κενόν : spq
κεφαλαιωδῶς : psq
κεφαλή : ryšʾ
κηρός : qry
κινέω : zwʿ
κίνησις : zwʿ
κινητός : zwʿ
κλίνω : ṣly
κοινός : gwʾ
κοινωνέω : šwtpʾ
κοινωνία : šwtpʾ
κοινῶς : gwʾ
κοσμέω : tqn
κόσμος : ʿlmʾ, ṣbt, tqn

κρᾶσις : mzg
κρείσσων : p''
κυρίως : mr'
λαμβάνω : nsb
λέγω : 'mr, mll, qry
λίθος : k'p'
λόγος : 'mr, mll, tḥwm'
λοιπός : mkyl
λύω : šry
μάθησις : ylp
μάλιστα : ytr
μᾶλλον : ytr
μέγας : sgy, rby
μέγεθος : rby
μέθεξις : šwtp'
μέλλω : ʿtd
μένω : ktr, pwš
μέρος : 'yn, mny
μέσον : mṣʿ
μέσος : mṣʿ
μετά : btr
μετα- : šḥlp
μεταβάλλω : ḥlp, šḥlp
μεταβολή : šḥlp
μεταξύ : mṣʿ
μέτειμι : šwtp'
μετέχω : šwtp'
μετουσία : šwtp'
μέτριος : špr
μέτρον : mšḥ, mtḥ
μηδαμοῦ : dwk
μήτηρ : 'm'
μίγνυμι : ḥlṭ
μικρός : zʿr
μῖξις : ḥlṭ
μόλις : ḥsn
μονάς : lḥd
μοναχῶς : ḥd
μόνος : lḥd
μόριον : mny
μορφή : dmy
μωρία : bwr
νεῖκος : zky
νῖκος : zky
νοέω : skl
νόημα : ḥšb
νόησις : ydʿ, rʿy
νοητός : ydʿ
νοῦς : hwn'
νῦν : hš'
ξηρός : ybš
ξηρότης : ybš
οἶδα : ḥkm, ydʿ
οἰκεῖος : byt'
οἰκείως : byt', mr'
οἶκος : byt'
οἴομαι : sbr
οἷον : 'yk, 'yn, m'
ὀλίγος : zʿr
ὅλος : kl
ὅλως : kl, swk
ὁμοιοειδής : dmy
ὁμοιομερής : dmy
ὅμοιος : dmy
ὁμοίως : dmy
ὁμολογέω : ydy, šlm
ὁμολογία : šlm
ὁμοῦ : tnn
ὄνομα : kny, šm'
ὀνομάζω : kny, šmh'
ὁρατός : ḥzy
ὁράω : ḥzy
ὁρίζω : prš, tḥwm'
ὁρισμός : tḥwm'
ὅρος : tḥwm'
ὅσος : mdm
ὁτέ : zbn
ὅτι : mṭl
οὐδαμῶς : swk
οὐδείς : mdm
οὐδέποτε : mtwm
οὐδέπω : hkyl
οὐκέτι : mkyl
οὐκοῦν : m'

οὖν : hkyl, mʾ
οὔπω : hkyl
οὐρανός : šmyʾ
οὐσία : ʾwsyʾ
οὕτως : kd
παγετώδης : qrr
πάθημα : ḥšš
παθητικός : ḥšš
παθητός : ḥšš
πάθος : ḥšš
παλαιός : qdm
πανδεχής : qbl
πανταχοῦ : dwk
πάντως : prs
πάνυ : sgy
παρά : brʾ, lpwt
παραδέχομαι : qbl
παραλαμβάνω : nsb
παραμένω : ktr
πάρειμι : nqp, qwm, qrb
πᾶς : ʾkḥd, mdm
πάσχω : ḥšš
πατήρ : ʾbʾ
παύω : šly
πεῖσις : pys
περαίνω : swk
πέρας : swk, tḥwmʾ
περί : mṭl
περιαιρέω : nsb, rwm
περιέχω : ḥbš
περιλαμβάνω : ḥbš, lbk
περιληπτός : ydʿ
περιτίθημι : rkb
πέτρος : kʾpʾ
πηγή : ʿyn
πίπτω : nzl
πιστεύω : hymn
πλείων : sgy
πλέκω : ʿzl, rkb
πλῆθος : sgy
πλημμελής : bll
πλημμελῶς : bll
πνεῦμα : rwḥ
ποιέω : ʿbd
ποιητής : pʾwṭʾ
ποιητικός : ʿbd
ποιός : ʾyn, znʾ
ποιότης : znʾ
πολύς : sgy
πορεύω : rdy
πόρος : prs
πόσος : kmʾ
ποσότης : kmʾ
ποτέ : mtwm
πρᾶγμα : ṣbw
πρέπω : pʾʾ
πρεσβύτερος : qdm
πρίν : qdm
πρό : qdm
πρό- : qdm
προαιρέω : rkb
πρόγνωσις : ydʿ, qdm
προηγέομαι : qdm
πρόθεσις : qdm
προνοέω : qdm, rʿy
πρόνοια : ḥšb, qdm
προοράω : ḥzy, qdm
προσ- : ʾkḥd
πρός : lwt, lpwt
προσδέω : snq
προσδιορίζω : prš
προσέρχομαι : ʾty, npq
προσεχής : qrb
προσημαίνω : šwdʿ
προσλαμβάνω : nsb
προστίθημι : ysp
πρότερος : qdm
προτίθημι : sym
προφητεύω : šʿy
πρῶτος : qdm, šry
πῦρ : nwrʾ
πυρώδης : nwrʾ
ῥέω : rdy
ῥῆμα : ʾmr, mll

ῥίζα : ʿqr
ῥίπτω : šdy
σαφής : ḥzy, nhr
σημαίνω : šwdʿ
σκέπτομαι : ʿqb
σκληρός : qšy
σκοπός : nyšʾ
σπέρμα : zrʿ
στάσις : qwm
στερέω : glz
στέρησις : glz
στηρίζομαι : ktr
στοιχεῖον : ʾsṭwksʾ
σύγκειμαι : sym
σύγκρισις : pḥm
συγχέω : plṭ
συλλογισμός : swlwgysmw
συμβαίνω : gdš
συμβεβηκός : gdš
συμπέρασμα : knš, ʿbr
συμπληρόω : šmly
συμπληρωτικός : šmly
σύμφωνος : šlm
συν- : ʾkḥd
συνάγω : nqp
συνᾴδω : knš
συναιρέω : rwm
συναναιρέω : bṭl
συνάπτω : nqp
σύνειμι : nqp
συνεχής : ʾmn
συνεχῶς : ʾmn
σύνθεσις : rkb
σύνθετος : rkb
συνθήκη : šlm
συνίστημι : qwm
συντίθημι : rkb
σύντομον : psq
σύστασις : qwm
σύστημα : qwm
συστοιχία : lḥm
σχῆμα : ʾskmʾ
σχηματίζω : ʾskmʾ
σῶμα : gšm, pgr
σωματόω : gšm
τάξις : ṭksʾ
τάσσω : ṭksʾ
ταχύς : qll
τελευταῖος : ʾḥr
τελευτή : šlm
τελέως : gmr
τέλος : nyšʾ, šlm
τέμνω : psq
τέσσαρες : ʾrbʿ
τέταρτος : ʾrbʿ
τίθημι : sym
τιθήνη : rby
τιμάω : yqr
τίς : ʾnšʾ, mdm, mn
τοιοῦτος : ʾyk
τόπος : ʾtrʾ, dwk
τρεῖς : mtḥ, tlt
τριχῇ : tlt
τριχῶς : tlt
τρόπος : znʾ
τροφή : sybr
τύπος : ṭwpsʾ
ὑγρός : rṭb
ὑγρότης : rṭb
ὕδωρ : myʾ
ὕλη : hwlʾ
ὑλικός : hwlʾ
ὑπάρχω : ʾyt, hwy
ὑπογραφή : tḥwmʾ
ὑποδέχομαι : qbl
ὑποδοχή : qbl
ὑπόθεσις : sym
ὑπόκειμαι : sym
ὑπολαμβάνω : sbr
ὑπομένω : ktr
ὑπόστασις : qwm
ὑποτίθημι : sym
ὕστατος : ʾḥr
ὕστερος : ʾḥr

ὑφίστημι : qwm
φαίνω : ḥzy
φανερός : ḥzy, ydʿ
φθείρω : ḥbl
φθορά : ḥbl
φιλία : rḥm
φιλοσοφία : pylswpʾ
φιλόσοφος : pylswpʾ
φλέβιον : wrd
φλέψ : wrd
φρονέω : sbr, rny, rʿy
φυλάσσω : nṭr
φυσικός : kwn
φύσις : kwn
φυτόν : nṣb
φύω : yʿy, kwn
χαλεπός : ʿsq
χαλκός : nḥšʾ
χείρων : sny
χθόνιος : ʾrʿʾ
χράω : ḥšḥ
χρεῖος : snq
χρόνος : zbn
χώρα : ʾtrʾ, dwk
χωρίς : blʿd
χωριστός : prš
ψυχή : npš
ψυχογονία : yld
ψυχρός : qrr
ψυχρότης : qrr
ὡσαύτως : dmy
ὥστε : gwn, mʾ

Proper Names

English	*Greek*	*Syriac*	*Reference*
Anaximenes	Ἀναξιμένης	ܐܢܟܣܝܡܢܝܣ	§7
Anaxagoras	Ἀναξαγόρας	ܐܢܟܣܓܘܪܘܣ	§10
Aristotle	Ἀριστοτέλης	ܐܪܝܣܛܛܠܝܣ	§14, 40
Atticus	Ἀττικός	ܐܛܝܩܘܣ	§73, 84
Boethus	Βόηθος	ܒܝܬܘܣ	§95
Democritus	Δημόκριτος	ܕܘܡܩܪܛܝܣ	§11
Diogenes	Διογένης	ܕܝܘ ܓܢܝܣ	§7
Empedocles	Ἐμπεδοκλῆς	ܐܡܦܕܘܩܠܝܣ	§13
Epicurus	Ἐπίκουρος	ܐܦܝܩܘܪܘܣ	§12
Heraclitus	Ἡράκλειτος	ܗܪܩܠܝܛܘܣ	§7
Hippasus	Ἵππασος	ܗܦܣܘܣ	§7
Leucippus	Λεύκιππος	ܠܘܩܝܦܘܣ	§11
Longinus	Λογγῖνος	ܠܘܢܓܝܢܘܣ	§95
Melissus	Μέλισσος	ܡܠܝܣܘܣ (ܡܠܝܣܝܣ)	§9
Oceanus	Ὠκεανός	ܐܘܩܝܢܘܢ	§6
Parmenides	Παρμενίδης	ܦܪܡܢܝܕܣ (ܦܪܡܢܝܕܝܣ)	§9
Plato	Πλάτων	ܦܠܛܘܢ	§16, 36, 40, 41, 68, 73, 75–77, 81, 85–87, 94, 95, 97
Plotinus	Πλωτῖνος	ܦܠܘܛܝܢܘܣ	§95
Plutarch	Πλούταρχος	ܦܠܘܛܪܟܘܣ	§84
Pythagoreans	οἱ Πυθαγορικοί	ܗܠܝܢ ܕܒܝܬ ܦܝܬ ܓܘܪܘܣ	§16, 36, 40
Severus	Σευῆρος	ܣܒܝܪܘܣ (ܣܒܝܪܣ)	§87, 94
Socrates	Σωκράτης	ܣܘܩܪܛܝܣ	§4, 40
Stoics	οἱ Στοϊκοί	ܐܣܛܘܐܝܩܘ (ܗܠܝܢ ܕܡܢ ܐܣܛܘܐ)	§15, 40, 42
Tethys	Τηθύς	ܛܝܬܘܣ	§6
Thales	Θαλῆς	ܬܐܠܝܣ	§5, 6
Timaeus	Τίμαιος	ܛܝܡܐܘܣ	§77, 87, 95
Xenophanes	Ξενοφάνης	ܟܣܢܘܦܢܝܣ	§8

Bibliography

Addai Scher (ed.), *Theodorus Bar Kōnī Liber scholiorum II* (Corpus Scriptorum Christianorum Orientalium, 69; Scriptores Syri, 26; Paris, 1954).
Adler, Ada (ed.), *Suidae Lexicon*, 4 vols. (Lexicographi Graeci, 1.1–4; Leipzig: Teubner, 1928–1935).
Algra, Keimpe, and Katerina Ierodiakonou, *Sextus Empiricus and Ancient Physics* (Cambridge: Cambridge University Press, 2015).
Allen, Pauline, and C.T.R. Hayward, *Severus of Antioch* (London / New York: Routledge, 2004).
Altheim, Franz, and Ruth Stiehl, "New Fragments of Greek Philosophers. II: Porphyry in Arabic and Syriac Translation", *East and West*, N.S., 13 (1962), 3–16.
Arnzen, Rüdiger (transl.), *Averroes on Aristotle's Metaphysics: An Annotated Translation of the So-called Epitome* (Scientia Graeco-Arabica, 5; Berlin: De Gruyter, 2010).
Arzhanov, Yury, "Greek Philosophers in Monastic Schools: Syriac Forms of Doxography" , in Andreas Lammer and Mareike Jas (eds.), *Received Opinions: Doxography in Antiquity and the Islamic World* (Philosophia Antiqua; Leiden / Boston: Brill, 2022), ch. 8, forthcoming.
Arzhanov, Yury, "Plato in Syriac Literature", *Le Muséon*, 132/1–2 (2019), 1–36.
Arzhanov, Yury, "Syriac Natural Philosophy in the Early Islamic Period", *Christian Orient*, New Series, 8 (XIV) (2017), 253–266 (Russian title: Юрий Аржанов, "Сирийская философия природы в раннеисламский период", *Христианский Восток*, 8 (XIV) (2017), 253–266).
Arzhanov, Yury, *Syriac Sayings of Greek Philosophers: A Study in Syriac Gnomologia with Edition and Translation* (Corpus Scriptorum Christianorum Orientalium, 669; Subsidia, 138; Leuven: Peeters, 2019).
Arzhanov, Yury, and Grigory Kessel, "Field Notes on Syriac Manuscripts III: A Previously Unknown Philosophical Manuscript from Alqosh", *Hugoye: Journal of Syriac Studies*, 23/1 (2020), 99–130.
Arzhanov, Yury, and Rüdiger Arnzen, "Die Glossen in Ms. *Leyden Or.* 583 und die syrische Rezeption der aristotelischen Physik", in Elisa Coda and Cecilia M. Bonadeo (eds.), *De l'Antiquité tardive au Moyen Age: Mélanges offertes à Henri Hugonnard-Roche* (Études Musulmanes, 44; Paris: Vrin, 2014), 415–463.
Assemanus, Stephanus Evodius, and Josephus Simonius Assemanus (eds.). *Bibliothecae Apostolicae Vaticanae codicum manuscriptorum catalogus in tres partes distributus: In quarum prima Orientales, in altera Graeci in tertia Latini Italici aliorumque Europaeorum idiomatum codices*, Pars I, tomus 3 (Vatican, 1759; reprinted Paris, 1926).
Aydin, Sami, "The Remnant of a Questions and Answers Commentary on Aristotle's Categories in Syriac (Vat. Syr. 586)", *Studia graeco-arabica*, 9 (2019), 69–106.
Aydin, Sami, *Sergius of Reshaina, Introduction to Aristotle and his Categories, Addressed to Philotheos: Syriac Text, with Introduction, Translation, and Commentary* (Aristoteles Semitico-Latinus, 24; Leiden / Boston: Brill, 2016).
Auffret, Thomas, "La doctrine de l'âme", in Riccardo Chiaradonna and Marwan Rashed (eds.), *Boéthos de Sidon – Exégète d'Aristote et philosophe* (Commentaria in Aristotelem Graeca et Byzantina – Series Academica, 1; Berlin / Boston: De Gruyter, 2020), 361–402.
Bakoš, Ján (ed.), *Le candélabre du sanctuaire de Grégoire Aboulfaradj dit Barhebræus* (Patrologia Orientalis, 22/4; Paris: Brepols, 1930).
Baltes, Matthias, "Zur Philosophie des Platonikers Attikos", in Horst-Dieter Blume and Friedhelm Mann (eds.), *Platonismus und Christentum: Festschrift für Heinrich Dörrie* (Jahrbuch für Antike und Christentum, Ergänzungsband 10; Münster, 1983), 38–57.
Baltes, Matthias, *Die Weltentstehung des platonischen Timaios nach den antiken Interpreten*, 2 vols. (Philosophia Antiqua, 30; Leiden: Brill, 1976).

https://doi.org/10.1515/9783110747027-004

Baltussen, Han, Michael Atkinson, Michael Share, Ian Mueller (transl.), *Simplicius. On Aristotle Physics 1.5-9* (Ancient Commentators on Aristotle; London: Bristol Classical Press, 2012).

Balty, Jean Charles, "Apamea in Syria in the Second and Third Centuries A.D.", *Journal of Roman Studies*, 78 (1988), 91–104.

Barnes, Jonathan (transl.), *Aristotle. Posterior Analytics* (Clarendon Aristotle Series; 2nd ed., Oxford: Clarendon Press, 1993).

Baumstark, Anton, "Griechische Philosophen und ihre Lehren in syrischer Ueberlieferung", *Oriens Christianus*, 5 (1905), 1–25.

Baumstark, Anton, *Aristoteles bei den Syrern vom V.–VIII. Jahrhundert.* Bd. 1: *Syrisch-Arabische Biographieen des Aristoteles; Syrische Commentare zur ΕΙΣΑΓΩΓΗ des Porphyrios* (Leipzig: Teubner, 1900).

Baumstark, Anton, *Geschichte der syrischen Literatur, mit Ausschluss der christlich-palästinensischen Texte* (Bonn, 1922).

Baumstark, Anton, *Lucubrationes Syro-Graecae* (Leipzig: Teubner, 1894).

Beck, Edmund, "Ephräms Rede gegen eine philosophische Schrift des Bardaisan übersetzt und erklärt", *Oriens Christianus*, 60 (1976), 24–68.

Becker, Matthias, *Porphyrios. Contra Christianos: Neue Sammlung der Fragmente, Testimonien und Dubia mit Einleitung, Übersetzung und Anmerkungen* (Texte und Kommentare, 52; Berlin / Boston: De Gruyter, 2016).

Bergsträsser, Gotthelf, *Ḥunain ibn Isḥāq. Über die syrischen und arabischen Galen-Übersetzungen* (Abhandlungen für die Kunde des Morgenlandes, 17/2; Leipzig: Deutsche morgenländische Gesellschaft, 1925).

Berti, Vittorio, "Libri e biblioteche cristiane nell'Iraq dell'VIII secolo. Una testimonianza dell'epistolario del patriarca siro-orientale Timoteo I (727–823)", in Cristina D'Ancona Costa (ed.), *The Libraries of the Neoplatonists: Proceedings of the Meeting of the European Science Foundation Network "Late Antiquity and Arabic Thought. Patterns in the Constitution of European Culture" Held in Strasbourg, March 12–14, 2004* (Philosophia Antiqua, 107; Leiden / Boston: Brill, 2007), 307–317.

Berti, Vittorio, *Vita e studi di Timoteo I († 823), patriarca cristiano di Baghdad: Ricerche sull'epistolario e sulle fonti contigue* (Cahiers de Studia Iranica, 41; Paris, 2009).

Bett, Richard (transl.), *Sextus Empiricus. Against the Physicists* (Cambridge: Cambridge University Press, 2012).

Borbone, Pier Giorgio, "*Marāgha Mdittā Arškitā*: Syriac Christians in Marāgha under Mongol Rule", *Egitto e Vicino Oriente*, 40 (2017), 109–143.

Bos, Gerrit, and Y. Tzvi Langermann, "An Epitome of Galen's *On The Elements* Ascribed to Ḥunayn Ibn Isḥāq", *Arabic Sciences and Philosophy*, 25/1 (2015), 33–78.

Boys-Stones, George, *Platonist Philosophy 80 BC to AD 250: An Introduction and Collection of Sources in Translation* (Cambridge, 2017).

Braun, Oscar, "Briefe des Katholikos Timotheos I.", *Oriens Christianus*, 2/1 (1902), 1–32.

Brisson, Luc, and Michel Patillon, "Longinus Platonicus Philosophus et Philologus", in Wolfgang Haase and Hildegard Temporini (eds.) *Aufstieg und Niedergang der römischen Welt*, Teil II: *Principat*; Band 36: *Philosophie, Wissenschaft, Technik*, 7. Teilband: *Philosophie* (Berlin / New York: De Gruyter, 1994), 5214–5299; Band 34: *Sprache und Literatur*; 4. Teilband: *Einzelne Autoren seit der hadrianischen Zeit und Allgemeines zur Literatur des 2. und 3. Jahrhunderts* (Berlin / New York: De Gruyter, 1998), 3023–3108.

Brock, Sebastian, *A Brief Outline of Syriac Literature* (Mōrān 'Eth'ō, 9; Baker Hill, Kottayam: St. Ephrem Ecumenical Research Institute, 1997).

Brock, Sebastian, "A Syriac Collection of Prophesies of the Pagan Philosophers", *Orientalia Lovaniensia Periodica*, 14 (1983), 203–246.

Brock, Sebastian, “Changing Fashions in Syriac Translation Technique: The Background to Syriac Translations under the Abbasids”, *Journal of the Canadian Society for Syriac Studies*, 4 (2004), 3–14.

Brock, Sebastian, “From Antagonism to Assimilation: Syriac Attitudes to Greek Learning”, in Nina G. Garsoïan et al. (eds.), *East of Byzantium: Syria and Armenia in the Formative Period* (Washington, 1982), 17–34 (reprinted with the same pagination in: Sebastian Brock, *Syriac Perspectives on Late Antiquity* (Variorum Series; London, 1984), Ch. VI).

Brock, Sebastian, “Some Notes on the Syriac Translations of Porphyry’s Eisagoge”, in *Mélanges en hommage F. Jabre* (Beyrouth, 1989), 41–50.

Brock, Sebastian, “Some Syriac Excerpts from Greek Collections of Pagan Prophecies”, *Vigiliae Christianae*, 38 (1984), 77–90.

Brock, Sebastian, “The Earliest Syriac Translation of Porphyry’s *Eisagoge*”, *Journal of the Iraqi Academy, Syriac Corporation / Maǧmaʿ al-ʿIlmī al-ʿIrāqī <Baġdād> / Hayʾat al-Luġa as-Suryānīya*, 12 (1988), 316–366.

Brock, Sebastian (ed.), *The Syriac Version of the Pseudo-Nonnos Mythological Scholia* (University of Cambridge Oriental Publications, 20; London: Cambridge University Press, 1971).

Brock, Sebastian, “Towards a History of Syriac Translation Technique”, in René Lavenant (ed.), *III Symposium Syriacum, 1980: Les contacts du monde syriaque avec les autres cultures (Goslar 7–11 Septembre 1980)* (Orientalia Christiana Analecta, 221; Rome: Pontificium Institutum Studiorum Orientalium, 1983), 1–14.

Brock, Sebastian, “Two Letters of the Patriarch Timothy from the Late Eighth Century on Translations from Greek”, *Arabic Sciences and Philosophy*, 9 (1999), 233–246.

Brock, Sebastian, and Lucas Van Rompay, *Catalogue of the Syriac Manuscripts and Fragments in the Library of Deir al-Surian, Wadi al-Natrun (Egypt)* (Leuven / Paris: Walpole / Peeters, 2014).

Brooks, Ernest W. (ed.), *Historia Ecclesiastica Zachariae Rhetori vulgo adscripta*, 2 vols. (Corpus Scriptorum Christianorum Orientalium, Scriptores Syri, series III, t. 5–6; Louvain: E Typographeo Reipublicae, 1919, 1921).

Busse, Adolfus (ed.), *Ammonius in Porphyrii Isagogen sive V voces* (Commentaria in Aristotelem Graeca, IV/3; Berlin: Reimer, 1891).

Butts, Aaron, *Language Change in the Wake of Empire: Syriac in Its Greco-Roman Context* (Linguistic Studies in Ancient West Semitic, 11; Winona Lake: Eisenbrauns, 2016).

Charlton, William (transl.), *Aristotle. Physics. Books I and II* (Clarendon Aristotle Series; Oxford: Clarendon Press, 2006).

Chase, Michael, “Porphyry”, in Harold Tarrant et al. (eds.), *Brill’s Companion to the Reception of Plato in Antiquity* (Brill’s Companions to Classical Reception, 13; Leiden et al.: Brill, 2017), 336–350.

Chiaradonna, Riccardo, “Porphyry’s Views on the Immanent Incorporeals”, in George Karamanolis and Anne Sheppard (eds.), *Studies on Porphyry* (London: Institute of Classical Studies, University of London, 2007), 35–49.

Çiçek, Julious Yeshu (ed.), *Mnorath Kudshe (Lamp of the Sanctuary) by Mor Grigorios Yohanna Bar Ebroyo* (Holland: Bar-Hebraeus, 1997).

Colonna, Maria Elisabetta (ed.), *Enea di Gaza. Teofrasto* (Naples: Iodice, 1958).

Cornford, Francis M., *Plato’s Cosmology: The Timaeus of Plato* (Indianapolis / Cambridge: Hackett Publishing Company, 1997).

Cureton, William (ed.), *Kitāb al-milal wa-l-niḥal: Book of Religious and Philosophical Sects by Muhammad al-Shahrastāni* (London, 1846).

Cureton, William (ed.), *Spicilegium Syriacum: Containing Remains of Bardesan, Meliton, Ambrose and Mara Bar Serapion* (London, 1855).

Daiber, Hans, *Aetius Arabus: Die Vorsokratiker in arabischer Überlieferung* (Wiesbaden: Steiner, 1980).

Daiber, Hans, "Die syrische Tradition in frühislamischer Zeit", in Ulrich Rudolph (ed.), *Grundriss der Geschichte der Philosophie: Philosophie in der islamischen Welt*, Bd. 1: *8.–10. Jahrhundert* (Basel: Schwabe, 2012), 40–54.

Daiber, Hans, "Hellenistisch-kaiserzeitliche Doxographie und philosophischer Synkretismus in islamischer Zeit", in Wolfgang Haase (ed.), *Aufstieg und Niedergang der Römischen Welt*, Teil II: *Der Principat*; Band 36/7: *Philosophie, Wissenschaften, Technik* (Berlin / New York: De Gruyter, 1994), 4974–4992.

De Haas, Frans A. J., *John Philoponus' New Definition of Prime Matter: Aspects of Its Background in Neoplatonism and the Ancient Commentary Tradition* (Philosophia Antiqua, 69; Leiden et al.: Brill, 1997).

De Lacy, Phillip (ed.), *Galeni De elementis ex Hippocratis sententia / Galen. On the Elements according to Hippocrates: Edition, Translation and Commentary* (Corpus Medicorum Graecorum, V/1/2; Berlin: Akademie-Verlag, 1996).

De Lagarde, Paul (ed.), *Analecta Syriaca* (Leipzig: Teubner, 1858).

Den Heijer, Johannes, "Les Patriarches coptes d'origine syrienne", in Rifaat Y. Ebied and Herman G.B. Teule (eds.), *Studies on the Christian Arabic Heritage in Honour of Father Prof. Dr. Samir Khalil Samir S.I. at the Occasion of his Sixty-Fifth Birthday* (Eastern Christian Studies, 5; Leuven / Paris / Dudley, MA: Peeters, 2004), 45–63.

Des Places, Édouard (ed.), *Atticus. Fragments* (Paris: Les Belles Lettres, 1977).

Des Places, Édouard (ed.), *Porphyre. Vie de Pythagore, Lettre à Marcella* (Paris: Les Belles Lettres, 1982).

Deuse, Werner, *Untersuchungen zur mittelplatonischen und neuplatonischen Seelenlehre* (Wiesbaden: Steiner, 1983).

Diehl, Ernst (ed.), *Procli Diadochi in Platonis Timaeum commentaria*, 3 vols. (Bibliotheca Scriptorum Graecorum et Romanorum Teubneriana; Leipzig: Teubner, 1903–1906).

Diels, Hermann (ed.), *Simplicii In Aristotelis Physicorum libros quattuor priores commentaria* (Commentaria in Aristotelem Graeca, 9; Berlin: Reimer, 1882).

Diels, Hermann, *Doxographi Graeci* (Berlin: Reimer, 1879).

Dillon, John (ed.), *Alcinous. The Handbook of Platonism* (Oxford: Clarendon Press, 1993).

Dillon, John, "Boéthos" [no. 43], in Richard Goulet (ed.), *Dictionnaire des philosophes antiques*, vol. 2 (Paris: CNRS, 1994), 122.

Dillon, John, *The Middle Platonists: A Study of Platonism, 80 B.C. to A.D. 220* (London: Duckworth, 1977).

Dorandi, Tiziano (ed.), *Diogenes Laertius, Lives of Eminent Philosophers* (Cambridge: Cambridge University Press, 2013).

Dörrie, Heinrich, *Platonica Minora* (München: Fink, 1976).

Dörrie, Heinrich, and Matthias Baltes, *Der Platonismus im 2. und 3. Jahrhundert nach Christus: Bausteine 73–100: Text, Übersetzung, Kommentar* (Der Platonismus in der Antike, 3; Stuttgart, 1993).

Drijvers, Han J.W., *Bardaiṣan of Edessa*, tr. Gertrud E. van Baaren-Pape (Studia Semitica Neerlandica, 6; Assen, 1966).

Dyck, Andrew R., "Notes on Platonic Lexicography in Antiquity", *Harvard Studies in Classical Philology*, 89 (1985), 75–88.

Edwards, Mark (transl.), *Neoplatonic Saints: The Lives of Plotinus and Proclus by their Students* (Translated Texts for Historians, 35; Liverpool: Liverpool University Press, 2000).

Endress, Gerhard, "Alexander Arabus on the First Cause: Aristotle's First Mover in an Arabic Treatise Attributed to Alexander of Aphrodisias", in Cristina D'Ancona et al. (eds.), *Aristotele e*

Alessandro di Afrodisia nella tradizione araba: Atti del colloquio La ricezione araba ed ebraica della filosofia e della scienza greche, Padova, 14–15 maggio 1999 (Padova: Il Poligrafo, 2002), 19–74.

Endress, Gerhard, "Philosophie und Wissenschaften bei den Syrern", in Wolfdietrich Fischer and Helmut Gätje (eds.), *Grundriss der arabischen Philologie*, Bd. 2: *Literaturwissenschaft* (Wiesbaden: Reichert, 1987), 407–412.

Fiori, Emiliano, "L'épitomé syriaque du traité sur les causes du tout d'Alexandre d'Aphrodise attribué à Serge de Reš'aynā", *Le Muséon*, 123/1–2 (2010), 127–58.

Fiori, Emiliano, "Un intellectuel alexandrin en Mésopotamie: Essai d'une interprétation d'ensemble de l'oeuvre de Serge de Resh'ayna", in Elisa Coda and Cecilia M. Bonadeo (eds.), *De l'Antiquité tardive au Moyen Age: Mélanges offertes à Henri Hugonnard-Roche* (Études Musulmanes, 44; Paris: Vrin, 2014), 59–90.

Fiori, Emiliano, and Henri Hugonnard-Roche (eds.), *La philosophie en syriaque* (Études syriaques, 16; Paris: Geuthner, 2019).

Flügel, Gustav (ed.), *Kitâb al-Fihrist*, 2 vols. (Leipzig: Vogel, 1871–1872).

Fortenbaugh, William W., et al. (eds.), *Theophrastus of Eresus: Sources for his Life, Writings, Thought and Influence*, 2 vols. (Philosophia Antiqua, 54; Leiden / New York: Brill, 1992).

Frankenberg, Wilhelm, *Evagrius Ponticus* (Abhandlungen der Königlichen Gesellschaft der Wissenschaften zu Göttingen, Philologisch-Historische Klasse; Neue Folge, Bd. 13, Nr. 2; Berlin, 1912).

Freimann, Aron (ed.), *Die Isagoge des Porphyrius in den syrischen Übersetzungen* (Inaugural-Dissertation; Berlin, 1897).

Furlani, Giuseppe, "Contributi alla storia della filosofia greca in Oriente: Testi siriaci, III: Frammenti di una versione siriaca del commento di Pseudo-Olimpiodoro alle Categorie d'Aristotele", *Rivista degli Studi Orientali*, 7/1 (1916), 131–163.

Furlani, Giuseppe, "Contributions to the History of Greek Philosophy in the Orient, Syriac Texts, IV: A Syriac Version of the λόγος κεφαλαιώδης περὶ ψυχῆς πρὸς Τατιανόν of Gregory Thaumaturgus", *Journal of the American Oriental Society*, 35 (1915), 297–317.

Furlani, Giuseppe, "Due scolî filosofici attribuiti a Sergio di Teodosiopoli (Rêš'aynâ)", *Aegyptus*, 7 (1926), 139–145.

Furlani, Giuseppe, "Il trattato di Sergio di Rêsh'ainâ sull'universo", *Rivista trimestrale di studi filosofici e religiosi*, 4 (1923), 1–22.

Furlani, Giuseppe (ed.), "Le Categorie e gli Ermeneutici di Aristotele nella versione siriaca di Giorgio delle Nazioni", *Atti dell'Academia Nationale dei Lincei, Classe di Scienze morali storice e filologiche, Memorie*, 6/5/1 (1933), 1–68.

Furlani, Giuseppe, "Sul trattato di Sergio di Rêsh'ainâ circa le categorie", *Rivista trimestrale di studi filosofici e religiosi*, 3 (1922), 135–172.

Furlani, Giuseppe, "Sur le stoïcisme de Bardesane d'Édesse", *Archiv Orientální*, 9:3 (1937), 347–352.

Genequand, Charles (ed.), *Alexander of Aphrodisias* On the Cosmos (Leiden: Brill, 2001).

Georr, Khalîl (ed.), *Les Catégories d'Aristote dans leurs versions syro-arabes* (Beirut, 1948).

Gertz, Sebastian, John Dillon, and Donald Russell (transl.), *Aeneas of Gaza: Theophrastus with Zacharias of Mytilene: Ammonius* (London: Bloomsbury, 2012).

Gioè, Adriano, "Il medioplatonico Severo: Testimonianze e frammenti", *Annali dell'Istituto Italiano per gli studi storici*, 12 (1991/1994), 405–437.

Gioè, Adriano, *Filosofi medioplatonici del II secolo D.C.: Testimonianze e frammenti. Gaio, Albno, Lucio, Nicostrato, Tauro, Severo, Arpocrazione* (Napoli: Bibliopolis, 2002).

Gottheil, Richard J.H., "A Synopsis of Greek Philosophy by Bar 'Ebhrâyâ", *Hebraica*, 3/4 (1887), 249–254.

Gottschalk, Hans B., "Boethus' Psychology and the Neoplatonists", *Phronesis*, 31 (1986), 243–257.
Goulet, Richard (ed.), *Dictionnaire des philosophes antiques*, vol. 2 (Paris: CNRS, 1994).
Goulet, Richard, "Severus", in Richard Goulet (ed.), *Dictionnaire des philosophes antiques*, vol. 6 (Paris: CNRS, 2016), 236–241.
Gourinat, Jean-Baptiste, "The Stoics on Matter and Prime Matter: 'Corporealism' and the Imprint of Plato's Timaeus", in Ricardo Salles (ed.), *God and Cosmos in Stoicism* (Oxford: Oxford University Press, 2009), 46–70.
Graffin, François (ed.), *Le Candélabre du Sanctuaire de Grégoire Abou'lfaradj dit Barhebræus. Troisième base: De la théologie* (Patrologia Orientalis, 27/4; Paris: Firmin-Didot, 1957).
Greatrex, Geoffrey, et al. (eds.), *The Chronicle of Pseudo-Zachariah Rhetor: Church and War in Late Antiquity* (Translated Texts for Historians, 55; Liverpool: Liverpool University Press, 2011).
Gregorić, Pavel, and George Karamanolis, *Pseudo-Aristotle*: De Mundo (On the Cosmos). *A Commentary* (Cambridge: Cambridge University Press, 2020).
Grillmeier, Alois, and Theresia Hainthaler, *Christ in Christian Tradition*, transl. by John Cawte and Pauline Allen, vol. 2, part 2 (London: Oxford University Press, 1995).
Guillaumont, Antoine, and Claire Guillaumont (eds.), *Le gnostique, ou A celui qui est devenu digne de la science. Édition critique des fragments grecs, traduction intégrale établie au moyen des versions syriaques et arménienne Évagre le Pontique* (Sources chrétiennes, 356; Paris: Cerf, 1989).
Gutas, Dimitri, *Greek Thought, Arabic Culture: The Graeco-Arabic Translation Movement in Baghdad and Early 'Abbāsid Society (2nd–4th/8th–10th centuries)* (London / New York: Routledge, 1998).
Gutas, Dimitri, "Paul the Persian on the Classification of the Parts of Aristotle's Philosophy: a Milestone Between Alexandria and Bagdad", *Der Islam*, 60 (1983), 231–267.
Hadot, Pierre-Henri, *Porphyre et Victorinus*, 2 vols. (Paris: Études augustiniennes, 1968).
Hadot, Pierre-Henri, "Fragments d'un commentaire de Porphyre sur le Parmenide", *Revue des Études Grecques*, 74 (1961), 410–438.
Hatch, William H.P., *An Album of Dated Syriac Manuscripts* (Boston: American Academy of Arts and Sciences, 1946).
Hausherr, Irénée, "Un grand auteur spirituel retrouvé: Jean d'Apameé", *Orientalia Christiana Periodica*, 14/1-2 (1948), 3–42.
Havrda, Matyáš, *The So-Called Eighth 'Stromateus' by Clement of Alexandria: Early Christian Reception of Greek Scientific Methodology* (Philosophia Antiqua, 144; Leiden / Boston: Brill, 2016).
Heimgartner, Martin, "Der ostsyrische Patriarch Timotheos I. (780–823) und der Aristotelismus: Die aristotelische Logik und Dialektik als Verständigungsbasis zwischen den Religionen", in Martin Tamcke (ed.), *Orientalische Christen und Europa: Kulturbegegnung zwischen Interferenz, Partizipation und Antizipation* (Göttinger Orientforschungen, I; Reihe: Syriaca, 41; Wiesbaden: Harrasowitz, 2012), 11–22.
Heimgartner, Martin (ed.), *Die Briefe 42–58 des ostsyrischen Patriarchen Timotheos I.: Textedition* (Corpus Scriptorum Christianorum Orientalium, 644; Scriptores Syri, 248; Leuven: Peeters, 2012).
Heimgartner, Martin (transl.), *Die Briefe 42–58 des ostsyrischen Patriarchen Timotheos I.: Einleitung, Übersetzung und Anmerkungen* (Corpus Scriptorum Christianorum Orientalium, 645; Scriptores Syri, 249; Leuven: Peeters, 2012).
Hein, Christel, *Definition und Einteilung der Philosophie: Von der spätantiken Einleitungsliteratur zur arabischen Enzyklopädie* (Europäische Hochschulschriften, 177; Frankfurt am Main: Peter Lang, 1985)

Henry, Paul, and Hans-Rudolf Schwyzer (eds.), *Plotini Opera*, Tomus I: *Porphyrii Vita Plotini. Enneades I-III* (Paris / Bruxelles, 1951).

Hespel, Robert (ed.), *Théodore bar Koni, Livre des scolies (recension d'Urmiah): Les collections annexées par Sylvain de Qardu* (Corpus Scriptorum Christianorum Orientalium, 464; Scriptores Syri, 197; Leuven: Peeters, 1984).

Hespel, Robert, and René Draguet (eds.), *Theodore bar Konai, Livre des scolies: Recension de Séert. II: Mimrè VI–XI* (Corpus Scriptorum Christianorum Orientalium, 432; Scriptores Syri, 188; Leuven, 1982).

Hicks, Robert Drew (transl.), *Diogenes Laertius. Lives of Eminent Philosophers, Volume II, Books 6–10* (Loeb Classical Library, 185; London / New York, 1925).

Hoffmann, Johann G.E. (ed.), *De Hermeneuticis apud Syros Aristoteleis* (Lipsiae, 1873).

Horstschäfer, Titus Maria, *'Über Prinzipien': Eine Untersuchung zur methodischen und inhaltlichen Geschlossenheit des ersten Buches der* Physik *des Aristoteles* (Quellen und Studien zur Philosophie, 47; Berlin / New York: De Gruyter, 1998).

Hugonnard-Roche, Henri, "Aux origines de l'exégèse orientale et la logique d'Aristote: Sergius de Reš'aina, médecin et philosophe", *Journal Asiatique*, 277 (1989), 1–17.

Hugonnard-Roche, Henri, "Die Schule von Keneschre", in Christoph Riedweg et al. (eds.), *Die Philosophie der Antike*, Bd. 5/3: *Philosophie der Kaiserzeit und der Spätantike* (Basel: Schwabe, 2018), 2469–2474.

Hugonnard-Roche, Henri, "L'épître de Sévère Sebokht à Aitilaha sur le *Peri Hermeneias*: À propos des propositions métathétiques et privatives, et de l'existence du possible", in A. Straface et al. (eds.), *Labor Limae: Atti in onore di Carmela Baffioni*, tomo I (Studi Magrebini, 12; Napoli: Università degli Studi di Napoli 'L'Orientale', Dipartimento Asia Africa e Mediterraneo, 2017), 337–366.

Hugonnard-Roche, Henri, "La scienza siriaca. IV. Matematica e astronomia", in Sandro Petruccioli (ed.), *Storia della scienza*, IV: *Medioevo Rinascimento* (Rome, 2001), 36–41, 69–70.

Hugonnard-Roche, Henri, "La constitution de la logique tardo-antique et l'élaboration d'une logique 'matérielle' en syriaque", in Vincenza Celluprica and Cristina D'Ancona (eds.), *Aristotele e i suoi esegeti neoplatonici: Logica e ontologia nelle interpretazioni greche e arabe. Atti del Convegno internazionale Roma 19–20 ottobre 2001* (Napoli: Bibliopolis, 2004), 55–83.

Hugonnard-Roche, Henri, *La logique d'Aristote du grec au syriaque: Études sur la transmission des textes de l'Organon et leur interprétation philosophique* (Textes et traditions, 9; Paris: Vrin, 2004).

Hugonnard-Roche, Henri, "Le corpus philosophique syriaque aux VIe-VIIe siècles", in Cristina D'Ancona (ed.), *The Libraries of the Neoplatonists* (Philosophia Antiqua, 107; Leiden / Boston: Brill, 2007), 279–291.

Hugonnard-Roche, Henri, "Les traductions syriaques de l'*Isagoge* de Porphyre et la constitution du corpus syriaque de logique", *Revue d'histoire des textes*, 24 (1994), 293–312.

Hugonnard-Roche, Henri, "Note sur Sergius de Rēš'ainā, traducteur du grec en syriaque et commentateur d'Aristote", in Gerhard Endress and Remke Kruk (eds.), *The Ancient Tradition in Christian and Islamic Hellenism: Studies on the Transmission of Greek Philosophy and Sciences Dedicated to H. J. Drossaart Lulofs on His Ninetieth Birthday* (Leiden: Brill, 1997), 121–143.

Hugonnard-Roche, Henri, "Porphyre de Tyr, Isagogè: Traduction syriaque", in Richard Goulet (ed.), *Dictionnaire des philosophes antiques*, vol. 5/2 (Paris: CNRS, 2012), 1450–1453.

Hugonnard-Roche, Henri, "Questions de logique au VIIe siècle: Les épîtres syriaques de Sévère Sebokht et leurs sources grecques", *Studia Graeco-Arabica*, 5 (2015), 53–104.

Hugonnard-Roche, Henri, and John Watt, "Philosophie im syrischen Sprachbereich", in Christoph Riedweg et al. (eds.), *Die Philosophie der Antike*, Bd. 5: *Philosophie der Kaiserzeit und der Spätantike* (Basel: Schwabe, 2018), 2445–2488.

Janáček, Karel, "Hippolytus and Sextus Empiricus", *Listy Filologické*, 82, Suppl. *Eunomia* 3 (1959), 19–21.

Kamil, Murad, *Catalogue of the Syrian Manuscripts Newly Found in the Monastery of St. Mary Deipara in the Nitrian Desert* (unpublished).

Karamanolis, George, *Plato and Aristotle in Agreement? Platonists on Aristotle from Antiochus to Porphyry* (Oxford: Clarendon Press, 2006).

Karamanolis, George, "Why Did Porphyry Write Aristotelian Commentaries?", in Benedikt Strobel (ed.), *Die Kunst der philosophischen Exegese bei den spätantiken Platon- und Aristoteles-Kommentatoren* (Berlin: De Gruyter, 2018), 9–44.

Karamanolis, George, *The Philosophy of Early Christianity* (Durham: Acumen, 2013).

Karamanolis, George, and Anne Sheppard (eds.), *Studies on Porphyry* (London: Institute of Classical Studies, University of London, 2007).

Keil, Henric (ed.), *Grammatici latini*, vol. 6, part 2 (Leipzig: Teubner, 1857).

Khoury, Joseph (ed.), *Le Candélabre du Sanctuaire de Grégoire Abou'lfaradj dit Barhebræus. Quatrième base: De l'incarnation* (Patrologia Orientalis, 31/1; Paris: Firmin-Didot, 1964).

Kindt, Bastien, Jean-Claude Haelewyck, Andrea Schmidt and Nicolas Atas, "La concordance bilingue grecque-syriaque des Discours de Grégoire de Nazianze", *BABELAO*, 7 (2018), 51–80.

King, Daniel, "Alexander of Aphrodisias' *On the Principles of the Universe* in a Syriac Adaptation", *Le Muséon*, 123/1–2 (2010), 159–191.

King, Daniel, "Origenism in Sixth Century Syria: The Case of a Syriac Manuscript of Pagan Philosophy", in Alfons Fürst (ed.), *Origenes und sein Erbe in Orient und Okzident* (Adamantiana, 1; Münster: Aschendorff, 2010), 179–212.

King, Daniel, *The Earliest Syriac Translation of Aristotle's Categories: Text, Translation and Commentary* (Aristoteles Semitico-Latinus, 21; Leiden: Brill, 2010).

Koch, Hal, *Pronoia und Paideusis: Studien über Origenes und sein Verhältnis zum Platonismus* (Berlin / Leipzig: De Gruyter, 1932).

Kroll, Wilhelm, "Ein neuplatonischer Parmenidescommentar in einem Turiner Palimpsest", *Rheinisches Museum für Philologie*, N.F., 47 (1892), 599–627.

Kutsch, Wilhelm, "Ein arabisches Bruchstück aus Porphyrios (?), Περὶ ψυχῆς, und die Frage des Verfassers der «Theologie des Aristoteles»", *Mélanges de l'Université Saint Joseph*, 31/4 (Beyrouth: Imprimerie Catholique, 1954), 265–286.

Lamberz, Erich (ed.), *Porphyrius. Sententiae ad intelligibilia ducentes* (Bibliotheca Scriptorum Graecorum et Romanorum Teubneriana; Leipzig: Teubner, 1975).

Lamoreaux, John C. (ed.), *Ḥunayn ibn Isḥāq on His Galen Translations* (Eastern Christian Texts; Provo, UT: Brigham Young University Press, 2016).

Leicht, Reimund, and Giuseppe Veltri, "The Study of Pre-Modern Philosophical and Scientific Hebrew Terminology – Past, Present and Future Perspectives", in Reimund Leicht and Giuseppe Veltri (eds.), *Studies in the Formation of Medieval Hebrew Philosophical Terminology* (Leiden / Boston: Brill, 2019), 1–35.

Lewis, Agnes S., *Catalogue of the Syriac MSS. in the Convent of St. Catharine on the Mount Sinai* (Studia Sinaitica, 1; London, 1894).

Lippert, Julius (ed.), *Ibn al-Qifṭī's Taʾrīḫ al-Ḥukamāʾ* (Leipzig, 1903).

Litwa, M. David (transl.), *Refutation of All Heresies* (Writings from the Greco-Roman World, 40; Atlanta: SBL Press, 2016).

Männlein-Robert, Irmgard, *Longin, Philologe und Philosoph: Eine Interpretation der erhaltenen Zeugnisse* (Beitrage zur Altertumskunde, 143; München / Leipzig: Saur, 2001).

Mansfeld, Jaap, "Doxography and Dialectic: The *Sitz im Leben* of the 'Placita'", in Wolfgang Haase (ed.), *Aufstieg und Niedergang der römischen Welt*, Teil II: *Der Principat*, Band 36/4: *Philosophie* (Berlin / New York: De Gruyter, 1990), 3056–3229.

Mansfeld, Jaap, *Heresiography in Context: Hippolytus' Elenchos as a Source for Greek Philosophy* (Philosophia Antiqua, 56; Leiden et al.: Brill, 1992).

Mansfeld, Jaap, *Prolegomena: Questions to be Settled before the Study of an Author, or a Text* (Philosophia Antiqua, 61; Leiden / New York: Brill, 1994).

Mansfeld, Jaap, and David T. Runia, *Aëtiana: The Method and Intellectual Context of a Doxographer*, vol. 1: *The Sources* (Philosophia Antiqua, 73; Leiden: Brill, 1996).

Mansfeld, Jaap, and David T. Runia (eds.), *Aëtiana V: An Edition of the Reconstructed Text of the Placita with a Commentary and a Collection of Related Texts*, 4 vols. (Philosophia Antiqua, 153; Leiden / Boston: Brill, 2020).

Marcovich, Miroslav (ed.), *Hippolytus. Refutatio omnium haeresium* (Patristische Texte und Studien, 25; Berlin: De Gruyter, 1986).

Markovich, Miroslav (ed.), *Pseudo-Iustinus. Cohortatio ad Graecos, De Monarchia, Oratio ad Graecos* (Patristische Texte und Studien, 32; Berlin / New York: De Gruyter, 1990).

McCollum, Adam, *A Greek and Syriac Index to Sergius of Resh'ayna's Version of* De Mundo (Gorgias Handbooks, 12; Piscataway, NJ: Gorgias Press, 2009).

McCollum, Adam, *The Syriac De Mundo: Translation, Commentary, and Analysis of Translation Technique* (Ph.D. dissertation, Hebrew Union College – Jewish Institute of Religion, Ohio, 2009).

McVey, Kathleen E., "A Fresh Look at the Letter of Mara Bar Sarapion to his Son", in René Lavenant (ed.), *V Symposium Syriacum, 1988: Katholieke Universiteit, Leuven, 29–31 août 1988* (Orientalia Christiana Analecta, 236; Roma: Pontificium Institutum Studiorum Orientalium, 1990), 257–272.

Merz, Annette, and Teun Tieleman (eds.), *The Letter of Mara bar Sarapion in Context: Proceedings of the Symposium Held at Utrecht University, 10–12 December 2009* (Culture and History of the Ancient Near East, 58; Leiden / Boston: Brill, 2012).

Meyerhof, Max, "Von Alexandrien nach Bagdad: Ein Beitrag zur Geschichte des philosophischen und medizinischen Unterrichts bei den Arabern", *Sitzungsberichte der Preußischen Akademie der Wissenschaften, Philosophisch-historische Klasse* (Berlin, 1930), 389–429.

Michalewski, Alexandra, "Atticus et le nombre des principes: Nouvel examen de quelques problèmes textuels du fragment DP 26 (= Proclus, In Tim., I 391.6-12 Diehl)", in Marc-Antoine Gavray and Alexandra Michalewski (eds.), *Les principes cosmologiques du platonisme: Origines, influences et systématisation* (Monothéismes et Philosophie, 23; Turnhout: Brepols, 2017), 119–141.

Miller, Dana R., "Sargis of Rešaina: On What the Celestial Bodies Know", in René Lavenant (ed.), *VI Symposium Syriacum, 1992: University of Cambridge, Faculty of Divinity, 30 August – 2 September 1992* (Orientalia Christiana Analecta, 247; Roma: Pontificio Istituto Orientale, 1994), 221–233.

Mitchell, C.W., et al. (eds.), *S. Ephraim's Prose Refutations of Mani, Marcion, and Bardaisan*, 2 vols. (London / Oxford, 1921).

Moreschini, Claudio (ed.), *Apulei Platonici Madaurensis opera quae supersunt*, vol. 3: *De philosophia libri* (Bibliotheca Scriptorum Graecorum et Romanorum Teubneriana; Stuttgart / Leipzig: Teubner 1991).

Moreschini, Claudio, "Attico: Una figura singolare del medioplatonismo", in Wolfgang Haase and Hildegard Temporini (eds.) *Aufstieg und Niedergang der römischen Welt*, Teil II: *Principat*; Band 36: *Philosophie, Wissenschaft, Technik*, 1. Teilband: *Philosophie* (Berlin / New York: De Gruyter, 1987), 477–491.

Mras, Karl, and Édouard des Places (eds.), *Eusebius Werke*, 8. Band: *Die Praeparatio Evangelica*; Teil 2: *Die Bücher XI bis XV, Register* (Die griechischen Christlichen Schriftsteller der ersten Jahrhunderte, 43/2; Berlin: Akademie-Verlag, 1983).
Mutschmann, Hermann (ed.), *Sextus Empiricus. Opera*, vol. 2: *Adversus dogmaticos. Libros quinque (Adv. mathem. VII–XI) continens* (Leipzig: Teubner, 1914).
Nau, François, "Le traité sur l'astrolabe plan de Sévère Sabokt, écrit au VIIe siècle d'après des sources grecques, et publié pour la première fois d'après un ms. de Berlin", *Journal asiatique*, 9/13 (1899), 56–101, 238–303.
Nau, François, "Le traité sur les constellations écrit en 660, par Sévère Sébokt, évêque de Qennešrin", *Révue de l'Orient Chrétien*, 27 (1929/30), 343–410; 28 (1931/32), 85–100.
Nimmo Smith, Jennifer (transl.), *A Christian's Guide to Greek Culture: The Pseudo-Nonnus Commentaries on Sermons 4, 5, 39 and 43 by Gregory of Nazianzus* (Translated Texts for Historians, 37; Liverpool: Liverpool University Press, 2001).
Nimmo Smith, Jennifer (ed.), *Pseudo-Nonniani in IV Orationes Gregorii Nazianzeni Commentarii.* Collationibus (Corpus Christianorum Series Graeca, 27; Corpus Nazianzenum, 2; Turnhout: Brepols, 1992).
O'Brien, Denis, "Plotinus on Matter and Evil", in Lloyd P. Gerson (ed.), *The Cambridge Companion to Plotinus* (Cambridge: Cambridge University Press, 1996), 171–195.
Osborne, Catherine, *Rethinking Early Greek Philosophy: Hippolytus of Rome and the Presocratics* (London: Duckworth, 1987).
Overwien, Oliver, "Der medizinische Unterricht der *Iatrosophisten* in der ‚Schule von Alexandria' (5.–7. Jh. n.Chr.): Überlegungen zu seiner Organisation, seinen Inhalten und seinen Ursprüngen", *Philologus*, 162 (2018), 2–14, 265–290.
Overwien, Oliver, *Medizinische Lehrwerke aus dem spätantiken Alexandria: Die Tabulae Vindobonenses und Summaria Alexandrinorum zu Galens De sectis* (Scientia Graeco-Arabica, 24; Berlin: De Gruyter, 2019).
Overwien, Oliver, "Secundus der schweigende Philosoph: Ein Leben zwischen Mythos und Kosmos", *Würzburger Jahrbücher für die Altertumswissenschaft*, N.F. 28b (2004), 105–129.
Phillips, George, *A Letter by Mār Jacob, Bishop of Edessa, on Syriac Orthography; Also a Tract by the Same Author, and a Discourse by Gregory Bar Hebræus on Syriac Accents Now Edited, in the Original Syriac, from MSS. in the British Museum, with an English Translation and Notes* (London / Edinburgh: Williams and Norgate, 1869).
Pognon, Henri, *Une version syriaque des aphorismes d'Hippocrate* (Leipzig: Hinrichs, 1903).
Possekel, Ute, "Bardaisan of Edessa: Philosopher or Theologian?", *Zeitschrift für Antikes Christentum / Journal of Ancient Christianity*, 10/3 (2007), 442–461.
Possekel, Ute, *Evidence of Greek Philosophical Concepts in the Writings of Ephrem the Syrian* (Corpus Scriptorum Christianorum Orientalium, 580; Subsidia, 102; Leuven: Peeters, 1999).
Rabe, Hugo (ed.), *Ioannes Philoponus. De Aeternitate mundi contra Proclum* (Leipzig: Teubner, 1899).
Ramelli, Ilaria, *Bardaisan of Edessa: A Reassessment of the Evidence and a New Interpretation* (Gorgias Eastern Christian Studies, 22; Piscataway: Gorgias Press, 2009).
Reich, Edgar, "Ein Brief des Severus Sēḇōḵt", in Menso Folkerts and Richard Lorch (eds.), Sic itur ad astra: *Studien zur Geschichte der Mathematik und Naturwissenschaften. Festschrift für den Arabisten Paul Kunitzsch zum 70. Geburtstag* (Wiesbaden: Harrasowitz, 2000), 478–489.
Reinink, Gerrit J., "Severos Sebokht", in Sebastian P. Brock et al. (eds.), *The Gorgias Encyclopedic Dictionary of the Syriac Heritage* (Piscataway: Gorgias Press, 2011), 368.
Reinink, Gerrit J., "Severus Sebokts Brief an den Periodeutes Jonan. Einige Fragen zur aristotelischen Logik", in René Lavenant (ed.), *IIIo Symposium Syriacum, 1980: Les contacts du*

monde syriaque avec les autres cultures (Goslar 7–11 Septembre 1980) (Orientalia Christiana Analecta, 221; Roma: Pontificium Institutum Studiorum Orientalium, 1983), 97–107.

Rist, John M., "Mysticism and Transcendence in Later Neoplatonism", *Hermes*, 92/2 (1964), 213–225.

Rodríguez, Carlos Quirós (ed.), *Averroes. Compendio de Metafísica: Texto árabe con traducción y notas* (Madrid: Maestre, 1919).

Rudolph, Ulrich, *Die Doxographie des Pseudo-Ammonios: Ein Beitrag zur neuplatonischen Überlieferung im Islam* (Abhandlungen für die Kunde des Morgenlandes, 59/1; Stuttgart, 1989).

Runia, David T., "What is Doxography?", in Philip J. van der Eijk (ed.), *Ancient Histories of Medicine: Essays in Medical Doxography and Historiography in Classical Antiquity* (Studies in Ancient Medicine, 20; Leiden: Brill, 1999), 33–55.

Runia, David T., and Michael Share (eds.), *Proclus. Commentary on Plato's Timaeus*, Volume 2, Book 2: *Proclus on the Causes of the Cosmos and its Creation* (Cambridge: Cambridge University Press, 2017).

Ryssel, Victor, *Über den textkritischen Werth der syrischen Übersetzungen griechischer Klassiker*, Teile 1–2 (Leipzig: Dürr, 1880–1881).

Sachau, Eduard, *Verzeichniss der syrischen Handschriften der Königlichen Bibliothek zu Berlin*, 2 vols. (Die Handschriften-Verzeichnisse der Königlichen Bibliothek zu Berlin, 23; Berlin: Asher & Co., 1899).

Saffrey, Henri-Dominique, and Leendert G. Westerink (eds.), *Proclus. Théologie platonicienne, Livre I* (Paris: Les Belles Lettres, 1968).

Ṣāliḥānī, Anṭūn (ed.), *Abū l-Farağ Ġrīġūriyūs Ibn al-ʿIbrī. Taʾrīḫ Muḫtaṣar al-Duwal* (Bayrūt, 1890).

Scholten, Clemens (ed.), *Theodoret. De Graecarum affectionum curatione: Heilung der griechischen Krankheiten* (Supplements to Vigiliae Christianae, 126; Leiden et al.: Brill, 2015).

Schulthess, Friedrich, "Der Brief des Mara bar Sarapion (Spicilegium Syriacum ed. Cureton p. 43 ff.). Ein Beitrag zur Geschichte der syrischen Litteratur", *Zeitschrift der Deutschen morgenländischen Gesellschaft*, 51 (1897), 365–391.

Share, Michael (transl.), *Philoponus. Against Proclus on the Eternity of the World 6–8* (Ancient Commentators on Aristotle, Bloomsbury Collections; London: Duckworth, 2005).

Siniossoglou, Niketas, *Plato and Theodoret: The Christian Appropriation of Platonic Philosophy and the Hellenic Intellectual Resistance* (Cambridge Classical Studies; Cambridge / New York: Cambridge University Press, 2008).

Smith, Andrew (ed.), *Porphyrii Philosophi Fragmenta*. Fragmenta Arabica David Wasserstein interpretante (Bibliotheca Sriptorum Graecorum et Romanorum Teubneriana; Stuttgart / Leipzig: Teubner, 1993).

Smith, Andrew, *Porphyry's Place in the Neoplatonic Tradition. A Study in post-Plotinian Neoplatonism* (The Hague: Nijhoff, 1974).

Smith, Andrew, "The Significance of 'Physics' in Porphyry: The Problem of Body and Matter", in James Wilberding and Christoph Horn (eds.), *Neoplatonism and the Philosophy of Nature* (Oxford: Oxford University Press, 2012), 30–43.

Sodano, Angelo R. (ed.), *Porphyrii in Platonis Timaeum commentariorum fragmenta* (Napoli, 1964).

Sokoloff, Michael, *A Syriac Lexicon: A Translation from Latin, Correction, Expansion, and Update of C. Brockelmann's Lexicon Syriacum* (Winona Lake / Piscataway: Eisenbrauns / Gorgias Press, 2009).

Strothmann, Werner, *Johannes von Apamea. Sechs Gespräche mit Thomasios, Der Briefwechsel zwischen Thomasios und Johannes und Drei an Thomasios gerichtete Abhandlungen* (Patristische Texte und Studien, 11; Berlin / New York: De Gruyter, 1972).

Stüve, Guilelmus (ed.), *Olympiodori in Aristotelis Meteora Commentaria* (Commentaria in Aristotelem Graeca, 12/2; Berlin: Reimer, 1900).

Takahashi, Hidemi (ed.), *Aristotelian Meteorology in Syriac: Barhebraeus, Butyrum Sapientiae, Books of Mineralogy and Meteorology* (Aristoteles Semitico-Latinus, 15; Leiden / Boston: Brill, 2004).

Takahashi, Hidemi, *Barhebraeus: A Bio-Bibliography* (Piscataway: Gorgias Press, 2005).

Takahashi, Hidemi, "Between Greek and Arabic: The Sciences in Syriac from Severus Sebokht to Barhebraeus", in Haruo Kobayashi and Mizue Kato (eds.), *Transmission of Sciences: Greek, Syriac, Arabic and Latin* (Tokyo: Organization for Islamic Area Studies, Waseda University (WIAS), 2010), 16–39.

Takahashi, Hidemi, "Syriac and Arabic Transmission of *On the Cosmos*", in Johan C. Thom (ed.), *Cosmic Order and Divine Power: Pseudo-Aristotle,* On the Cosmos (Scripta Antiquitatis Posterioris ad Ethicam Religionemque pertinentia, 23; Tübingen: Mohr Siebeck, 2014), 155–169.

Takahashi, Hidemi, "The Greco-Syriac and Arabic Sources of Barhebraeus' Mineralogy and Meteorology in *Candelabrum Sanctuarii*, Base II", *Journal of Eastern Christian Studies*, 54 (2005), 191–209.

Takahashi, Hidemi, "The Mathematical Sciences in Syriac: From Sergius of Resh-'Aina and Severus Sebokht to Barhebraeus and Patriarch Ni'matallah", *Annals of Science*, 68 (2011), 477–491.

Tanaseanu-Döbler, Ilinca, "Bemerkungen zu Porphyrios und Bardaiṣan", *Zeitschrift für Antikes Christentum / Journal of Ancient Christianity* , 19/1 (2015), 26–68.

Tannous, Jack, *The Making of the Medieval Middle East: Religion, Society, and Simple Believers* (Princeton, NJ / Oxford: Princeton University Press, 2018).

Tannous, Jack, "*You are What you Read*: Qenneshre and the Miaphysite Church in the Seventh Century," in Philip Wood (ed.), *History and Identity in the Late Antique Near East* (Oxford, 2013), 83–102.

Taylor, Thomas (transl.), *Proclus' Theology of Plato* (The Thomas Taylor Series, 8; London: Prometheus Trust, 1995, reprint of the 1816 edition).

Thom, Johan C., "Introduction", in id. (ed.), *Cosmic Order and Divine Power: Pseudo-Aristotle,* On the Cosmos (Scripta Antiquitatis Posterioris ad Ethicam Religionemque pertinentia, 23; Tübingen: Mohr Siebeck, 2014), 3–17.

Trabattoni, Franco, "Boéthos de Sidon et l'immortalité de l'âme dans le *Phédon*", in Riccardo Chiaradonna and Marwan Rashed (eds.), *Boéthos de Sidon – Exégète d'Aristote et philosophe* (Commentaria in Aristotelem Graeca et Byzantina – Series Academica, 1; Berlin / Boston: De Gruyter, 2020), 337–346.

Verrycken, Konraad, "Porphyry In Timaeum Fr. XXXVII (Philoponus *De aeternitate mundi contra Proclum* 148 9–23)", *L'Antiquité classique*, 57 (1988), 282–289.

Villey, Emilie, "Ammonius d'Alexandrie et le Traité sur l'astrolabe de Sévère Sebokht", *Studia Graeco-Arabica*, 5 (2015), 105–128.

Villey, Emilie, "Quadrivium dans la tradition syriaque", in Houari Touati (ed.), *Encyclopédie de l'humanisme méditerranéen* (<http://www.encyclopedie-humanisme.com/?Quadrivium-dans-la-tradition-syriaque>, assessed on 01.10.2020).

Wachsmuth, Curtius, and Otto Hense (eds.), *Joannis Stobaei Anthologii Libri duo priores* (vols. I–II; Berlin, 1884); *Libri duo posteriores* (vols. III–V; Berlin, 1894–1912).

Walbridge, John (ed. and transl.), *The Alexandrian Epitomes of Galen.* Vol. 1: *On the Medical Sects for Beginners, The Small Art of Medicine, On the Elements According to the Opinion of Hippocrates* (Provo: Brigham Young University, 2014)

Watt, John, "A Portrait of John Bar Aphtonia, Founder of the Monastery of Qenneshre", in Jan W. Drijvers and John W. Watt (eds.), *Portraits of Spiritual Authority: Religious Power in Early*

Christianity, Byzantium, and the Christian Orient (Religions in the Graeco-Roman World, 137; Leiden / Boston / Köln: Brill, 1999), 155–169.
Watt, John, "Sergius of Reshaina on the Prolegomena to Aristotle's Logic: The Commentary on the Categories, Chapter Two", in Elisa Coda and Cecilia M. Bonadeo (eds.), *De l'Antiquité tardive au Moyen Age: Mélanges offertes à Henri Hugonnard-Roche* (Études Musulmanes, 44; Paris: Vrin, 2014), 31–57.
Watt, John, "Syriac Philosophy", in Daniel King (ed.), *The Syriac World* (London / New York: Routledge, 2019), 422–437.
Watts, Edward, *City and School in Late Antique Athens and Alexandria* (Berkeley et al.: University of California Press, 2008).
Whittaker, John, "Atticus", in Richard Goulet (ed.), *Dictionnaire des philosophes antiques*, vol. 1: *Abam(m)on à Axiothéa* (Paris: CNRS, 1989), 664–665.
Whittaker, John (ed.), Pierre Louis (transl.), *Alcinoos. Enseignement des doctrines de Platon* (Paris: Les Belles Lettres, 1990).
Wiessner, Gernot, "Zur Handschriftenüberlieferung der syrischen Fassung des *Corpus Dionysiacum*", *Nachrichten der Akademie der Wissenschaften in Göttingen I; Philologisch-historische Klasse*, 3 (1972), 165–216.
Wissowa, Georg (ed.), *Paulys Real-Encyclopädie der classischen Altertumswissenschaft*, Neue Bearbeitung, 5. Halbband: *Barbarus — Campanus* (Stuttgart, 1897).
Wright, William, *Catalogue of Syriac Manuscripts in the British Museum, acquired since the Year 1838*, 3 parts (London, 1870–1872).
Wright, William, with an introduction by Stanley A. Cook, *A Catalogue of the Syriac Manuscripts Preserved in the Library of the University of Cambridge*, 2 vols. (Cambridge, 1901).
Zonta, Mauro, "*Nemesiana Syriaca*: New Fragments from the Missing Syriac Version of the *De Natura Hominis*", *Journal of Semitic Studies*, 36/2 (1991), 223–258.

General Index

https://doi.org/10.1515/9783110747027-005

References

a) Ancient Authors

Aeneas of Gaza, *Theophrastus* (ed. Colonna)
46.16–47.2: 60

Alcinous, *Didaskalikos* (ed. Whittaker)
8.2: 54
8.3: 54–55
9: 53

al-Shahrastani, *Kitab al-Milal wa-l-nihal* (ed. Cureton)
345–346: 77

Apuleius, *De Platone et eius dogmate* (ed. Moreschini)
I.5: 55

Aristotle
Analytica Posteriora
71b32–72a5: 47–48
Analytica Priora
24a10–11: 33
Metaphysica
988a18: 30
1033a–1033b: 54
Book Alpha: 42
Book Lambda: 21
Physica
184a10–184b14: 48
184b15–25: 42, 48
192a15: 70
Ch. 7: 21

Atticus, *Fragments* (ed. des Places)
Fr. 1–9: 57
Fr. 1: 49
Fr. 4: 50
Fr. 23: 58
Fr. 24: 58
Fr. 26: 59
Fr. 38a–39: 61

Averroes, Epitome of Aristotle's *Metaphysics* (ed. Rodríguez)
76.6–11: 77

Diogenes Laertius (ed. Dorandi)
VII.134: 52

Eusebius, *Praeparatio Evangelica* (ed. Mras & des Places)
XI.1.2: 49, 57
XI.27–28: 64
XIII.17.1–7: 61
XIV.10.3: 64
XIV.14: 42
XV.6.2: 50
XV.10–11: 64
XV.11.2: 65
XV.15–16: 64

(Ps.-)Hippolytus, *Refutatio omnium haeresium* (ed. Marcovich)
X.6.1–3: 43

Homer, *Iliad* (ed. West)
XIV.246: 87

Ibn al-Nadim, *Fihrist* (ed. Flügel)
1.253: 46, 68

(Ps.-)Justin Martyr, *Cohortatio ad Graecos* (ed. Markovich)
Ch. 3–4: 42
Ch. 12: 36

Olympiodorus, *In Arist. Meteor.* (ed. Stüve)
126.14: 35

Philoponus
Contra Proclum (ed. Rabe)
VI.2: 71, 73
VI.14: 75–76
XIV.3: 73

Plato, *Timaeus*
27c–30a: 47
28a: 111
28a1–2: 91, 111
28a1–3: 47
28a2–3: 91, 111

https://doi.org/10.1515/9783110747027-005

26.11–13: 53
149.11–18: 46
163.16–20: 46
165.8–10: 46
166.3–5: 46
181.7–10: 52
188.32–189.1: 46
229.16–230.14: 74
231.5–24: 69–70

Stobaeus, *Eclogae* (ed. Wachsmuth)
I.11.5: 55
I.3.96: 16

Suda (ed. Adler)
2098: 64, 69

Terentianus Maurus, *De Syllabis* (ed. Keil)
1286: 80

Theodoret, *De Graecarum affectionum curatione* (ed. Scholten)
§95: 45

Theophrastus (ed. Fortenbaugh)
Fr. 230: 53

Timothy I, *Letters* (ed. Heimgartner)
Letter 43: 4

b) Syriac Manuscripts

Alqosh, Chaldean Diocese, Syr. 61: 25, 68
Baghdad, Chaldean Monastery, ms. 171: 27
Baghdad, Chaldean Monastery, ms. 509: 3
Berlin, Petermann I 9 (Sachau 88): 19, 68
Berlin, Syr. 190 (Sachau 81): 11
Cambridge, Add. 2812: 27, 68
Dayr al-Suryan, Syr. 20: 16
Dayr al-Suryan, Syr. 27: 5–14, 24, 34, 38, 62, 66–69, 79, 80, 83
Dayr al-Suryan, Syr. 28: 25
Jerusalem, St. Mark's Mon., Syr. 135: 11
London, BL Add. 12151: 26
London, BL Add. 12155: 24
London, BL Add. 12167: 7
London, BL Add. 12170: 80
London, BL Add. 14620: 17
London, BL Add. 14650: 7
London, BL Add. 14658: 8, 9, 20, 24
London, BL Add. 14668: 7
London, BL Add. 17130: 7
London, BL Add. 17156: 27
London, BL Add. 17194: 7
London, BL Add. 17215: 25
London, BL Add. 18819: 7
London, BL Add. 18821: 24
Mardin, Church of the Forty Martyrs, 404: 8
Paris, BnF Syr. 210: 11
Sinai, Syr. 16: 8
Vatican, Syr. 158: 67
Vatican, Syr. 168: 11
Vatican, Syr. 586: 33

www.ingramcontent.com/pod-product-compliance
Lightning Source LLC
Chambersburg PA
CBHW052330100426
42737CB00055B/3295

* 9 7 8 3 1 1 1 2 7 4 6 6 9 *